⚛Mixed Bag⚛

Mixed Bag

JIM RIKHOFF

FOREWORD BY GENE HILL

ILLUSTRATED BY GORDON ALLEN

Published by the
National Rifle Association of America
Washington, D.C.

Library of Congress Catalog Card Number 79-83761

Printed in the United States of America

Published by National Rifle Association of America
1600 Rhode Island Avenue, NW
Washington, D.C. 20036

Mixed Bag was originally published by The Amwell
Press and is reprinted by Agreement.

First NRA paperback edition, September 1980.

ISBN 0-935998-35-7

It has been said by others
Children are always the young strangers
Coming from some place
Travelling the journey we all must go

This child was such a young stranger
Coming from some place
In the time of crabapple blossoms in cold rain
Flowering briefly
Blossoming in those bitter hours of false spring
Losing to the cold burning of decay

Perhaps we hope too much
Perhaps our hurt is too much hope
Perhaps we find our children a brief denial of
our deaths

And on this cloudless April morning
Touched with red and ochre and olive high
    in the branches
It seems impossible that anything could die

We loved you these past months
Growing deep inside your mother's unfathomed depths
Echoing our timeless origins
Moving with ancient stirrings and awakenings

Forever new
Blossoming in the time of magnolias
Failing while we watched
Helplessly

It has been said by others
Children are always the young strangers
Coming from some place
Travelling the journey we all must go

Ernest Schwiebert
April 25, 1970

Contents

Foreword

The purpose of a foreword is fairly arbitrary. Some use it to explain the author's place in the scheme of things literary. Others try to verify the authenticity of the author's point of view or simply to praise him. No one ever asked an antagonist to write a foreword.

The writing here speaks for itself. It's not my purpose to justify it, explain the metaphors or translate a message. None of that is needed in this case since Jim's writing is much like Jim: straight talking, intelligent, wry, humorous and basically honest. His writing is all that good writing should be—trusting that someone else will be responsible for spelling, punctuation and the niceties of grammar. I have no doubt that you'll like it, nor any doubt that you'll come away knowing a good deal about Jim and liking him.

I never liked the phrase "outdoor writing." It always reminds me, being a simplistic person, of someone scribbling under a tree or alongside a brook. Good writing is just that; good stories or essays on the out-of-doors must be evaluated on their quality—not their environment. None of these pieces will improve your skills at the pursuit of sport but almost all of them will add to your appreciation of the understanding of the quality that we must all aspire to in living our way of life if we are to find those greatest of satisfactions—an understanding of who we individually are, what meaning our lives have, what enrichment we have gained from our high adventures and our simple larks.

I have been fortunate enough to have been involved in many of these outings—even those I haven't admitted to in public. Jim and I have travelled together from near the Arctic Circle to the Equator—and covered many a neighboring woodlot and swamp in between. We have eaten each other's bread and sung each other's song. And I consider myself privileged to have done so.

Jim's oft-stated philosophy is "nobody's perfect." But, like most simple phrases, that isn't what it seems to mean. Other writers have said the same thing in more resounding terms. ". . . no man is an island . . ." "Marching to a different drummer." "Man is an unfeathered biped." To paraphrase a few who come quickly to mind. Jim's stories here, as does his eloquent lifestyle, reflect a gentle goodness of purpose; a self-less understanding that we are all trying to do our best, have a good time, and follow that basic precept of medicine, "Do no harm."

I said that I wouldn't explain this book and I'm really not. I'm just trying to say that I'm sorry if you've never known Jim personally—and that his book will pleasure you with his unending, boundless enthusiasm for all the things we enjoy in common, only slightly less than if you'd actually been along, which is more the way Jim really would have liked it.

Jim likes parties, planned or spontaneous. A mixed gathering of friends, acquaintances and captivated strangers find themselves warmed by his presence. I have been involved in enough of them—in Nairobi, Colorado tent camps, roadside taverns, and even duck blinds and bass boats—to have seen his missionary skills work under the most incredible of circumstances. I see this book as one of Jim's parties, once or twice removed. He wants you to enjoy yourself, whatever your definition, and he's doing his best to make that happen. He doesn't expect any of us to be perfect and will do his best to help us forget that we're not—or better yet, to not care.

So, let me speak for Jim and say, "glad you're here . . . and have a good time."

GENE HILL
January, 1979

Introduction

After writing about a dozen forewords to other people's books over the last few years, it seems a bit strange to sit down to put forth an introduction, which after all is the author's own foreword, to one's own book. An introduction, properly speaking, should tell the reader what the book is all about, maybe why the writer wrote it and, perhaps, acknowledge a few debts of gratitude to various and sundry friends and associates.

On first glance, such a task should be a fairly easy one to accomplish, but on further reflection, the job is more complicated than originally envisioned. In the last analysis, I believe, you have to be a bit crazy to want to write a book—unless, as in this case, it is a pretty painless process, having been constructed of bits and pieces that have been written over the past twenty years.

This book is called *Mixed Bag* because that is just what it is—a very "mixed" collection of articles, essays, fiction and oddities that have appeared over a long period of time in a most varied number of periodicals. Strangely, I have included nothing from the most prestigious magazine I have ever written for (Arnold Gingrich's old *Esquire*) and, conversely, have selected stories from some relatively obscure publications. There's a good reason for this. Some of the bigger books so mess about with your prose (they call it "edit") that you can barely recognize the outcome as one's own progeny. On the other hand, the smaller magazines allow you more freedom of expression to make up for the paucity of pay.

The reader will find quite a variety of subjects included in this collection. There are stories on horses, dogs and children. There are fishing stories, a piece or two on foxhunting in the old-fashioned sense of the word. Mostly they are stories about hunting and, I guess, just people. People I have known and, in some cases, are no longer with us. A lot of my friends had to leave early, so you will have to indulge me a bit if my memories sometime take on a bittersweet cast.

I have included quite a bit of fiction, which we all know is becoming increasingly rare these days. It seems that the major outdoor magazines are obsessed with stories on "how-to-kill-a-bear-rabbit-bass-marlin-woodchuck faster and cheaper than my neighbor" and recoil in horror from anything that resembles fiction or fancy. There are exceptions, of course, but they are becoming increasingly few and far between. Good creative outdoor writing may be the next endangered species.

Yet when someone remembers—if, indeed, anyone cares—the best outdoor writers and writing twenty-five years from now, who and what will be brought to mind and what forgotten? Who will recall "I Caught the Monster Bass of Pelican Pond on $1.98" or "Me and Joe Got Our Buck the First Day?" They will remember Nash Buckingham, Havilah Babcock, Ed Zern, Bob Ruark and Gene Hill, to name a few of the very best. And how about Corey Ford, John Madson, George Bird Evans and a handful of others? You don't (or didn't) see them grinding out grist for anyone's mill. Well, not often, at least.

The above small sermon in no way implies that this writer counts himself in the same class as the gentlemen mentioned, but he hopes that he can be judged as one of those who is trying. Hence, you will find a goodly portion of fiction, and, hopefully, some humor. (There are those who say *all* of my work is fiction, but we ignore small minds.) Most of the stories included have already appeared in magazines, but there are one or two pieces that are still looking for a berth. Maybe they never will be published again, so you will have a "collector's item," whatever that is.

Part One of the book is comprised of the first year's twelve monthly columns that I have done for *The American Rifleman* since taking over the last page in July of 1978. That monthly column, entitled, fittingly enough, *Mixed Bag*, was the idea of George Martin, the head man for the National Rifle Association's publications, who had either enough guts or, some would say, stupidity to give me a free hand to write what and how I wanted in a magazine not previously known for its latitude in editorial matters. George got me writing on a steady basis again after many years of procrastination and for that I owe him more than he will ever know or that I can repay in kind. In the same token, I am also indebted to Gene Hill for his unswerving—even in the face of some fairly hefty adversity—support of my writing over the years. Lastly, I would be remiss if I didn't mention the interest and help offered by my wife, Jan, during the good times and the bad since I first started to try to write outdoor material out in Arizona over twenty years ago.

xii

I hope you get as much pleasure out of this book as I have had gathering the experiences upon which it is based and even in writing it.

JIM RIKHOFF
Speakeasy Hill
High Bridge, New Jersey
January 1, 1979

Acknowledgments

Most of the articles, stories and essays that appear in this volume first appeared in the magazines and books listed below. Although I have always retained all book rights to my work, I would like to extend my appreciation to both the editors and publishers involved who first put these tales in print.

All of the stories that are in Part One were first published as untitled "Mixed Bag" columns in *The American Rifleman*, July, 1978, through June, 1979 issues.

"Grand Slam in Big Game," *True Hunting Yearbook*, No. 13, 1962 edition.

"Taking Your Chances in the High Country" first appeared as "Elk with the .264 and .308," *Gunsport*, January, 1962.

"Crazy Sport for a Sporty Bird," *True*, September, 1964.

"Big on Pigs," *Outdoor Life*, August, 1964.

"Biggest Bird Bonanza in the U.S.," *True Hunting Yearbook*, No. 19, 1968 edition.

"First Buck," *Field and Stream*, February, 1979.

"Long Stalk for a Sly Sable," *True Hunting Yearbook*, No. 15, 1964 edition.

"Full House On Leopards," *Outdoor Life*, October, 1965.

"Lions Are Deadliest Just Before They Die," *True Hunting Yearbook*, No. 18, 1966 edition.

"Kenya's Game," *Guns*, January, 1967.

"More Down There Than the Lusitania" first appeared as "We Fished the Lusitania Wreck," *Sportfishing*, April, 1966.

"Fishing, Money and/or Wives," *Fishing World*, July-August, 1965.

The following columns (originally untitled) appeared as "Wranglin' East" columns in *Horse and Rider* magazine on dates indicated. "City Mice and Country Cousins," July, 1969. "Saddle Sore Memories," August, 1969. "Saddle Up!", May, 1969. "Here Come De Judge!" August, 1968. "The Loser's Circle," June, 1969.

"Scars" is an original article.

"The Demon Dog of Deacon's Draw," *The American Field*, December 3, 1977.

"Remember Tolliver Guilford?" is an original story.

"The Man With the Cardboard Suitcase" is an original story.

"The New Year's Entry," *Horse and Rider,* January, 1970.

"The Friday the Thirteenth Hunt," *The American Field,* December 2, 1978.

"Epilogue to a Hunting Moment of Truth" first appeared in *Hunting Moments of Truth,* Winchester Press, New York, 1973.

I

MIXED BAG

The First Year

A Note on Part One

I received a phone call from George Martin the Spring of 1978. George had recently moved from California, where he was a big man in Petersen Publications, to Washington, D.C., where he was to be an even bigger man with the National Rifle Association. Specifically, he was to head up all NRA publications. Among his primary early tasks was the renovation of *The American Rifleman*, the venerable major magazine of the 100-year-plus organization.

George wanted a back page column that would be diametrically opposite of the general content of the magazine's inner pages. *The Rifleman* has always leaned to the technical, no-nonsense school of outdoor writing and, indeed, it still largely—and, I feel, correctly—subscribes to that format. It should; that's what the readership wants—most of the time.

George felt that the readers might also like a little comic, or at least different, relief on its back page. He wanted Gene Hill to do the job— as only Gene can—as that aging gentleman had inaugurated his first column many years before on the back page of *Guns & Ammo* under George's tutelage. Since Gene was already tied to *Field & Stream*, poor old George had to settle for thirty-second best.

In any event, we've been there a year and, despite dire predictions from some of the old guard who were horrified by my approach to certain sacred subjects, have even received a certain measure of acceptance from the readership. So the mail would seem to indicate. Read on and see for yourself. The first twelve columns follow.

First Shot

I can't remember when I read my first *American Rifleman*. I'm 47 years old now, so I know it must be at least 35 years ago. I believe it was some time in the early 'Forties, during the opening years of the Second World War, when paper was scarce, magazines slim and Americans passed along well-thumbed periodicals and newly hatched paperback pocketbooks like treasured rare volumes.

We were all starved for entertainment of any kind. Gas rationing had cut the traditional "Sunday drive" in the country; trains and planes were crowded, with priority given to servicemen on the first and government and business bigwigs on the latter. Vacations were largely out of the question—and unpatriotic to boot—for the duration. Everyone worked. The men too young, old or infirm for active duty took the places of those who did serve in the armed forces. As for women, it was the day of "Rosie the Riveter" or volunteer work with the Red Cross or "Grey Ladies." Kids held down odd jobs or collected tin foil, paper or scrap for the war effort.

As for the shooting sports, well, there was more serious business to be done with guns and ammunition those days. Beginning with the drive to collect firearms of all types for the British Home Guard after the Dunkirk evacuation, Americans of all ages and persuasions knew that our time was coming. Old duck guns and deer rifles were going to be hung up for a Springfield 03A3 or one of those new-fangled, fast-shooting Garands. There was no talk then of gun control, "Saturday Night Specials," the innate evil of firearms, the bad influence of guns in American history or any other such nonsense. Farmer and worker, city dude and country cousin, we all damn well knew what guns were for and everyone was pretty proud that Americans, by and large, knew how to handle them, had always used them to protect our liberties, both collective and personal, and were ready to do so again. Outside of Jeannette Rankin, a pacifist congresswoman from out West, few raised a dissenting voice, and she wasn't around following the next election after Pearl Harbor.

As a youngster just broaching my teens—the traditional time when a lad receives his first gun, usually a .22 single-shot—it was a tough time

4

to come of firearms age. Sure, there was gun activity all around, but very little of it applied to an eleven-year-old in 1942. Maybe, if the war held on long enough, the youngsters would get a crack at ROTC training, but there wasn't ammunition to spare for idle plinking or even target practice. In the war's early years, before our giant industrial plant was fully geared up to mass produce small arms by the millions, our new soldiers trained with wooden guns and learned to shoot with .22's. As for commercial shotgun or sporting rifle ammunition, forget it. A few dedicated hobbyists and hunters started the War with considerable ammo, but even that was gone by the end of the hostilities in August, 1945. A limited amount of shotshells, .22 rimfire and a very little centerfire sporting ammunition was released to designated stores where farmers, who had to show cause for vermin control or other good reason, were rationed small amounts. Obviously, some of this ammunition found itself in guns pointed at pheasants, rabbits and deer, but by and large, American sportsmen were pretty well starved of new products, especially new sporting guns. Winchester, Remington, Colt, Savage, all the traditional firearms makers of New England, were concentrating their efforts on military arms and, in this, were joined by typewriter, automobile and other mass production companies.

I finally got my first gun in 1945. I don't think that I will ever forget that day. My Dad took me down to Vonnegut's Hardware store in Indianapolis and bought me a Savage 3C .22 rimfire, bolt action, single-shot. I still have it in my gun cabinet. My wife learned to shoot with it and it was my son's first rifle. (I guess it will go to his son in some future year—if we still are allowed to give our sons and grandsons their first .22 rifles.) Since then I have owned over a hundred guns—some ranging in price so different from that first gun (I think it cost 13 bucks) that I won't commit myself in print on the off chance my wife might read my column—but I'd no more part with that little cutdown Savage than I would my other most valued possessions, if I could think of any more valuable!

My parents were divorced when I was three, so my father lived in Cedar Rapids, Iowa, and visited my sister and me in Indianapolis occasionally. During summers, we visited him in Iowa, first in an apartment, then a house and, finally, but best of all, a small farm outside of town. An ardent hunter, fisherman and horseman, my father longed for us to follow in his footsteps, but while the fishing and horse ends were easy to handle during our summer vacation months with him, the hunting part was almost impossible to manage because we were back with our mother for the school year.

Also, one must remember that the game situation was vastly different in those days. Most of the Middlewestern states hadn't had a deer season in years. Wealthy sports went off to Michigan, Wisconsin or Canada for deer and—unbelievable to us—moose and bear! I never saw a deer in Indiana, Iowa, Illinois or Ohio in all the years I was growing up and going to school through college. When I saw my first deer during a summer fishing trip in 1938 to the North border-lake country of Minnesota, I almost had a fit from excitement. Later, I heard wolves across Lake Kabetogama on another trip in 1945 and I have never forgotten that first sound. To this day, the cry of a loon and the howl of a wolf mean the wilderness, my youth and my father.

I also remember the first time I heard, then saw, a flock of Canadian geese passing way overhead one crisp Fall day towards dusk. I was passing a football with a friend on New Jersey Street, a little used road behind Washington Boulevard where I lived on the North side of Indianapolis, when I heard this haunting, alien honking series of crys, first faint and then steadily growing, but still distant because of the great height of the flock's flight. I recall Bobby Goldberg and I stood, slack-jawed like two village idiots, gaping in silence as the large strung-out V-formation slowly flapped over us and then was gone. Everytime I hear or see a Canada goose now—and we have many using our rural area of New Jersey year-round—the same thought still courses through my mind that I had that first day: From where do they come and to what distant place are they going? I want to get into a car, leave everything and follow the flock.

I have never forgotten that first .22 rifle, that first deer seen or that first goose heard, that first *American Rifleman* read. All of those things —plus my father, other relatives and many friends—pointed my unknowing feet on the first faint path leading towards what has become the main corridor of my life, the outdoor field sports of shooting, hunting and fishing. In the years since that first gun and that first *American Rifleman*, the accidents of history, a lot of luck and a little talent have guided me through some of the most enjoyable—and some sad—times a man could experience in almost half-a-century of varied living. I have hunted and fished all over the world, worked for a great firearms manufacturer for sixteen years, written hundreds of articles and edited a few books, started two outdoor publishing companies, worked and sweated with some fine conservation and hunting organizations, raised a fine family and am starting something new once again.

As you may have guessed by now, this is the first of what, hopefully, will be a regular monthly column in *The American Rifleman*, the good Lord, my editors and you, our readership, willing. *The American Rifleman*, as with everything in life, is changing. As we all know, change ain't necessarily progress, but I think the people in charge of this transition know what they are doing. I think they are going to make the *Rifleman* a more vital, responsive magazine, closely allied and identified with the interests of our readers. I hope to be a positive, albeit somewhat different, part of what is always called "a new look" by magazine publishers. In this case, this column *will* be something new, at least for this magazine. I've tried to give you a small hint of my background; more, maybe too much, will come later. One might say my shooting experience has been a "mixed bag"—and so this column will reflect, again hopefully, to everyone's occasional interest. We—the trusting editors and I—will try to bring some rather unusual stories and sidelights on shooting and allied subjects to these pages. Our success will depend on your response. In the last analysis, after all, a column and its columnist have to reflect the wishes of its readership. Let us know what you think, what you like and also what you don't particularly enjoy. Maybe we'll change but, human nature being what it is, I doubt it.

7

The Happy Hunting Home

As the old saying goes, it's hell getting old but consider the alternative. The aging process and its problems were the subject of a recent discussion with my good friend Joe Hudson, who has achieved a certain distinction over the years by managing to remain chairman of South Carolina's Department of Wildlife and Marine Resources Commission under both Democratic and Republican Governors. Such a feat indicates something more than mere wisdom garnered by age.

In any event, both of us were sadly contemplating the inevitable ravages of time, some of which seemed more evitable lately than others. I bemoaned the fact that my offspring had taken to mocking their elder in public places when I found my arms were no longer long enough for me to read the average menu. My son had been impertinent enough to suggest that I not bend my head before company —as in pouring a drink, for instance—as an unsightly amount of skin was showing through my carefully combed remaining hair. Joe allowed as how, by bits and pieces, he too was slowly falling apart and it was probably only a matter of time, after all, before he would be reduced to decrepitude. Joe is only 44; I am 47. It made me morose.

At this point a younger companion, Floyd whats-his-name (I find it increasingly difficult to remember names) offered the unsolicited opinion that Joe and I would soon be spooning each other pablum, hopefully laced with a little bourbon for taste, in the local Bide-A-Wee Rest Home for Sporting Gents. What was offered in passing jest kindled an intriguing possibility. What about a retirement home for aging hunters and fishermen? Outdoor Sportsmen. Not crashing bores like geriatric golfers, tremulous tennis freaks or yawning yachtsmen. We could call it "The Happy Hunting Home," it being perhaps unnecessary to point out that the next stop for most inmates would be the fabled felicitous hunting grounds of Indian legend.

As anyone knows who has ever attended a rod and gun club dinner, sportsmen are a sociable, if not downright garrulous, bunch who delight in each other's company and the opportunity to exchange accounts of past, present and planned exploits, some of which even bear a faint semblance to the truth. When the time comes when the daugh-

8

ters and sons-in-law can no longer stomach grandpaw's presence cluttering up the Danish modern decor of their suburban split-level, what better solution for all concerned than to pack up the old boy's worn Bean boots, battered tackle boxes, Case knife collection and stuffed moose head and haul them all off to the local Happy Hunting Home where they will be given proper appreciation.

A marvelous, born again (if I may borrow the term) sporting life awaits the dispossessed aging sport. All hunters and fishermen love the challenge of the chase with all of its attendant rewards for achievement in the field. A whole series of awards programs could be devised culminating, perhaps, in the supreme accolade—"The Weathering Big Name Trophy," which would be given to that sportsman who inflicted upon his peers the most consistently outrageous name dropping in any given year. A mere passing reference to a record book trophy or a casual cocktail with an unemployed Hollywood actor (or even actress) would hardly measure up.

A winning combination might well go something like this: "I'll never forget when Prince Philip suggested I stop over for a spot of red deer stalking at Balmoral on my return from my 47th African

9

Safari when I shot my world-record elephant with the last Governor-General of the Sudan, but, of course, Ava and I couldn't make it as Jackie insisted we stop over in Washington before our Asiatic cruise."

Another popular series could be the annual "Bernie Krocket Awards," named after the noted Brooklyn sportsman-tippler who killed seven six-packs of beer before tumbling off a party boat in Sheepshead Bay, thus leap-frogging his long-planned sojourn at the Happy Hunting Home for a rather more abrupt reunion with some previously departed buddies at the aforementioned H. H. G. (Grounds, that is).

The "B. K." Record book—hereafter always awesomely referred to as "The Book"—would contain a meticulous archive of various ratings within special areas of competition. For instance, awards through four positions (plus honorable mention for fifth place) might be given for the length and decible rating of after-dinner snores in front of the TV set. A preliminary competition could be programmed on a monthly basis with a "snore-off" set each January which would pit the previous twelve months' winners for the annual championship. If sufficient interest were generated—and enough contestants would last out the year —a special category could be established for mid-day snorers and so on. As one can see, the possibilities are endless—what with yawns, post-prandial belches (and other noises I leave to your imagination) to be evaluated.

For those of a more scholarly bent, the Home would sponsor an official media monitoring team whose special task would be to screen all of Marlin Perkins' "Wild Kingdom" episodes and the Walt Disney Show for episodes of obvious nature-fakery. Another team would be responsible for keeping track of all the anti-gun, anti-hunting and, ultimately, anti-fishing editorials and stories in *The New York Times*, *Washington Post* and other founts of enlightened urban game management. The more aggressive members of this elite team would be assigned the honor of writing letters of rebuttal and ridicule (thus, the term "R & R") to the editors or television networks involved.

Naturally, the Home would provide an abundance of badges, pins, emblems, blazer patches, certificates and scrolls of merit and other tangible means of rewarding the efforts of their sportsmen. In this manner, life will have meaning and the old sports kept young in heart, spirit and mind, if a bit feebler in body. All in all, a worthy cause and one deserving of all of our support if, for no other reason, that with a bit of luck we may all be candidates for membership in the honorable ranks of the newly (just now) formed National Association of Senior Sportsmen (N.A.S.S.) in the future.

The horizons are without limit and we welcome your suggestions. You may direct all inquiries to the editor of this magazine as this writer will be making a prolonged tour of possible Happy Hunting Home sites throughout the Greek Isles and Polynesia. As one last point of interest, we should mention that there should be serious consideration given to the possibility of co-ed Homes, thus following the example so enthusiastically embraced by the undergraduates of our colleges in recent years. After all, as has often been forcefully put to me, it is not necessary to hunt and fish to have a good time. I can just barely remember girls, but what was it we used to do with them? Ah, yes, I recall—we used to put their pigtails in inkwells!

Amwell

It's August. Dog days. That halfway time of the year when our trout fishing is dribbling out with low water and the first bird hunting is yet to begin. New Jersey's first wild upland shooting is a special early woodcock season in mid-October; the regular small game season doesn't open until the second week in November. Only those lucky to have access to semi-wild shooting grounds (legal from about September 1 to mid-March in our state) can take advantage of almost six weeks of early training and gunning with old Blue. The Amwell Shooting Preserve makes September livable for me.

My fondness for Amwell was recently reawakened by reading George Bird Evans *Recollections of a Shooting Guest*, fittingly published by—what else—Amwell Press of Clinton, New Jersey. You will find that much of the book centers upon George's shooting trips some twenty years ago at Amwell with the late Dr. Charles Norris, a distinguished sportsman and author of *Eastern Upland Shooting*. They enjoyed some fine pheasant shooting, excellent dog work and, not the least, had the pleasure of the company of Duncan Dunn, the genial Scottish-American proprietor of Amwell.

Dr. Norris—well into his eighties by then—had to give up his hunting by the time I arrived on the Amwell scene the fall of 1959. I had missed him by about one season and George Bird Evans by a year. I heard about both of them, but never met either one. Dr. Norris died in February of 1961, and G. B. E. and I, at this writing, still have been confined to telephones and typewriters.

Duncan Dunn soon became one of the friends of my life. He was about ten years older than I and had started Amwell some years after coming back from World War II. The late Colonel Foran, a local power in Hunterdon County politics, had taken the young gamekeeper under his wing and Amwell, which had been the Colonel's private shooting lodge, was made a semi-private shooting club, open to a limited membership. Amwell was—and is—dedicated to a quality shooting experience and bears little resemblance to the "put-and-take" public shooting preserves one too often encounters. As one might guess, Amwell became famous throughout the East as one of the premier shooting grounds of the country.

It was no wonder. Duncan Dunn boasted an unusually appropriate background for the owner of Amwell. His grandfather had been gamekeeper to the Duke of Argyle in Scotland and had been brought over by the Stuyvesant family to run the large shooting establishment on their estates at Allamuchy, New Jersey. This same Dunn, also named Duncan, was the man who introduced the Scottish method of raising pen-held pheasants into North American game breeding circles. In turn, his son (the latter Duncan's father) ran the state game farm at Toms River, New Jersey. As far as anyone knew, the Dunns had always been involved with game and gamebreeding.

Duncan Dunn and I had many good years. We shot a lot of birds, had some refreshments together and shared a few tragedies and many pleasures. His heart started to weaken in physical strength, but never in spirit, in the early 1970's and he was, as they say, supposed to take it easier. He was lucky in that his oldest son, Malcolm, had come home to become a partner at Amwell. Duncan did slow down a bit, and it was then the great dream was born: Duncan, Gene Hill and Lamar Underwood and I would all go to Kenya for a three-week safari the spring of 1972.

After the first enthusiasm wore off and the time came closer to turn the dream into reality, Duncan became filled with doubt. He questioned that we—some years younger—would want him along. More important, he questioned whether he—and he always had a modest approach to his very superior qualities—would "belong" on an honest-to-gosh, full-blown, traditional East African safari with all the trimmings. Between his son, wife and the rest of us, we bulldozed him onto the airplane and off to Nairobi. He had the time of his life.

One night, when it was dusk and Gene and I were returning with our professional hunter, David Ommanney, in the Landrover, we caught sight of the campfire flickering in the Acacia trees many miles distant across the plain. As we approached, we could make out a circle of camp chairs about that fire and one figure, square and sturdily built, slumped comfortably in one chair in the middle. I asked Dave to let me out some distance from the campsite and walked in alone toward the seated figure who, of course, was my old friend from Amwell. He was holding a glass of scotch in his hand, his eyes were closed and he was gently humming "Scotland the Brave." I said nothing as I approached and sat down beside him. He did not open his eyes but

13

simply said: "I've been looking for this place fifty years, Jim. I can die happy now." It was a long way from Amwell but yet not so far at all.

Duncan took a busmans holiday shortly prior to Christmas, 1973, and went goose hunting with his younger son, Mike, and an Amwell member who had good shooting in Delaware. It was a bluebird day and no geese were shot, but Duncan enjoyed being out in the pits as always. After the day was done, the party retired to the lodge for social hour and while reminiscing about his African trip, he suddenly placed his head on his great chest and left us. No noise, no fuss. It was not his way.

When they placed Duncan in the rescue squad ambulance, Mike looked down at the license plate and the first three letters were "Mac" —his father's nickname. As the ambulance speeded toward town, a lone Canada goose flew into the front of the vehicle. It was killed instantly and I am told that Mike murmured to his father—"We got your goose after all." It was a long way from Africa but yet not so very far at all.

Malcolm Dunn runs Amwell now and it is much as before. Some things have changed, of course, but not so much that George Bird Evans would feel a stranger in front of the fire. Dr. Norris and "Mac" Dunn are gone, but there are still those who love good bird dogs, fine flying birds and a glass by the fireplace. It has been twenty years since George and Kay Evans have walked the fields of Amwell. That's too long. I think I better give them a call and have them up next month. After all, there should be some further reflections of that "shooting guest." He writes too well about the things most of us enjoy to allow him too much spare time in his last years. If George Bird Evans, a mere stripling in his seventies, is going to match Dr. Norris, he's got ten more productive years ahead of him, and we want our share.

Timberdoodle Talk

The woodcock is a wondrous bird.

Literally here today and gone tomorrow, the woodcock maintains its numbers by the very nature of its gypsy life. While grouse can be overshot and the species is prey to cyclical fluctuations, the woodcock seems immune to these deadly pressures. There are "good" and "bad" years, but they are more in our eyes than from increase or decline in local woodcock flights.

A lot of hunters talk about grouse hunting when they really mean they are going after grouse *and* woodcock. Somehow the grouse takes on more importance among upland shooting folk. Maybe it's because the ruffed grouse is more difficult for a dog to handle and a man to hit on the wing. Yet, I'd wager a Parker double-gun against a Sears single-shot that, if the truth were both known and admitted, most hunters are really secretly pleased when Old Blue points a woodcock rather than inadvertently flushes a grouse. Woodcock hold better to dogs than grouse—and most men hunt for their dogs more than for themselves.

We're lucky in New Jersey. We have both an abundance of birds and good woodcock ground. Cape May could be the best woodcock county in the East. If one gets a call from a Cape May buddy announcing "the flight's in—you better get down here right away"—well, one gets. If the flights are really coming through, it isn't necessary to journey to Cape May for good shooting. It's right next door in most of the rural areas of the state.

The last time I hunted woodcock with Gene Hill, another outdoor scribbler of some talent, occurred several years ago. The memory illustrates both the nature of woodcock hunting and the aptness of my comments about New Jersey.

I was hunting our club grounds at Amwell, some 1,000 acres of prime upland country. It was a Sunday and while one could legally shoot released birds, any migratory or non-stocked birds were forbidden by state law. One of the members returned and, proving an occasionally honest man still exists, bemoaned the fact that he had never before encountered so many woodcock in so short a time. His dog had gone

16

from point to point, then to frustration and finally lapsed into bewilderment. His master had withstood temptation and hadn't fired a shot or so he said.

This little poignant vignette produced quite an effort on the hunters assembled around the fire that evening. It was one of the few times I have seen that bunch struck dumb. When the full significance of the story finally settled over the group, I noted with some interest and a bit of panic that some members were casting sly glances at their watches and at the encroaching twilight. Saved by the proverbial bell, we were delivered from the temptation of illegal gunning by the setting sun.

I had unavoidable business in New York the next day, but soon found that my tasks would be completed about midday. It took about five minutes of sustained brooding before my course became brilliantly clear. I called Gene and told him birds were in and I knew where. He took no second urging to drop everything, get in his car and head for home and shotgun. We would meet at the Amwell Cabin at 3:00 p.m.

sharp. For once in our lives, we were both fairly on time. We were on the edge of the favored covert—a woodlot surrounding one side of the old Foran cabin—in another half-hour.

Most of the birds had left or, perhaps, other members had worked the covert over earlier in the day, but my setter, Cherokee Jim, made game constantly from the moment we entered the briars. Woodcock spatter was everywhere and it was only a few minutes before Jimmy glided into point. The tail was solid still so I knew the odds were heavily weighted that the bird was close and holding. It was, but we couldn't get a shot when the bird flushed through the brambles. At least that's my story and I'm sticking to it!

As woodcock will do, it flew only a few score yards before coming down again. As Gene and I made our way through the almost impenetrable thicket, we flushed another bird which Gene marked down on the opposite side of the covert. When we reached Jimmy, he was on point on the far edge of our woodlot. I walked past him, the bird flushed, flying along the side of the tree line, and I managed to drop him with my 20-gauge. After Jimmy retrieved the bird—expertly found, but disdainfully carried—we quickly swung back to the spot Gene had marked for the other bird, which was found by Jimmy and roundly dispatched by Gene in short order. And that was the sum total of all of the woodcock we found in that covert!

We had driven some sixty-five miles, rushed through New York traffic and half a business day, driven another sixty-five miles home to get our guns and my dog, and added a final twenty additional miles to get to Amwell and the whole thing was over in about an hour-and-a-half. Worth it? Of course. We'd both do it again any day we had the chance—because it was one of the finest afternoons of our lives. It was a beautiful fall day with the season's foliage at its best. The dog worked well. The woodcock both held and flew well. And, for once, we both shot well. I might add that the refreshments tasted better back in front of the cabin's fire that night than they would have in the best beanery in New York.

That's what a good woodcock day—or even hour—can do for you.

No One's Perfect!

Everyone has a bad luck animal. You can be the luckiest man in the yearly hunting camp; the proverbial happy hunter who always brings something back for the pot during small game season. But casually mention one animal to a certain person and the blood pressure rises, the eyes cloud over and with groans and sighs, defeat—nay, despair—commands. Elk—more specifically, a good six-point bull—are my bad luck animals.

I went on my first elk hunt in 1961—a ten-day pack trip with Wendell Copenhaver's outfit in Montana's Bob Marshall Wilderness area. We covered a lot of ground, up and down, back and forth, from 4:00 a.m. until sometimes 10:00 p.m. at night. Finally, after not seeing *any* elk for nine days, my guide, Larry Fite, and I came across three cow elk just at dusk, when we were heading in to our horses on the last night. We dropped two and we had our elk meat for the winter. I didn't know it, but that was the last elk I was to kill for fifteen years!

In the interim, I must point out that I didn't ignore elk hunting in favor of more rewarding pursuits. On the contrary, I figure I spent about another hundred days and several thousand dollars pursuing my particular will-of-the-wisp. I covered countless miles by airplane to get to elk states from my home in New Jersey; many more by truck, horseback and shank's mare after I got there.

I cajoled, lured and blackmailed any number of friends, both old and new, to accompany me on trips to Montana's Bitterroots, Idaho's Salmon River, various spots in Colorado and Wyoming's Gros Ventre Valley. I mention "new friends" as well as "old" because after an elk trip with me, I *had* to get new recruits because even my oldest friends avoided the subject of elk hunts like poison. All I had to do was bring the subject up and I'd clear the room like a finance man looking for derelict debtors. I was the Jonah of elk country.

The word soon got around. Not only was I the world's unluckiest elk hunter, but my mere presence in an elk camp was enough to cast a pall on everyone's hunting. I went on four successive elk trips in four states in four different years and NO ONE got an elk in any of the

19

camps. After a wipe-out elk hunt with Gene Hill, Davy Call, Davy Olyphant, Bill Kissel, Howard Symonds (who is even *more* unlucky than I am on elk) and me, plus *seven* others in camp for a total of fourteen hunters, Cotton Gordon, the outfitter and former president of the Colorado Outfitter's Association, gave up hunting in America and shifted his activity to Zambia.

In the meantime, I had already pretty well used up Idaho and Montana too. First, I took Johnny Falk, who worked with me at Winchester, on his first elk hunting trip, which, I believe after ten years, has also been his last. That was the Bitterroot hunt in Montana and, needless to say, no one saw an elk.

The next hunt was with the late Jack and Eleanor O'Connor, Bob Chatfield-Taylor and the also late Peter Alport at Dave Christianson's excellent elk camp in Idaho's Salmon River country. Bluebird weather kept the elk so far into the black timber even the deer flies couldn't find them. I volunteered to go with Dave and another guide below a ridge where we had the O'Connors, Bob and Pete on stands.

After plowing through blowdowns and thick brush for about two hours, I heard elk going out ahead of me over the ridge, but no shots. When I finally got to the top to find a comfortable spot to have my cardiac arrest, I found that Bob and Pete, bored after fifteen or so minutes—and knowing that with me involved, there was no hope anyway—had gone back to camp to talk ballistics with the cook. The next day a heavy fog settled in and that was the end of that hunt. Score: elk .999; us'uns, zero.

I next headed for Wyoming in company with the late Warren Page, long-time shooting editor of "Field & Stream." He knew a spot that was elk heaven! Loring Woodman's Darwin Ranch on the Gros Ventre has got to be one of the finest elk camps anywhere. I soon fixed that up. We saw scores of moose (no permit) and even a pair of beautiful big horn rams (ditto), but nary an elk—cow or bull. When we left and I mentioned we ought to try again next year, Warren mumbled something about "don't call me, I'll call you."

Things were pretty slim for the next year or so, but finally, in 1976, I figured the stories had died down enough that I could organize another elk trip. Slyly hiding my involvement to almost the last, I was able to trap the boys into another trip to the Darwin. After I killed a five-point bull the first night, everyone figured the luck had finally turned.

Six-pointers would be stacked up like cordwood. Loring and his guides were dancing in the pasture. The grand celebration was already planned for the last night.

Well, we still had the party, but it was more like an Irish wake. There wasn't another elk killed in the remaining nine days of our hunt. It was rather forcefully mentioned that it was bad enough when *NO ONE* killed an elk, but when I had the effrontery to take the only one, it was simply too much.

This year the guys have organized a really superb hunt for early December in New Mexico. I pointed out that I had never hunted elk in that state. They pointed out that it was unlikely I would, if they— and the New Mexico Guides Association, the Department of Game and Fish, and the organized rod and gun clubs of the state—had their way.

No one's perfect.

A Christmas Gift

Know ye all gentlemen by these presents that this being the season of good will and holiday cheer that we, the sportsmen of all lands, but especially those who cherish the traditional shooting sports in these United States, do petition that august and benevolent personage known by many names, but who, in all cases, simply embodies the spirit of Christmas in all men's minds, that we be granted the following gifts so that the coming year surpasses the last, to wit:

Ability to pursue our individual sports in a fashion to bring no one harm and many men pleasure; to inflict no damage or careless pain in our hunting; to improve our marksmanship in the field and on the range.

Beauty in our perception of the great outdoors, so that we can protect and maintain the unspoiled plains, forests, wetlands and waters that provide the necessary life-sustaining habitat of our wildlife.

Charity to the majority of those who do not understand our sports so that we may create a climate of communication in order that mutual understanding and a full knowledge of the positive facts of our positions may be advanced.

Devotion to our cause from all sportsmen so that we may maintain the credibility of our sport as well as unswerving opposition to that minority of opposition that demands our total defeat.

Energy to maintain constant vigilance against the unceasing campaign to undermine sound game management and our Constitutional rights.

Fairness in our approach to those great numbers of well-meaning citizens who have been misled about sporting firearms and hunting by the distortions of a small vocal minority, and who may be open to counter-argument.

Grace in our perception of our responsibility to our fellow men in the field and in our acceptance of the wildlife trust so that our critics must forever abandon the term "slob hunter."

Hope that by our actions the soundness of our logic and the morality of our ethics will gain credence with the majority.

Integrity of performance so we need never be ashamed of either our individual or collective deeds as sportsmen.

Justice from our peers, enforcement and judicial officials who each day control more and more the private actions of all citizens and in whose hands our freedoms are delicately balanced.

Kindness to all, including those who never ask, but perhaps need it most—the new shooters, unfamiliar and embarrassed, on our ranges and clay target fields.

Love for our fellow man and all of the Creator's creatures so that we place a proper value on those animals we do take in harvest and form an appreciation for life and death on all levels.

Maturity of judgement so that we are not tempted, through temper, intemperance, cupidity, greed, gluttony or unthinking action, to debase ourselves and other sportsmen by behavior that brings discredit on our sport.

Nobility of character so that the balance scales of public opinion will be tilted in our favor in any honest evaluation of the constitutional rights of private citizens to bear and keep arms and, also in defense of hunting as a legitimate game management and recreational process.

Objectivity in our evaluation of our own shortcomings and weaknesses so that we can most effectively resolve our own problems before others, less concerned with our well-being, usurp our right to govern our own sport.

Purity of purpose so that our time, talent and treasure are not diluted in irrelevant causes to the detriment of our major mandate—the defense of our rights and privileges in the outdoor sports.

Quality of argument so that our persons and programs are not held up to ridicule and our cause destroyed by our own ill-prepared and poorly presented positions.

Responsibility of action so that no man casually or slovenly approaches his sport in the belief that "one man doesn't count" or that one chance to answer a critic won't matter.

Strength to pursue our ideals and our goals in the face of sometimes seeming overwhelming opposition.

Thoughtfulness, temperance and tolerance in our relations with others, non-sporting or not, young or old, urban or rural, rich or poor, white or black, male or female, so that our position gains by contact rather than is demeaned by the exposure of our people and their arguments.

Unanimity of all sportsmen so that we provide a united front to all of our detractors and thus present an unbroken wall upon which their lances will be shattered.

Vitality to maintain the drive to meet all contests, be they on National, state or local levels, so that it is our opposition that finally falters and fails.

Wisdom to meet all challenges in a rational and understanding fashion so that our enemies are separated from the vast majority of citizens who are open-minded and reasonable.

Xmas in coming years so that we may be free to follow our joys and hopes for our family and friends, pursuing our lives and our sports in peace and harmony.

Youth so that our sport will be regenerated and expand as new generations learn the pleasure of a day in the field or on the range as countless Americans have done for over four hundred years.

Zest, last but not least, to follow the will-of-the-wisp, the unattainable, the golden fleece, the Holy Grail—the perfect score, the 1000 straight targets, the big buck with no name, the phantom bear of the swamp, the double on woodcock, the triple on dove, the perfect twilight shot, the dream pack trip to the Far North, the fantasied safari to Africa, the look in a youngster's eyes some Christmas morning when that first rifle is found under the tree, all these and finally, also those secret hopes and dreams in each reader's deepest thoughts.

I wish you all a most Merry Christmas and the best of coming years.

The Last Hunt

Very few men are legends in their own lifetimes, which is probably a pretty good thing when one considers the possible consequences of too many egos abroad at one time. A lot of people think they are legends, but very few are genuine bonafide "living legends," and even fewer are nice about it. Jack O'Connor, who died a year ago this month, was one of the rare last ones.

It's taken me that year to sit down at this typewriter and write an obituary on Jack. And now that I'm at it, I guess I'll have to admit that this short, inadequate piece isn't going to be any sort of a conventional obituary. When Jack had his first and last heart attack on board a cruise ship coming back from Hawaii last winter, he was working on his last book. Yes, I mean the last book he intended to write, not just "last" because death made that decision for him. That book will be his definitive memorial because it is something different than anything he ever wrote.

I knew Jack for some twenty years. We hunted quite a number of states and a couple of Canadian Provinces. We also hunted Mexico, Scotland, Spain and Italy—sometimes even with a little success. We always planned to take an African safari together but somehow the years passed and we never did. While Jack hunted the world over—from Alaska to Zambia—his primary identification was always with his native Arizona and the Southwest, including, very significantly, Northern Mexico. He was an expert on African safaris and Indian shikars, but old timers and young whippersnappers alike still picture Jack's familiar Hibernian mug peering through wirerimmed glasses out from under an old beat-up cowboy hat. And well it should be for, regardless of all of his world travel and sophisticated cultural and educational achievements, he remained the quintessential Southwestern hunter.

Few of his fans knew that Jack served in both the United States Army and Navy for some years at the tail-end of World War I, including a memorable stint as a 15-year-old, obviously under-age, private in the Arizona National Guard, activated as the 158th Infantry. He was known as "Cactus Jack, the Ass-less Wonder"—a description, I might add, that remained incredibly apt right up to the end. (One recalls an historic occasion a few years back when Winchester took the gun writers to Italy to view their new ammunition plant; on the way over we were standing in the plane's aisle discussing ballistics when a stewardess had to go by Jack, who promptly pulled in his stomach to allow this pleasant passage and found to his dismay that his pants fell down.)

Perhaps Jack was most closely identified with his many years (starting in 1937) with *Outdoor Life*, primarily as Arms and Ammunition Editor from 1941 until his retirement from that position in 1972. He stayed on as Hunting Editor after his retirement until 1973 when he grew weary of changing editorial policy and took his talent and prestige to Peterson. He still contributed a full feature article every month right up and past his death, because he always stayed well ahead on his assignments, something his editors cherished.

Jack died just two days short of his seventy-sixth birthday; strangely, his old rival-friend, Warren Page, the long-time shooting editor of *Field & Stream*, had died on Jack's seventy-fifth birthday the year before. Jack and I were hunting sheep together in the Cassiar range of British Columbia and the Pellys of the Yukon when he was in his early seventies. We both took a stone sheep in the Cassiars, but Jack never fired his gun in the Yukon on what was to be our last hunt together, which I think now we both knew.

We were with a brand new outfit, Teslin Outfitters, who had just taken over a country that had not been hunted for six years. They also had not had a chance to do much more than put in an excellent base camp on Francis Lake, so when we took off from there with our pack string, we were really striking out into new country. It was just as if we were old mountain men pushing around that next bend, through that next stream, over that last ridge. Jack was exhilarated. After a day or two on the trail, as we made camp at dusk, he told me that of all the places he had hunted—from Africa to India and beyond—he guessed that he loved the high country of the Northwest the best.

We pressed on for five days and saw no game. Finally even the last rudimentary man-made trails petered out and we followed increasingly narrow and steep game paths. There were so many blowdowns and so much buck brush that we had to get down off our horses and cut our way through. It soon became obvious that Jack, partially crippled from a bad automobile accident years before and circulatory problems from plain old age, couldn't make it any further in that country.

26

He insisted that we make a camp by a stream in the open and that I go on with one guide while he remained with the rest. I went off and a couple of days later took a sheep. We returned and Jack was overjoyed. We had made the trip a success—for myself obviously, but also for Teslin's first hunt and lastly for him on what he knew might be his last trip to his beloved high country. We packed up and headed back and once almost got another sheep for Jack. He didn't care about not getting the shot, but seemed strangely content to be once more on horseback, with friends, in another country, with a river to cross and maybe some trees to rest under.

I have no doubt that he has found those trees.

Illegal Cat House Raided in Jersey

TRENTON, N.J., February 30, 1984 (AP)—Agents of the Department of Agriculture's Bureau of Ass, Tiger and Felines (BATF), acting on uncollaborated information from anonymous informants, today arrested fourteen feline fanatics in a surprise raid on an illegal cat house in the rural Amwell area of New Jersey's Hunterdon County. The surprise attack at dawn, the first authorized by the so-called Federal "Fugitive Feline Law" recently passed by Congress and signed by President Billy Carter, was co-ordinated with some 187 local, state and Federal law enforcement personnel.

"While no actual contraband cats were found on the premises, we did impound almost eight ounces of cat nip and one 'Kutzy Kitty' rubber toy, amply demonstrating conspiracy to violate the Federal statutes covering clandestine cat activity," Merlin "Tex" Mavis, BATF Director, reported in the special press conference convened after the raid. Over seventy national and regional representatives of all media were present, including the major TV networks.

Also present were Ms. Cleva Aimless and Alex Hummingbird, co-directors of "Save our Asses" (SOA) the national organization credited with the passage of the new cat control legislation. Ms. Aimless pointed out the Federal legislation was needed because individual states, primarily in rural areas, had been recalcitrant in facing up to the national cat crisis and had been "derelict in their duty" to the citizens of other states in enacting and enforcing effective laws to curb cat movement across their state lines.

Background

"Save our Asses," now mainly concerned with illegal cat ownership at all levels of the American body politic, was first formed by Ms. Aimless and Mr. Hummingbird to combat the epidemic import of various species of the then endangered five species of Asiatic wild asses (Equus hemionus) that had been encouraged by preservationist groups in the late 1970's.

28

"Other groups, well-meaning perhaps, *but totally misguided* and *certainly ill-led*, mistakenly believed that the only way to save the Asiatic wild asses was to provide a new habitat in the United States, which has an environment unusually hospitable to the propagation of all kinds of asses," Ms. Aimless stated. "What they didn't realize was that these imported species would thrive too well and put serious pressure on our less hardy strain of native American asses, (Equus asinus americanus) especially in areas adjacent to Eastern urban centers, the most favored breeding grounds of our home-grown species."

Tiger Trouble

"Fortunately, that battle was won early in this decade," Mr. Hummingbird said, "and our native-born ass population was not only maintained, but indeed has increased. We then turned to the problem of the international status of the tiger, a subject close to the heart of every right-thinking American."

"It was our feeling that the position of the shooting lobby—namely, that the closing down of legal tiger hunting in India has contributed to the severe decline in tigers through lack of interest, anti-poaching patrol, and funding—was totally wrong, regardless of the facts presented by so-called scientific study," Mr. Hummingbird continued. "We therefore launched a campaign to *remove* the tiger from American consciousness, working on the theory that the less said about the animal, the better and the problem would go away."

"I must say we were most successful in our program," Ms. Aimless added. "We were able to *persuade* barber shops to stop using *Lucky Tiger* shampoo, drugstores to drop *Tiger Balm* and radio and television networks to ban the playing of 'Hold that Tiger.' After a series of high-level meetings with concerned alumni and faculty, strongly reinforced by spontaneous organized student demonstrations, we prevailed upon Princeton University to drop the tiger as its mascot."

"Yes, first they were known as the 'Princeton Pussycats'," Ms. Aimless said, "but when the true nature of the evils of catdom became fully known by an aroused American public, the name was finally changed to the 'Princeton Pussyfoots'."

When questioned as to the ultimate results of the tiger campaign, Mr. Hummingbird pointed out that it had been "eminently successful as the American public had completely forgotten about the tiger." Upon further query, Mr. Hummingbird also admitted that the problem had "indeed gone away too, because there were no longer any tigers left to concern one's self with."

Cat Campaign

"It was then we realized that our energies should be harnessed to attack the biggest problem of all—the exploding cat population in the United States," Ms. Aimless stated.

"For years we had believed that the blood-thirsty hunter was the major cause behind the decline in wildlife, but further study, inaugurated and monitored after the ban of most hunting in 1981, convinced us the *real* culprit was the domestic cat," Mr. Hummingbird said.

"This was our finest test; I might say, our finest hour," Ms. Aimless continued, "for it was now that we were finally able to muster our total effort and convince the Federal Government that *our* problems were *their* opportunity."

"Yes, in no time at all they saw the light and organized another Federal agency just to handle all of our left-over ass and tiger problems as well as the continuing battle against the misled feline fanatics, who persist in harboring outlaw cats."

"I'm pleased to report that there are now over 1,700 statutes governing not only cat, but *all* pet, ownership, transportation and sales transactions." Mr. Hummingbird produced a sheaf of papers measuring over a foot in height. "The Bureau of Ass, Tiger and Felines has over 4,000 agents divided between its seven-story Washington headquarters, six regional offices and 50 state co-ordinating sections, all with a budget of approximately $370,000,000.68."

"We feel this first BATF raid is a symbol of a new age for America. No longer must we be in thrall to pet owners. The first battle against cats has been won. Today cats, tomorrow dogs!", Ms. Aimless proclaimed.

There were no dog owners available for comment.

Nowhere to Go . . .
And Nothin' to Do . . .

I've got nowhere to go and nuthin' to do when I get there. It's March, that in-between time. The last near-by hunting season was over in February and Pennsylvania's turkey season isn't until May. I'm sitting here with a pile of guns I should have cleaned earlier, a bored bird dog and a wary wife. She knows I'm going into one of my "difficult periods." The kids are smart. They've disappeared, knowing full well that this is the time I sign up work parties for idle hands.

I don't even feel like reading any of the four dozen or so sporting catalogs accumulated over the winter. That's the trouble with March. It's too nice. It's not like January or February, when it's colder than any sane man wants to tolerate, the wind is whistling and the snow is flurrying. Then you're grateful for the fire and bemoan the circumstances that prevent you and faithful Old Blue from chasing the wily old grouse of Changewater Mountain. (Old Blue, by the way, is grateful too, being curled up like Cleopatra at your feet.)

You want to be outside *doing* something, anything, in March. The snows gone, the winds are drying out the ground, a few warm days give an occasional hint of the Spring to come and, pardon the expression, the sap at least feels like it's ready to run. It's no time to be indoors reading or just puttering—and it certainly isn't the time to be wandering aimlessly around outside, bouncing from noplace to nowhere.

I suppose I could be a birdwatcher or something, but I've never been much of a spectator. I've always been a participant sportsman. No watching TV football or baseball for me. If someone took me birdwatching, I'd probably get us into a lot of trouble. I'd want to shoot the rosybreasted sapsucker or something.

I suspect I'm not alone in this either. I've read a lot of other outdoor writers enraptured by the beauty of nature. I certainly can't fault either their sentiment or style, but I sometimes wonder if perhaps they don't dish up a rather self-serving and one-sided version of the picture they

31

see. Don't get me wrong, I take second place to no man in my love of outdoor beauty, but I just think that there is more to man's communing with nature than some of us want to admit. After all, man *is* a predator. Without becoming overly long-winded on the subject, let it suffice to say man is, has always been and always will be a hunter. Beauty perceived or not, that's how man sees nature—as a backdrop to his own life and pursuits.

Let me relate a story to back my point. Some years ago I was duck hunting with the late Gene Smith and that bard of the bayous, Grits Gresham, at Win Hawkins' Oak Grove Club in Louisiana. The Oak Grove is one of the finest traditional duck hunting clubs in the country and, under Mr. Win's serene supervision, things are done right. Early morning—like four a.m.—I was awakened, had quail on toast for breakfast (not all bad!) and was deposited in an airboat to be taken out to my blind. We whished through the narrow channels of the surrounding swamps, dropping off the various hunters with Cajun guides waiting in pirogues, which are long shallow-drafted wooden boats that were pushed through the reeds to blinds.

When it came my turn, I found a long lanky good ol' boy leaning on his pole like some sort of South Louisiana Ichabod Crane. After I managed to move my paraphernalia and creaking body into his pirogue with a minimum of clumsiness, we pushed off into the early mist as the sound of the retreating airboat gradually drifted away in the distance. In a few minutes we broke into a patch of open water of several hundred square feet in which a carefully constructed blind was perched on stilts. We tied up the pirogue, covered it with reeds and took our places, still silent, in the blind. My companion rearranged a few reeds in the front of the blind as all guides do to show how utterly helpless you would be without their expert eye and superior craftsmanship.

The first faint streaks of dawn were edging over the horizon, but it was still largely dark in the swamp. But it wasn't silent. The wings were starting to whistle past our heads, by our blinds, and occasionally we would hear a "plop" as one or another would drop into the open water about us. Then one would voice a tentative, sort of inquiring quack; another would plaintively quack-quack back; a more garrulous old-timer would vent his irritation with the younger set with a whole stream of indignant chortles, gurgles and quacks. The sun continued to fight its way through the Spanish moss, lush swamp grasses and reeds. Finally, some rays broke through to reflect over the face of

the pond surrounding us just as a flight of green-winged teal swept through out of nowhere and dropped in among our decoys.

"It's just plain beautiful. Fantastic. You know, I don't have to shoot a duck today and I'd be perfectly satisfied. It's something just to be here seeing this dawn in the swamp," I rhapsodized to my Cajun friend, who was thoughtfully picking his nose.

"Wal, I'm-a-tol you wan ting, Lil' brother," were his first words, "Ol' Jean Richard, me, take lotsa you dudes out here for shoot de duck and most of dem fellas speak to me jus lak you. Yeah, so trés bien. So trés belle. Be-yu-tee-fool. But I gonna tell you wan more ting. Come day after de duck saison over, ain't wan dude come down here wit ol' Jean Richard at fo' clock any morning!"

Well, that says it all. Being a spectator isn't enough. You've got to be a piece of the action to want to get up at four o'clock in the morning for anything. And, oh yes, that just brought something else to mind. I know what to do in March now. If I can't go hunting or fishing and don't feel like reading about it, then I guess I'll just have to call up some of the boys—Davy, Joe, Hilly, Harry or maybe even George in Washington—and talk about it. I always could kill more ducks over a telephone or, better yet, a refreshment, than I could leaning over a blind anyway. See you in April. Things are looking up.

Closing the Puppy Gap

It's time to close the puppy gap. We're down to two labradors, two setters and a Jack Russell (that's right) terrier. We don't count the 25 plus-or-minus foxhounds, because we are only part-owners and, besides, they are all down at Bill Read's anyway.

As for the Jack Russell terrier, well, that's my wife's personal body-guard, confidant, canine confessor, true-blue buddy and all-time companion, day or night. In fact, if the truth were admitted, I am convinced that Bobby has no doubts that Jan is his real mother. Worse, I half suspect that Jan subconsciously subscribes to the same belief.

Now a Jack Russell terrier, ounce for ounce, is probably the fiercest creature alive outside of a rogue bluegill. The breed—still jealously unregistered by its zealous small band of owners—was developed by the Reverend Jack Russell, a foxhunting parson of early Eighteenth Century England, who wanted a small terrier-type "hole-dog" that would go down holes to do battle with foxes who had gone to ground. Since the foxes usually outweighed the terrier about two to one, the Jack had to make up in sheer ferocity and courage what it lacked in weight. He does.

When the average person pets a Jack Russell, said dog—if in a good mood—emits a series of purr-like growls. If really benevolently disposed, Bobby will even offer a snarl or two. Those unacquainted with terrier talk take these noises as anti-social behavior, not realizing that these are happy sounds for the well-adjusted Jack Russell. Needless to say, the "Senior Terrier" views me with ill-disguised contempt and merely tolerates my presence as a gesture to Jan.

My labradors are hunting dogs or so it says in all the books. The youngest lab—named "Solo" because she was the only puppy in her litter—is without question one of the great retrievers of all time. A big female of 100 pounds or so, Solo looks like some sort of prehistoric black monster when she hits the water and bears down on a hapless duck. The only problem is that she has never really grown up, tho' she's now cracking five.

When she brings the duck back to shore or finds on land, she thinks it's all a grand game and it's my job to catch her rather than her bring-

ing the bird back to me. Don't tell me it's a lack of training: I've spent a small fortune with two of the best trainers around. One almost gave up dog training after a six-week session with Solo. We put an electric collar on her that would have galvanized an elephant and she thought she was being tickled. She's now known as that "advertisin' dawg" of the Rikhoffs. You know, put her down in one county and advertise for her in the next.

As for her mother, that lab is so dumb that, honest to gosh, when she had the one and only puppy of her life, she didn't know she was pregnant. My wife looked out the window one day and there she was straining as if constipated. Jan had to run and pull the puppy out. When the mother saw her puppy, she almost fainted dead away in astonishment. No wonder Solo has always been neurotic, what with a mother like that.

Bravely named "Simba Negra"—a hopefully, tho' improbable, hybrid mixture of Swahili and Latin meaning "Black Lion"—Solo's mother is generally considered to be worse than worthless, never having deigned to participate in anything resembling the field sports. This ten-year pensioner of the Maison Rikhoff spends a good deal of time lying around on the sofa watching *The Guiding Light* and such on daytime T.V. She also munches the occasional bon-bon, and I fear, reads *Movie Mirror* on the side. Simba is convinced she is a member of the family, an unusual anthropomorphic consideration amply encouraged by other members of the clan. Fat chance of ever getting rid of her.

In fact, she is, hands down, the dominant personage of the house. If there were any showdown between Simba and me, I know who'd have to hike it to the barn. The fact that she contributes absolutely zero to society has nothing to do with her past, present or future. It has long been apparent that we run the biggest social welfare program for animals in Hunterdon County. All a dog, cat or even horse has to do is stagger onto the property and he (she, it) is fixed for life.

Now, I've owned some good labs in my day. One, Chula, ended up with only three legs in her last years and became a small legend, scrambling over stone fences in the deep snow after grouse or plunging into the water for wounded ducks. Another, a chocolate lab from Bert Carlson's kennel out in Washington, came from a litter of nine that, I'm told, was the first in which *all* of the pups were liver-colored. When Mocha arrived, she looked like a warm Hershey bar. Unfortunately, she was killed by a car just as she started to come along in the hunting field.

I've had my best luck with my setters. Now, if you are all good and do as your mothers, fathers, wives, husbands, sons and daughters say, I'll tell you about them in some future time. That way maybe you won't think I'm totally incompetent in the dog handling area. Only nine-tenths. In the meantime, I think I had best put out some exploratory feelers for a new puppy. We're running a little low.

Setters That Have Owned Me

There are bird dogs and then there are English setters. I've always been lucky with my setters. Things were made plain right from the start. As soon as I accepted the fact that they owned me, we never had any trouble at all.

My first dog, "Jack," was a tri-colored setter of the big rangy type rarely seen in the field today. I was seven years and he was seven weeks old. It was, of course, love at first sight, back in Indianapolis in 1938. There have been a lot of dogs since—cocker spaniels, a chow (the only dog I ever hated), some great old hounds (both large and small), and a six-pack of Labradors—but somehow I guess I've always been a setter man.

"Bootlegger Belle" was the first honest-to-gosh hunting dog that I owned all by myself. All of my previous dogs had been "family," either half-owned with my sister or really my Dad's hunting companion. Belle was mine. I got her from Gene Hill about twenty years ago, after our first hunting trip.

Belle was the Marilyn Monroe of the dog world. The essence of femininity, she none-the-less was all business in the field. As any good bird dog should, she loved to hunt and, thanks be offered, she loved to hunt with me. (Well, most of the time.) She was a white setter, dappled with orange, what we would call an orange-belton today. There was a good deal of Ryman blood in her, so she was a good mixture of both Lavarack and Llewellyn strains.

I can't remember the number of fine days she gave me in the field, the birds pointed, the ones luckily brought to bag, the pleasure and zest for living she offered my friends. Then in one month, ten years ago, Belle went first of cancer; then my faithful old Lab, "Chula," with the carcinoma that had taken one of her legs previously; and lastly, to sort of really get my attention, my father lost his brave bout with the same disease the night of July fourth. It was not my favorite summer.

I didn't look for another setter for several years. I don't know why I held back on the breed; I went out and got two more Labs right away. I hunted those dogs, more-or-less, the next couple of years. I found I was hunting upland birds less and less. It took a while for me to admit it, but I simply missed walking over a point and I didn't get the same kick out of working behind someone else's dog. It just wasn't the same, so I didn't go.

Finally, one day I was visiting George Schielke at his fine gunsmith shop at Washington's Crossing and, knowing that all manner of pilgrim passed his way, casually mentioned that if, by chance, he should hear of a "made" bird dog, pointing persuasion, I was in the market. I didn't expect to hear from George, but one morning Gene Hill woke me up to tell me he had my dog at home. It seems he had visited George the day before and our friend had two dogs—a little setter and a scrawny pointer—that an itinerant Cherokee construction worker had left with him to sell.

Gene had taken to the little setter right away, carried it home and put it down in one of his back fields. As he reported with a bit of awe, the "little fella pointed seven pheasants in a half-hour!" Since this particular dog had just come up from North Carolina and had been quail-trained almost exclusively, we were both mightily impressed. I jumped into my car, headed for Gene's, picked up the little setter— again another orange and white—and drove to our Amwell shooting grounds. Malcolm Dunn put out a mixed batch of pheasant and quail. "Jimmy" (for coincidently, that was his name) moved off, tail and nose high, and in short order moved through that bird field like he had quartered it a dozen times. He went from bird to bird, handling each species as they came, like a little hunting machine. I bought the dog.

Jimmy is nine or ten now. We don't know exactly how old he was when we bought him, but we figure he had to be at least three to handle like he did. The Indian disappeared and we never got any papers, but the birds don't seem to know that Jimmy's unregistered. He handles pheasant, quail, chukar, woodcock and ruffed grouse with equal skill. He retrieves doves. He points ducks and retrieves them from land or water. More than anything else, he—to the rest of the family's disgust—worships me. He thinks I am just great. I think he is a dog of rare discerning taste!

In the last year or so, Jimmy has slowed up—maybe even a little more than his master. Arthritis has started to stiffen and occasionally lame his joints. I'm afraid that the milkiness slowly clouding his eyes are cataracts. He has a hard time finding me in heavy coverts. I'll see him straining his ears to find me, his eyes bewildered as he casts his head in frustration looking, but not seeing.

I guess Jimmy will one day join Belle, Chula, Mocha and even Jack. But this time I won't have to wait a couple of empty years before I walk into another point over a dog of my own. We've got young "Pat," Jimmy's son and marked just like him, coming on fine at age fifteen months. Pointing and retrieving, working with his father like some sort of younger brother, Pat doesn't have papers either, but somehow I figure he's got a hunting heritage that few champions can match.

On Wisconsin!

It's June and the mind turns back to summers spent many years ago in Wisconsin. Since my parents had split the blanket early in my toddling years, my sister and I always spent summers with my Dad. After the Second World War ended, he moved from Iowa to Madison, Wisconsin, where he entertained the fantasy of becoming a root beer tycoon. Part of that plan envisioned his son and heir learning the business, as they say, "from the bottom up" and his idea of bottom was quite low indeed. I finally graduated to the exalted status of "route salesman," which meant that I now drove a "Dad's Old Fashioned Root Beer" truck through the back country of lower Wisconsin, Eastern Iowa and a bit of Northern Illinois. It was an educational experience.

I soon found that being a "King of the Road" was a heck of a lot more fun than being at the mercy of the plant foreman eight hours a day in Madison. Contrary to popular myth, being the boss' son isn't always what it's cracked up to be. I loved the freedom of being on my own, responsible only to my own conscience, setting my own priorities and time schedule.

Those were the days before the Interstate highway system and a great deal of time was spent on secondary roads reaching towns like Black Earth, Sun Prairie, Richland Center and Fort Dodge. Of course, I had some big towns—like Janesville and Beloit—but mostly I hit the byways rather than the highways. My customers were located in country grocery stores (I. G. A. and the like), crossroads gas stations, neighborhood taverns and, the center of all teenage activity in those days, the local drive-in snack stand. In no time flat I fell madly in love with two Norwegian-American girls, one Switzer (German Swiss) miss and a black-haired, green-eyed Irish lass. I also was pleased to note that Wisconsin was a sportsman's paradise compared to Indiana.

Fishing was the major summer outdoor activity, but shooting wasn't completely eclipsed. I soon learned it paid to carry a rifle behind the seat in my cab. As soon as the first hay started to be "made," it was open season on woodchucks. As with farmers everywhere, the Wisconsin variety was not overly enamored of their groundhog population.

40

All it took was a courtesy call for permission and the occasional "Papa" size gallon jug of Dad's finest. Some pretty fine relationships were established and I often wished I could have stayed through the Fall for pheasant and rabbit hunting.

My favored firearm at that time was the newly introduced Winchester Model 43 in .218 Bee caliber. Prior to the Bee's introduction about the only commercial varmint loads were the old standby .22 Hornet and the awesome .220 Swift, both of which were chambered in the Winchester Model 70. Since the Model 70 was a bit rich for my blood, I was very interested when Winchester brought out the less expensive Model 43 early in 1949. I was to get three summers of chuck shooting with that gun and I really don't know how many varmints it accounted for, but let it be said that I didn't lack for shooting and the farmers seemed satisfied!

I probably would have been just as well off with an old Hornet, but the Bee was a little hotter. What I really wanted was a .220 Swift, but I was smart enough to know that the Swift's fearsome noise would win very few friends among the conservative farmers of southern Wisconsin. My Model 43 had a Lyman micrometer peep sight and a bead front. It wasn't the greatest sight combination in the world but it did the job up to about 125 or so yards, which was about the most distance involved.

As all good things must, my Wisconsin summer shooting ended in 1951. The next summer found my shooting activity upgraded courtesy of the United States Army. My father gave up on my following in his

41

footsteps, sold the business and, some years later, passed away. When I returned from the Army, I went back to college and have been East ever since 1957. When I was with Winchester for some sixteen years, I did a lot of traveling but for some strange reason I never set foot in Wisconsin. Until last year.

The Ruffed Grouse Society was holding its annual meeting in Minnesota in prime grouse and woodcock country. Suddenly one day I knew I was going to drive back for it. I would load my setter, Jimmy, and 20 gauge Model 21 in the station wagon and head West. In the back of my mind I was turning back the years.

I hit the outskirts of Madison about dusk the second day out. The city had grown so much that I could hardly find the root beer plant and Bee's tavern, the old stamping ground for the "Dad's" crew. I finally found S. Park Street and the plant. A false wall covering (yellow, I think) covered the outside. Bee's was still there, but had been "modernized." The shuffle board tables were gone and wood paneling covered the walls. It was a nice, sedate neighborhood bar. I hated it.

When I let Jimmy out for an early morning run before we set off for Minnesota, he wandered into a patch of swampy cover adjacent to our motel on the town's far outskirts, started to make game and, wonder of wonders, put up a pheasant. As Tom Wolf wrote years ago, "you can't go home again"—but you can at least make an effort. I'll try again some day—maybe during the hunting season I never had a chance to enjoy so long ago in another time.

II

NORTH AMERICAN JAUNTS

A Note on Part Two

As one might guess from the title, this section deals with North American hunts—both for small and large game.

The first two stories cover my first major big game trip out West some eighteen years ago. I spent about a month in Montana and it was one of the great times of my life. I was some younger and could climb mountains a lot better in those days! I was field-testing the new .264 Winchester Magnum in the Model 70 Westerner.

Luckily, I had spectacular hunting and ended up with several mule deer and antelope plus my first elk. I also met some fine people who were to become even better friends . . . Ralph Shipley and Bill Browning of Montana. And, of course, who could forget the late Larry Koller, who—along with Jack O'Connor, John Amber, Warren Page, Pete Kuhlhoff and Jack Knight—was to be my mentor during my fledgling years with Winchester.

You will also find a piece on New Jersey rail bird shooting that shows that (one) we still have some fine, unusual shooting in that state and (two) it helps to be a little crazy to do it. The other bird hunting story centers on how it *used* to be in Arizona (before the Corps of Engineers and the developers ruined all the habitat and nesting grounds) when a man went out for September dove hunting and took home 37 birds after a couple of hours in the morning. No more. The limit hangs around twenty now—ten each of mourning dove and whitewing—if you can find any of the latter to shoot. It never ceases to amaze me how man delights in fouling his own nest.

The last tale in this part relates the story of my son's first deer back when he was a pint-sized ten-year-old. He is now seventeen, his hands are about an inch longer than mine and he wears a size twelve shoe. I also treat him with considerably more respect than I used to.

Grand Slam in Big Game

The three of us lay, belly-down, on the near side of the ridgeline. I was forward, my cheek pressed to the Model 70's stock; my eye concentrated on the antelope slowly parading past my scope on the plain below. One by one, gently raising dust in the morning sun as they casually proceeded single-file up a small incline, the antelope herd passed by until the biggest buck came into my 'scope's field. They were about 250 yards away.

"Is that the one?" I whispered. "The second buck?"

"Yeah, I think so," Ralph Shipley lowered his glass. "He's—let's see —one, two, three—fourth from the rear."

"I can't get them all in my 'scope, but I think I'm on him. How big do you think he runs? Is he bigger than the one we glassed last night?"

"Well, I dunno—let me take another look. No, I think he might even run a little smaller. Maybe 12 to 12½ inches. Do you want him?" Ralph queried.

My finger was on the trigger; my thumb rested on the safety. I took a long breath, then slowly—and, admittedly, a little unevenly—released it. My finger was stiff as I slowly relaxed and uncurled it from the trigger. It really didn't want to quit before it had finished the job. I had already missed one excellent antelope. It had been the first day and our stalk brought us only about 600 yards from our chosen buck— a magnificent head with 15-inch horns or so—as dusk fell. A strong wind had arisen and I misjudged the drift of my .264 Magnum's 140-grain bullet. It was a sad moment for Ralph, who had put me onto his ranch's prime antelope.

For me—on my first Montana antelope hunt—it was sadder still. Later, we had glassed a great many more antelope—and had even made three stalks. But, infatuated by the first day's big buck, we had turned them all down.

"No," I slowly exhaled, "I guess I'll give him a free ride this time. Let's move out." Crawling backwards, I managed to pick up a small collection of cactus spines in a number of delicate areas best left unmentioned. This did not improve my general morale.

Along with Larry Koller—the other member of the hunting party described above—I had arrived at Miles City the previous Monday. Larry had hunted with Ralph Shipley before and he had warned me that no man loved hunting more, or knew more about antelope and mule deer in this part of the county.

"Are you here to drink and hell around, or hunt?" were practically Ship's first words. His eyes loomed balefully out from under the brim of his Stetson as he awaited my answer.

"Hunt," said I, attempting to match his stare. My little Tyrolean sports hat was no match for his Stetson, however, and I lost the exchange.

"Okay, let's get on with it then. You guys follow with Bill Browning over there in his station wagon and I'll lead the way to the ranch in my Power-Wagon." He hitched up his pants and was halfway to the truck before we could answer.

Ship's Teepee Ranch is some 20 miles south of Miles City. It runs about 20,000 acres, but he has hunting rights with a number of his neighbors so that he actually ranges over many thousands of additional acres during hunting season. Since the Tongue River runs through his land, there is ample water—supplemented with strategic reservoirs—for a good head of game. Mule and whitetail deer, beavers and other water animals, antelope, sage hens, grouse and pheasant—and, of course, predators like bobcats and coyotes—abound. Not satisfied with this, Ship has imported five buffalos for future release in special naturally enclosed areas. Few remember, but the last great buffalo herd was slaughtered a few miles from the Teepee Ranch in the 1880's. It's traditional buffalo country and Ship reasons that it could be again with proper management and protection. He and his son, Robbie, can provide both on the Teepee Ranch. God help any man who would poach one of his buffalos.

Our antelope hunt started practically the minute we arrived at Ralph's ranch. A few minutes were begrudged by the ranch's owner for changing clothes and grabbing a fast bite of lunch and then we all climbed into the Power-Wagon. Ship figured we had just enough time to squeeze in an antelope reconnoiter before the mule deer began to sally forth for their evening promenade and dinner.

We patroled the ranch for about a half hour before the Power-Wagon lurched to a halt and Ship clambered from the cab with his binocular. He concentrated on a far-away patch of white specks for a moment or two and then motioned for the spotting 'scope. A few min-

47

utes of fiddling for proper range adjustment, a second or two of intense observation, and with a grunt of satisfaction he turned to me and indicated that I should take a look at his find. One look was enough: there was a prime antelope buck gently taking its leisure a mile or so in the distance.

He was accompanied by about a dozen does and lesser bucks. Ship looked at me quizzically, pointed to my rifle and jerked a thumb in the general direction of the antelope herd. We were off on our first stalk approximately 40 minutes from the moment we left the ranch house.

I followed Ship through a patchwork of coulees and dry washes toward the concealment of a butte situated on our right, three quarters of the way to the antelope. We moved swiftly, steadily and silently. Many times the top of the dry wash's banks were over our head. As we approached the butte, Ship whispered that we might get a shot from it if our luck held out. It didn't.

We were making slow, careful progress around the side of the butte when Ship suddenly froze ahead of me. Barely moving his head, he motioned to the valley below. We were "rimrocked." The antelope— equally concealed to us as we had been to them during our approach —had moved down valley as they fed. Luckily they had not seen us yet, but we didn't dare move. We stood out on the side of the butte like the proverbial set of sore thumbs. The big buck was obscured by brush. We sat there for about 20 minutes before Ship muttered that we had one chance: we could play "cow." The antelope were used to seeing cattle. One more cow—or what appeared to be a cow—wouldn't matter, if we could put on a convincing act. Ship started down the side of the hill. I followed him with my rifle across his half-bent back and my one hand on his waist. As the rear-end—a role some have remarked I was admirably suited for—I hunched over and trotted along in my best cow-fashion.

Believe it or not, it worked. At first the antelope hesitated as the "cow" came strolling across their line of vision, but somehow we filled the bill and they returned to their food gathering. We soon came to a concealing wash and, dropping from sight, were able to resume normal posture and gait. We ran along for a hundred feet or so and then pulled ourselves up for a fast shot. They were gone.

They had not spooked, however, but had merely meandered over a ridge. We caught sight of the last few as they slid quietly over the ridge-line. We ran up the hill with as much speed as we could muster at this stage of the game and, dropping to our stomachs, eased up to the horizon-line. The antelope were out of sight once more, having dropped into a small ravine leading down to the plain below. When they appeared again, they were about 600 yards away. Dusk was fast falling. There was no time for another stalk; we had to take our chances now. We noticed that the wind—gentle in its stealth—had quietly stirred and was now steadily pushing across our faces.

I got into position and placed my scope on the herd as they wandered up from the creek bed and on up the plain. They halted some 600 to 700 yards away and, after milling around a bit, began to graze once more. Trying to judge the wind as best I could—it was gusty and gave no sustained sense of velocity, I lined up the big antelope—allowed for windage—and touched the rifle off. The crack of the magnum made a muffled snap in the wind and, simultaneously, the big buck jumped in the air. The other antelope peeled off around him like petals of a spreading flower. Dust kicked up behind his tail as he left the country. As mentioned earlier, horns well in the record class. We never saw him—or his like—again on that hunt. Slowly, we got up. Silently, we returned to the truck. It was dark now and we started back for the ranch. The hunting was over for that day.

The next morning—and the next four—we were off again. We saw literally hundreds of antelope and mule deer. The other members of our party—Larry, Bill Browning and Ship's son, Robbie—filled out their antelope permits plus a few deer tags for good measure. I held off, still waiting for an antelope to measure up to the first one. As mentioned earlier, we made a few stalks, but on careful evaluation, decided against taking the animals concerned.

On the morning of the sixth day we spotted about 65 antelope moving around in two or three different bunches, but there were no bucks to satisfy our high standards. After driving around for an hour or two more. Ship suddenly stopped the Power-Wagon and spent a few minutes studying the side of a small hill about half a mile away. There was a solitary antelope buck bedded down on the hillside. The spotting scope showed him to be a good head—the best since the first day. We decided to try and get him for me.

We made our stalk on the opposite side of the hill from the antelope's bed. We used the coulees and dry washes as cover for our approach. Moving swiftly—as our cover permitted—we were able to cover the first three-quarters of our sneak in 10 or 15 minutes. Our main worry was the wind: typically, it was constantly switching on us—and changing in intensity. I could not forget what the wind had done on that first antelope. Our second concern was the very distinct possibility of spooking other antelope that might be bedded down in the general area. If we inadvertently bounced an unknown midmorning sleeper out of his bed, we would spook every other animal in the vicinity.

We slowly made our way up the hill. Cautiously we inched our way to the crest and—removing our hats first—eased our vision over the rim to survey the other side of the hill. There was nothing there!

"Well, I'll be da—" I started to say. Ship gripped my arm and motioned for quiet.

"There he is!" he whispered. I didn't see anything.

"Underneath us! Look, down there! Shoot, dammit."

I dropped my eyes and still didn't see anything. Then I lowered them to the immediate area in front of us. There was the antelope—a scant 75 yards from where we were standing—with its head cocked on alert, tense and expectant before it leaped to its feet in alarm. It jumped up as I made a fast offhand shot. It was a miss. I missed another offhand running shot, firing too quickly after my first miss. I ran to the other side of the hilltop as Ship yelled encouragement and advice. The antelope was circling the hill below the crest line and was beginning to put an increasing amount of territory between its hide and the hunters on the hill. I dropped to a prone position and lined him up in my sights as he ran along a fence. I squeezed the trigger and he dropped in almost the same instant.

"Why didn't you do that the first shot? Now look how far we're going to have to carry that blame 'annalope.' Here's a souvenir," and Ship handed me the brass from my last shot. A big grin slashed the bronzed tan of his face. If there was one thing Ship liked better than bagging game himself, it was the pleasure of seeing his guests connect.

We paced off the distance from where I took my last shot to where the antelope lay. It was 248 yards. The antelope had been hit through the shoulders and the 140-grain .264 Magnum slug had done its job before the animal had hit the ground. When we measured its horns, we found each outside curve ran 13½ inches and found it totaled 72 4/8 points according to Boone & Crockett qualifications—just 2 4/8 out of the records. While it couldn't match the trophy antelope I missed the first day, it was a good representative head and I was—and am—quite pleased with it.

The next week was spent covering various game areas in Montana. We visited the Roundup territory in Musselshell County for two days and Bill Browning took a nice mule deer buck. Later we moved into Cascade County south of Great Falls.

On the morning of the second day in Cascade, we piled into the Power-Wagon and headed for the hill and range country outside of town. A 40-minute ride brought us within the fences of the Sieben Livestock Company's large ranch. Each year a certain number of hunters—both resident and nonresident—are allowed to hunt in specified areas throughout the local season until a predetermined number of deer are harvested. The deer herd is kept in reasonable balance; the lucky hunters get a chance at some excellent deer hunting. A passing check of a number of parked cars at ranch headquarters showed seven states represented. Not bad for one hunk of deer property—even if the property in question does run into the tens of thousands of acres.

We hunted throughout the morning by covering the ranch roads leading back into the reefs and valleys of the high country surrounding the ranch. When we would come upon a likely area, we would dismount and glass the countryside for deer. There were no lack of does and smallish bucks, but we were looking for the best we could expect to find in the few days we had left. About midmorning we spotted a fairsized herd of 15 or 20 deer on a hillside. Ship and I crawled up on the side of a twin ridge and glassed them. They were

now below us—with a small valley dipping between our two ridges. It didn't appear that we would be able to get any closer. A terrific wind whipped across us from right to left. The deer were bunched up in two clusters about 650 yards away. There was a fair-sized buck in one group. We decided to take a shot since I had not taken a deer yet. It was a clean miss.

The deer milled around for a second or two. The confusion of their behavior obscured the buck and another shot was impossible. Finally, one more courageous—or perhaps ignorant—than the others broke from the herd and took off down the side of the hill and into the dip that led to the valley road below. The rest followed. For an instant or two the buck was left in the open. Another hasty shot. Another miss. A group of does again closed about the buck as they all moved down the valley. It almost seemed as if they were protecting him. The lead deer were crossing the road now, the adventurous doe in the lead. They started up another hill and soon began to drop over the ridgeline across from us. The buck was now well out of range—some 800 or 900 yards. We watched them until the last dancing tail dropped over the horizon. We walked back to the truck.

After lunch we decided to make a drive across the face of a long, sweeping ridge bordering one side of our section of the ranch. There was a vast expanse of trees—pines, firs and other conifers, mostly—across the top third of the ridge, and we had spotted a couple of bucks bedded down in these woods. Undoubtedly there were many more invisible to both our naked eye and our binoculars. We drove up as far as the truck would go. It went places I thought no vehicle—outside of a helicopter—could possibly navigate. When we finally lurched to a halt, it seemed as if we were on a 45° angle with the world.

The ground had been relatively barren of trees the first two-thirds of the way up. It was, after all, really pasture land and was used as such by both cattle and deer. We came to a halt just below the wooded top third. Two members of our party had been left below to make their way up a ravine to the top of the same reef, only about a mile further to the left. They would drive toward our stands. Since they were going straight up and were good climbers—and we had to proceed at an angle with the truck, we did not have to wait long until our rendezvous time. We moved up the ridge, dropping Larry Koller just below the trees so that he could command a good shot at anything breaking out of the woods. Ship took a place in the center of the woods.

I decided to make for the top of the ridge. There was a clearing just under the ridgeline and it looked like a good spot for deer to cross over the ridge to the other side. Bill Browning followed me. Since he had taken both of his deer, he carried his camera.

There were no paths and a good deal of snow covered the ground. Blowdowns and thickets made the going difficult. I trudged on, pausing now and again for breath, bearings and a worried glance at my watch. My companions should be beginning their drive at any minute. I kept on until I came to the edge of the small clearing near the top. It was about 175 yards long and about half again as wide—with the width largely dissipated by the sharp elevation of the ground as it crested at the summit. Just as I approached the last clump of trees before the clearing, I caught sight of a buck rigid as a statue a few feet below the top. Poised for retreat, he had obviously crept out ahead of the drivers and made his way to this escape pass. I raised my rifle, but my sights were obscured by branches. Frustrated, I dropped down but found I was still blocked. Behind me Bill tried to get in position for a picture. Finally, stumped by the trees, I took a chance and made a dash to the clearing and threw myself down for a shot. All I succeeded in doing was to fill the end of my scope with snow. Bill said the buck was over the ridge before I hit ground.

"If there's one thing I've learned about hunting Montana muleys, it's that you can't outrun them," Bill sadly commented as he surveyed my prone shape, two-thirds sunk in a snow bank. He helped me up and I cleaned the snow out of my scope. We could hear one of the drivers coming through the brush. He was shouting, but we couldn't make out his words. If any deer were in front of him, they would be breaking out any second. On the edge of the woods we took a stand that commanded an open field of fire for anything leaving the timber on the other side of the clearing. We heard a slight rustle and a fat three-point buck trotted out of the woods and stopped for a second in the middle of clearing with ears alerted. Eating meat! I dropped him with one shot through the shoulders.

"Boy, he dropped like a ton of bricks—how come you took him? We've turned down better heads," Bill said.

"Maybe better heads, but not fatter. Did you see the gut on that boy?" I replied with gluttonish appreciation. "You don't eat the antlers, you know. I'll save my other permit for a rack. I can just see the steaks and chops I'll get off that one."

I got up and we paced off 125 yards to the buck. As Bill continued to take pictures, I got prepared for the dirty work.

"Heads up!" someone to our right shouted. It must be one of the drivers. "Two bucks are coming out! They're right in front of me. I just turned them with a couple of shots," the voice continued. We could hear crashing through the woods somewhere below and to the right of us. We were caught in the middle of the clearing. I dropped my knife and picked up my rifle. A rustle of leaves, muffled hoof beats, and a buck wheeled around a tree below us and slid to a frightened halt as we loomed into view. He was a big four-pointer. I dropped to one knee as another four-pointer, twin to the first ground to a standstill behind the first. I fired and the first buck dropped. The other buck disappeared into the trees. Stunned, I sat by my first deer and stared at my second buck a scant 40 yards away. My Montana deer hunting was over for this season. I had filled out both of my tags in a little less than seven minutes. I had my meat and my rack. I emptied my rifle and picked up my knife. We had a full afternoon's work ahead of us. Twelve days later I took an elk in the Bob Marshall Wilderness area above Ovando (but thats another story) and clipped the last tag from my nonresident $100 license. I had a grand slam—one antelope, two mule deer and an elk.

Taking Your Chances in the High Country

Near the end of the third day, Wendell Copenhaver and I sat on the top of "Whiskey Ridge" and surveyed the country below and across from us. We were about five miles from our camp, on the Dry Fork of the North Fork of the Blackfoot River in the Lolo National Forest of Montana's Rockies. Our horses were down trail two miles by the base of the ridge. It had been a long climb to the top, through snow drifted—in some places—five or more feet, but the "Ridge" had almost always produced elk in the past. It was fabled in local lore: hard to climb, but worth it since a perservering hunter was very likely to get a shot at a decent bull.

The season before, Wendell related, two hunters had each collected a six-pointer on the ridge on their first day out of camp. This was a different year and this hunter had a different sort of luck. Three days out and we had yet to see an elk—or even get close to one.

But this was elk hunting. Hunter success on elk is very low compared to other members of the deer family. Only about 22 per cent of Montana's hunters bag an elk and they have one of the best herds and success ratios in the country. Deer, moose and caribou hunters generally do much better throughout the continent. Men hunt elk for years without ever connecting. While a good bull is certainly the most desirable bag from a trophy point of view, the vast majority of hunters will settle for anything—if they only get that chance.

There was no disgrace, I found, in taking a cow or even a good calf. In fact, local residents—who were more concerned with four or five hundred (or more) pounds of good meat rather than their pride, preferred to take a dry cow above all others. As they said, "You don't eat the antlers, you know!"

I wanted a bull, however, as it was my first elk hunt and I was primarily concerned with taking a trophy. I had spent two weeks in Montana prior to embarking on my pack trip for elk with the Copenhaver Brothers. During that period, I had hunted—quite literally—from one end of the state to another. I had filled out most of my special non-resident big game license and had taken an excellent buck ante-

55

lope and two good mule deer bucks. I had put frosting on the cake by taking part in some excellent Hungarian partridge shooting. It was now time to top the trip off with the best trophy of all—a good elk.

My appetite had been whetted by the sight of five bull elk during a mule deer hunt near Cascade, Montana. Ralph Shipley, who owns the Teepee ranch near Miles City in the eastern part of the state, had just killed an excellent mule deer buck with a long shot from his .44 Magnum Ruger. We had brought up his Dodge Power truck to load it when he looked up and across the valley to the opposing ridge. There rimrocked on the side of the hill were five bull elk making for a patch of timber above and to the right. A fine six-pointer led the way; a pair of scraggly antlered bulls and two spikes followed in single file.

They had been moving at a steady pace from the bottom of the valley and the big boy had laid his fine set of antlers back across his shoulders as his tongue protruded from the exertion of his climb. Ralph knew I had never seen elk before and that I had my license with me. They were fair game—and beautiful fair game at that. "You'll never get a chance at a better trophy," he quietly said. The bulls glistened with an orange-tinged glow in the late morning sun. "No," I slowly replied, "my money's down with the Copenhavers and I'm scheduled for a ten-day pack trip next Tuesday. If I take this one now, my trip will be over—it isn't worth it." Whether or not this was a wise decision remained to be seen. In fact, it is still an undecided question in some minds—including my own.

A week later found me on the top of Whiskey Ridge after three days of hard hunting. Spoiled by the comparatively easy antelope and mule deer hunting Montana offers, I was somewhat discouraged by the relative scarcity of game. We had seen some 2,000 head of big game—antelope and deer—in the ten days of hunting prior to my pack trip; we had not seen one single head in these first three days since we had packed in to the Dry Fork.

It was a different country; high, barren yet bountiful, cold, windswept and often rainy. Ours was the Copenhavers' last pack trip and the November weather was often nasty—filled with snow, rain, sleet and, it sometimes seemed, a mixture of all three compounded by a biting wind. The trout streams meandering through the mountain valley meadows had long since frozen over for the most part and we were forced to cut through a layer of ice for our camp water. Other hygenic necessities were even less pleasant, but could hardly be

avoided. It was indeed a different brand of hunting than we had encountered previously.

The day spent packing in from the Copenhavers' ranch outside
Ovando was a beautiful one, however; a bit of snow clung to the lowlands, while the high lands were fairly well covered with old drifts
crusted over with a hard, noise-producing surface layer. The sun was
out and the wind down, so our seven-hour trip over the pass and into
the Dry Fork valley camp was a pleasant enough journey. That night
produced a different variety of weather, however, and—as a consequence—a decision I had not planned on.

I had brought two rifles to Montana: a new Winchester Model 70
Westerner in .264 Win. Magnum and, as a reserve for my elk hunt, a
Model 70 Alaskan in .338 Win. Magnum. I knew what the .338 Magnum would do; I had killed two moose with it in the past. But I was
excited by the new .264 Magnum, and had used it exclusively on the
first part of my Montana hunt. It was scoped with a 4X Lyman and
sighted in for 200 yards.

I had done a lot of shooting with the scope sights and made some
rather decent shots for my antelope and mule deer with that set-up.
The iron sights were sighted in for 100 yards, but I had not had an
opportunity to shoot over them since the gun had been delivered to me
but a few days prior to my departure. I had been told that a good
many elk shots—in fact, the vast majority—were over a hundred yards,
with many extending to two or three hundred. A scope was a definite
advantage for such shooting, but the weather made this sort of sighting
highly impractical.

In the first place, the visibility was extremely poor (it was snowing
steadily). Secondly, it appeared we would have to try to still-hunt our
elk as the bugling season was long since over. This meant we would be
tracking through all sorts of cover, blowdowns, forests, mountain bogs
and other similar unpleasant country. No place for a scope. It would
become fogged or, worse, its ends clogged with snow.

Besides, Wendell pointed out, our shots would probably be considerably under one hundred yards on this hunt because of conditions
—if we were lucky to get any shots. Off came the scope.

I would use my regular iron sights—a large buckhorn rear and out-
size front post that Judson Darrow, the Connecticut gunsmith, had
installed. I decided to use the .264 Magnum since I wanted to take
all of my game with it on this trip. I was curious to compare the performance of the 140-grain Power Point bullet on species as widely

varied as antelope, mule deer and elk. I knew what it would do (and it was favorable) on the first two animals.

The first day out was a miserable one. Wendell Copenhaver and I crossed over the ridge bordering our valley into another bottom land. The rest of our party with Larry Fite, the other guide, went down toward the Danaher part of the Bob Marshall Wilderness Area some nine miles or so farther in the Flathead National Forest adjoining the Lolo. Wendell and I left the horses after four or five miles and proceeded on foot. We hunted the bottom blowdown-bog country between the valley's ridges. There were many tracks, but none were fresh enough to stimulate much excitement.

After following tracks—with the hope of perhaps jumping an elk in its bed—for a few hours, we came to the conclusion we were getting nowhere fast and started back toward the horses. When we came to a wide clearing a few hundred yards from our horses, we found a new set of elk tracks, from appearance a cow with calf. They cut directly across our older tracks leading into the bogs.

Obviously, the elk must have sat up on the ridge watching our progress with great amusement and, when we were out of sight, they had calmly trotted down and across the meadow to the opposite ridge. We took off after them and followed their tracks practically to the top of the ridge. Unfortunately, they were running and appeared to continue over the ridge into another valley complex.

Wet and tired, we gave up and trudged back down the ridge after two more hours of climbing. It was almost four p.m. and the sun was beginning to fade, so we headed back to the horses and then to camp. It was an educational day for everyone concerned; the other party had equalled our luck.

The next day the whole party took off for the Danaher area. The Danahers were an old ranching family that had homesteaded the mountain meadows of that country before the government had turned it into the Bob Marshall Wilderness Area. It had been a good ranch on fertile range, but along came the First World War and after that the Spanish Influenza epidemic, that swept the world.

In those days (and even now) people didn't travel the passes after mid-November until spring. When the first party went into the Danaher in the Spring of 1919, they found the Spanish flu had left two people out of 17. That was the end of the Danaher ranch; soon it became part of the Bob Marshall Wilderness Area, forever closed to

58

homesteading or, for that matter, any man-made permanent structure. It remains a monument to wilderness—its beauty and its harsh code of living and dying.

We left Louie Lineaweaver (one of the other hunters) and Larry Fite at an old camp site while Louie's son, Chuck, went with Wendell and myself up and around a surrounding ridge. Our plan, after reaching the top of the ridge, was to separate and drive whatever game there was down toward the valley and the two hunters stationed there. All our efforts produced was a fleeting glimpse of one cow elk for Louie and Larry. They didn't have enough time for a shot before the elk was lost again in the brush. Another two hour ride took us back to our main camp on the Dry Fork. It rained all night; sleeted the next morning.

Wendell and I had chosen the "Whiskey Ridge" hunt on the third day while Larry and Chuck returned to the general area around the Danaher. The higher we went on Whiskey Ridge, the more powdery —and, hence, silent—the snow became. We were in good spirits and filled with anticipation because we had seen one fresh set of bull tracks—and, later, droppings and urine—as we came in to the Whiskey Ridge area. We had followed that set of tracks, but had been unable to run that particular bull elk down. It was the only sign we saw. For some unfathomable reason, the top of the ridge was barren of tracks, where usually there were many.

Wendell and I sat on the ridge's top and silently munched our sandwiches. The country lay around us in quiet, magnificent splendor. Its vastness commanded respect and admiration, but nothing—at least to our sight and hearing—moved except the wind and an occasional creaking pine or scolding bird. Silence and solitude.

We separated on our way down. Wendell indicated a pattern for me to follow as part of a drive downward. He would work down and across and perhaps scare something over towards my path. It was a pleasant trip down. The sleet and wind had long since drifted away, but there was no sign of game. I cut Wendell's trail and soon saw him and our horses ahead of me on the trail. Discouraged—but undaunted as they say, we returned to camp. We found Larry and Chuck had moved some elk in the timber, but had been unable to get a shot.

The fourth day Louie Lineaweaver had to return to Ovando. We said goodbye and he mounted up for the long 18-mile trip back to the Copenhaver ranch. Chuck, Larry, Wendell and I headed for the Danaher. The only game that had been sighted had been in that region and we figured that this was certainly better than the blank we had drawn in other directions. For a change, Larry paired off with me while Wendell guided Chuck. We took one creek area and Chuck and Wendell took another on the opposite side of the valley. It seemed that our luck wouldn't be affected by the transfer in guides as Larry and I failed to come across a single fresh track during the morning.

Later—about 1:30 p.m.—as we rested after lunch, we heard a single shot bounce across the valley. Larry turned to me and said, "Well, there's only one shot—I bet that's it for Chuck; Wendell's got him an elk. Let's see what I can do for you now." I allowed as how this would

60

be all right with me and we got ourselves together for our afternoon hunt.

Spurred on by Chuck's single shot, we worked hard the rest of the afternoon. We criss-crossed back and forth across the small valley that housed our creek; we traversed trail and path on either ridge; we glassed country behind, in front and beside us. We didn't see a movement; we couldn't find a fresh track. When we got back to camp it had been dark for two hours and the boys were almost finished with supper. Wendell had almost begun to worry about us. Our luck had begun to change: a bull calf elk had stood up about 50 yards in front of Chuck and he had dropped him with one shot. For the first time since we had "packed-in" five days before there was fresh meat in camp.

The next day—the fifth hunting day—Wendell and Chuck took a string of pack mules back to the site of their kill to bring out the carcass after they quartered it. Larry and I headed back up to the Danaher. About three-fourths of the way we cut across fresh elk tracks from the valley meadow below up to the ridge bordering the trail. We tethered the horses and followed the tracks up the side of the hill. They were fresh and Larry silently indicated—after a five-minute walk—that we should begin to move cautiously. They might be bedded down anywhere ahead after we topped the first rise on the side of the ridge.

They looked to be a small herd of cows with calves. Suddenly Larry stopped. He motioned me to freeze. Too late. I caught a fast glimpse of swift movement and a rustling of brush several yards above us. Larry sighed and said, "Well, that ties it. They had a sentinel placed in that small hollow up there. Well, they're long gone now." We climbed up to where they had been bedded down. Five hollowed indentations in the snow indicated where they had been lying down, quietly digesting their breakfast. Unhappily we trudged back down to the horses and mounted up.

We proceeded down the trail, past the remains—a few leaning fence rails and a piece or two of rusted machinery—of the old Danaher ranch. You could barely make out where the building—long since torn down by the government—had once stood. We kept to the main trail through the wide meadows of the valley as it jutted between opposing ridge lines. Soon the meadow spread out until it was a mile or so wide. We followed the trail as it bisected the middle. Presently I noticed a fresh set of tracks cutting the trail ahead of us. Larry stopped and, after carefully examining them, stated they were a bull's and they were fresh enough to follow. We followed the tracks by horse until they started to head through some thicket into a spread of bogs before rising up the side of ridge. We left the horses and went on by foot.

We made a long stalk through the bogs, over a small rise, down a creek bed, up another rise and continued to climb as we started up a ridge, steep and heavily wooded with both trees and thickets—a veritable jungle as it turned out. We simply couldn't proceed with any speed and not make noise, but we tried. Snow dropped down our necks as low-hanging branches were swept clear of their white burden as we pushed upward. Once again I realized the futility of carrying a scoped rifle through such cover and thanked providence that I had taken my scope off.

Finally, we came upon droppings and urine. He wouldn't be far ahead. And then we came upon a small knoll and there was his bed—still stinking with the smell of him, but he himself long vanished. We looked up from his bed at the path his tracks took. They went right over the top of the ridge a few hundred feet above us. He had heard us coming thirty or so minutes before and had simply taken his time to retreat. He was long beyond our reach now.

Larry and I stopped for a cigarette. This didn't seem to be our day, but he suggested we work our way back to the horses in a round-about fashion from the direction we had trailed our long-lost bull. That way we would have a chance to either cut his trail if he circled back (small chance!) or find new tracks if other elk were moving in the area.

We moved on for fifteen or so minutes and, as luck would have it, came upon fresh tracks of a small herd of cow elk, perhaps four in number and, strangely, without calf. We followed their tracks carefully and quietly. They must have known we were on them for they would never settle down to bed. It was evident from their tracks that they were milling about ready to bed, and once we came across a place where one had actually lay down for a moment or two, but they were skittish and kept on. Casually feeding, never running, occasionally urinating or dropping excrement—all the preparations to bedding down.

After two hours of steady pursuit, Larry called a halt. "I don't think those ladies are ever going to settle down this afternoon," he complained, "and, I hate to say it after all this, but it's going to get dark pretty soon. We had best head back to the horses and get on our way back to camp before Wendell sends a posse out looking for us." We headed down the side of the hill without regard to noise or commotion, kicking snow and sliding as we went.

We walked back until we found our old tracks leading in for our stalk on the bull we had spooked from his bed. Soon, tired and discouraged, we were once again trudging across a small meadow sandwiched between a horseshoe series of three ridges. It was about 5:15 p.m. and the sun was in its final stages. We were about half-way across the open meadow when Larry looked up and whispered, "Hold it! Look! There, down at the end of the meadow. Three cows! They're just now trotting out into the field from that patch of woods. No. More to the right, Yeah, right there. See them." The last few phrases were in answer to my excited questions. We were frozen. They were about 500 yards away.

Without caution, they trotted onward—and toward the two frozen figures caught dead center in the middle of the meadow. What a spot for a telescopic sight! And here I was caught with iron sights that I had never fired over. A perfect clear-distance shot. No obstructions and just enough light left to gather in a scope. We waited. The moments seemed endless as the elk still trotted forward. Finally they began to hesitate, then nervously mill about before finally halting, heads lifted in the air.

"The wind is blowing up from the creek bed where we just came from and they smell us," Larry murmured, "We better get ready to take them. You take the big one on the left and I'll take the one on the right. The one in the center gets a free ride. O.K.? You still aren't waiting for a bull are you?"

"Not this trip," I replied, "All I want right now is that great big beautiful cow elk in front of me."

"They're going to take off any minute. When I give the word, throw yourself down and take your time on a good prone shot," he continued, "Now!—and fire when you're ready." They were about 200 yards away.

We dropped and I lined up the big elk on the left in my iron buckhorn sight. The front post pinpointed her shoulder and I touched off the .264 Magnum, automatically throwing the bolt back after the shot and thrusting another shell in the chamber. The elk staggered and turned, heading aimlessly back toward the end of the meadow. Larry's .308 Winchester Model 88 barked beside me and his elk's hindquarters spun a quarter turn. The unscathed member of the trio was in the lead now. They didn't know what had happened or from where (they still hadn't really seen us or gotten the full strength of our scent), but they knew things would be better somewhere removed from the immediate vicinity.

They took off—the wounded elk doing amazingly well (a testimony to that animals innate vitality)—at a brisk trot for the rear of the meadow. We both fired again, seemingly with no effect. Then it seemed—on his third or fourth shot—that Larry hit the elk (I had originally hit) with a shot through her hindquarters. It was the only part she was presenting. She went down in a fast crumble, indicating a fatal hit either through the spine or, perhaps as it passed through, the heart.

Meanwhile, I was on my last shell. The sound elk had broken from the meadow and was entering the bordering timber. The other elk, wounded in the rear left leg by Larry's first shot, was right behind her. If she got in the timber, we faced a long stalk—and, perhaps, an impossible one since darkness was rapidly approaching. I held a foot over her back as she half-turned momentarily to check her fallen companion before ducking into the concealing thicket. I pulled the trigger; she took three steps, staggered and fell.

Larry and I got up and paced it off his elk. It was 375 paces to the spot where she dropped. We walked on to where the other elk lay. It was exactly 410 paces. She had been hit diagonally from the rear of the rib cage forward through the lungs and heart. I turned to Larry and exclaimed, "I sure could have used a scope on that last one." He grinned and rejoined, "Well, you have to take your chances in the high country. You got your elk, didn't you?"

Crazy Sport for a Sporty Bird

"Well, don't just stand there, get me out!"

The good doctor's voice was a mixture of mournful reproach and desperate entreaty. He was waist-deep in muck with no foreseeable escape. One would think he had not received proper warning of what to expect on a south Jersey clapper rail shoot.

I carefully picked my way—slowly—until I was almost in reach of his outstretched hand. Almost. I stopped for another moment to view the slowly sinking form of my old friend.

"You know, you remind me of a beached whale, wallowing around like that," I remarked.

"Cut the comedy. The other guys are a mile away by now. Come on, give me your hand." He was right: the other hunters—a long ragged line of sodden, bedraggled skirmishers—were two channels ahead of us. The sound of a shot, and then another, decided me. I grabbed his arm and helped him from the tidal ooze. He was no pretty sight.

"Some hunt! You'd think I'd have learned by now," said David Lee Call, M.D., ear, nose and throat specialist, with some bitterness. Dave and I had been roommates and fraternity brothers at Ohio State University some 10 years before and possibly he hadn't listened too closely when I proposed this hunt. "It's rough as hell," I warned him as I tossed out the bait.

"Yeah," he said suspiciously, "what is it?"

"Rail shooting."

"Rail? You're putting me on! Sounds like some sort of 'snipe hunt' gag."

But after reference to a few books I finally convinced him that there were such creatures as "rail" and that we were going to hunt them next season in the marshes around Tuckerton, New Jersey.

He was fascinated by the descriptions of various rail birds that we mined from my library. We were after clapper rail—marsh hens, if you're a southerner—one of the largest of the clan. While they are a fairly popular bird in the South, they have been largely overlooked in the Northeast, with the great exception of the south Jersey salt marshes.

Rail are long legged, grayish birds about the size of a large woodcock and have that bird's longish bill. They breed in salt marshes from Connecticut south to the Caribbean and the Gulf of Mexico. Clappers are migratory and highly sensitive to the first onslaughts of cold winds in September—they'll move out suddenly. Rail present a strange, almost ethereal quality in flight. Deceptively slow, their lazily flapping long wings fool many a hunter into missing.

When Dave asked what kind of equipment to bring and I told him nothing he wanted to use again—and a water-ski life belt—he gave me a strange look and nodded his head slowly. I think he knew even then that there was more to rail hunting than just the shooting.

Sure enough, along came the tail end of August and Dave appeared with a pair of moth-eaten sneakers, a disreputable pair of pants that looked as if they'd been cadged from a morgue, and an old seedy-looking white dress shirt.

He also had a timeworn 16 gauge Model 97 Winchester shotgun—the old exposed-hammer "knuckle-buster." My father used to have a 12 gauge version of the same gun and I have a lot of affection and respect for the model.

"Where's your water-ski belt?" I accused.

"Don't need one. We're—at least *I'm*—not going swimming and, even if we were, I swim pretty damn good," he added in a defensive tone.

Dave's gun was a good choice for rail—16 gauge and an open choke —but I was afraid it was almost too good a gun to take into the marshes. The salt and muck wreak havoc with both the finish and the functioning of any firearm. Pumps and automatics are particularly vulnerable and have a tendency to develop stoppages due to the mess that accumulates in such actions. The best bet is an old double—inherited from someone's great uncle or from the nearby pawnshop. As long as it's got good barrels and fires when you pull the trigger, you're in business. The best gauges are the smaller ones—16 or 20. If you can handle a 28 or .410 gauge, so much the better. As with quail and woodcock, it's almost a crime to bring a big 12 bore down on a rail. As befits the smaller gauges, a rail hunter should lean toward the lightest loads with the smallest shot.

Dark and early the next morning, I hauled his protesting body from the bed in our guest room, shoved a cup of coffee and a roll at him and pushed him into the station wagon. We had to meet Dick Wolters and Ed Zern with their small pack of Labradors at 7:30 in order to hunt the high tide. Since rails will skulk, run and refuse to flush when the tidal beds are exposed during low tide, a hunting party has to time its rendezvous accordingly. It was a three-hour drive to Tuckerton from my home near High Bridge.

Ed and I had hunted the year before with Pete McLain, senior wildlife manager of the Division of Fish and Game, New Jersey Department of Conservation and Economic Development, and a group of his old rail-hunting buddies. We had a fine hunt, with practically everyone taking close to a limit. The action had moved fast because the birds seemed to prefer to run more than fly—even at high tide. We had to push them hard with sprinting charges until . . . But I'm getting ahead of my story.

Pete McLain was the unquestioned captain of our hunt because he knows clapper rail as few men do. Since rail birds are largely unknown to most hunters, few professional game men spend much time with them. Pete is one of the exceptions, however, and his applied knowledge and promotional work has helped to make New Jersey one of the most rail-bird conscious sections of the country.

As the clapper rail is a migratory bird, it is governed by federal regulations and while a duck stamp isn't required, the possession, hunting and transportation of all rails, gallinules and Wilson's snipe are subject to federal law with the individual states setting their hunting seasons and limits within the framework laid down by the Fish and Wildlife Service.

Generally the service prescribes that seasons shall lie between September 1 and January 15 of the following year.

New Jersey's season almost always opens on the first day of September—if it is not a Sunday, when no hunting is allowed—and legally closes on about November 10, but for all practical purposes the actual hunting is long gone. As noted previously, cold weather pushes the birds south and it is a rare year when any rail are around after the first of October. Federal bag limits in all states are 15 clappers daily with a possession of 30. Shooting is from sunrise until sunset except on opening day when the season begins at 12 noon standard time.

We turned off the main highway and onto the road which becomes a sandy, built-up causeway to the Coast Guard station and fish factory. The roadbed drops away a few feet from the pavement and from there on it's good, old-fashioned Jersey tidal marshland—sand, mud, muck, old sea shells of all manner and size, grasses, shore birds and mosquitoes. It is fit land for neither man nor dog, but from all appearances as we drove out, this Labor Day, both species seemed to be crazy about it. Hunters in all types of fantastic garb and dogs of all breeds (though mostly Labradors) were seen traversing the marshes as far as the bay on one side and the ocean on the other.

We found Pete's car; they had gone on without us. We dismounted and adorned ourselves with the strange paraphernalia identified with rail hunters. I put on a rope for a belt with two cloth bags hanging on it, one plastic lined for shells and one for birds. Over it all I tied on a six-inch-wide yellow water-skiing life belt of polyurethane foam. I was pleased to see both Ed and Dick had similar life belts, though admittedly not quite as dashing as mine.

"My, you're pretty," Dave murmured.

"Come on, let's get with it. I think I see Pete and the other guys out there beyond that first channel," Ed said.

Five or six men were pushing through the grass and water from one channel to another. The channels were like canals crisscrossing the marshes. Some were rather small, hardly more than two or three-foot ditches; others were large—20 to 40 feet across and of unknown depth. Many were navigable, so we knew we had some swimming ahead of us. At least, Ed and I knew. Dave was beginning to get some idea about it and wasn't noticeably overjoyed by the prospect.

Ed charged down the side of the road bank, his two Labradors ranging in joyous fashion about him. I followed with Dick. All three of us were soon calf-high in muck. I looked back and motioned Dave to catch up. With a game look of despair, he plunged toward us. After the first two or three steps, he gave up trying to avoid sinking at least ankle deep every other step.

We heard a shot ahead of us. One of Pete's party gave a whoop and we saw a Labrador bound forward, seize a drowned-looking something and head back toward its owner. We could make out four other Labradors besides Ed's.

Ed Zern is a great connoisseur of rail birds. While a majority of hunters—and their wives—are somewhat baffled about what to do with a bag of clappers the first time they bring one home, Ed greedily maneuvers for other men's birds at the end of a day's hunt. He maintains that they are "horrible—inedible—dirty—unpalatable" yet he may be seen secreting a number of birds (more than his limit, I suspect) in devious nooks and crannies of his station wagon. Confronted by this evidence and pressed for a recipe, he grudgingly admits that he "supposes" rail can somehow be got down the gullet if one were to first skin and clean them well, brown in a skillet with bacon fat—with maybe a dash of cognac—then bake or broil with a strip of bacon wrapped around the breast and a piece of orange inside the body cavity.

About 20 steps more and I heard a loud swat followed by a curse from behind me. "Wow! Where did these hellish mosquitoes come from? I'm being devoured," Dave complained.

"I told you to put on a lot of that bug goo, but you wouldn't listen," I smugly answered. "And it'll get worse before it gets better, but you'll be numb by then."

Suddenly—no, that isn't the right word, but with something like a lazy "who cares?" jump from the grass—a grayish bird flapped into the air and laboriously flew away. Dave gaped first at the bird and then at me as I threw my gun to my shoulder, swung on the bird and pulled the trigger. A silent curse, a jerky continued swing and another shot spurred on the airborne hobo, unhurt and apparently even unruffled.

I jammed in two more shells. Dave gave me a funny grin and I noted his step seemed a bit lighter as we continued across the marsh in pursuit of Pete's platoon of hunters. We hit the first channel—the one separating us from Pete and the main bunch—and Ed waited until all four of us were together.

"Well, nothing like a refreshing dip in the sea, I always say. Shall we, gentlemen?" and Ed slid down the bank until he was knee-deep in mud and water. His Labs pounced happily in beside him.

"You're kidding," Dave said in an awestruck little voice.

"Nope, see you on the other side—I hope," and I followed Ed. Dick gave his water-ski belt a reassuring tug, girded his ammo and game belts a bit more tightly around his hips and with a heaven-directed last glance, stepped off the bank into the channel. He hit a deep spot and was up to his neck in seconds. Remarkably undismayed for a first timer, he proceeded to dog paddle toward the opposite bank.

Quite professionally, he copied Ed's and my experienced crawl with one hand holding the gun above water like a torch of liberty and the other strenuously paddling below the surface. I looked at Ed who just managed to grin before swallowing a small wave of salt water. Dick would make it. I was less sure of Dave.

"I ought to go back right now, while the getting's halfway good." But he warily lowered himself into the channel.

"Lord, that's cold!—Especially NOW!" His water level had reached a delicate area sensitive to sudden chill. The rest of us were more than halfway across by now so there was no turning back. Dave kept com-

69

ing, slow and not too sure. His gun-holding arm kept getting lower and lower. Finally the gunstock was touching water. Then it was about three inches submerged. The water level was just about chin high, but he was making it. One of the Labs, perhaps temporarily overcome with mercy, decided to swim back and see how the rear guard was doing. Anxiously it licked the swimmers face to show commiseration.

"Don't make waves!" the swimmer gulped frantically. Too late. Dave shot his head up three or four inches in a desperate, coughing explosion, spewing sea water. The dog turned and swam toward our shore. Dave followed.

"Here, let me give you a hand," I offered in a rare moment of compassion.

"Never mind! Where were you when that black beast tried to drown me?" Dave sounded a bit peeved, but then he grinned. "Boy, those shells really weight a guy down. I could have used one of those life belts at that, even a yellow one."

"How many shells have you got?"

"Two boxes."

"Good Lord! no wonder you almost drowned! Here, give us some. We'll divvy 'em up and spread some of that weight around," I said.

"Yeah, and quit making cracks about my dog," Zern said. "Wool was only trying to help you. Why didn't you grab his tail and let him pull you in?"

"The humiliation of it! Pulled in by a dog's tail." Dave shook his head in wonder. Water sprayed his shoulders. The Labradors vigorously shook themselves in sympathy.

After everyone had his wind back we started off again. Pete and his bunch were waiting for us some 100 yards ahead. They had obviously derived much amusement from our tortuous progress.

Pete runs a tight, well-organized hunt at a fast, tough pace, a world away from the leisurely turn of the century pursuit of rail when the sportsman, firmly enthroned on a chair in the prow of a flat-bottomed boat, was eased through the marshes by a professional pusher guide.

We were spread out in an irregular skirmish line for approximately 100 yards. Occasionally this line would bend, stretch, bulge or contract when an obtrusive patch of water—pothole or stream—would intervene. Through it all, Pete maintained contact with the outlying points so we could resume our steady push as soon as circumstances permitted. The Labradors—all six of them—ranged back and forth in front of us.

Suddenly a shot cracked out to the right of us. Two Labs were

70

racing for a partly seen quarry that seemed by the motion of the reeds to be scampering ahead toward the next wide channel, indistinguishable even in the short distance separating us from the dogs. We could not truly make out what the winning Lab was carrying triumphantly back to its master. We pushed on. Soon we were nearing the last 30 or so yards of tidal marsh before the channel waters began.

"Let's push this one hard! They're running on us!" Pete called.

Looking ahead, I saw a grayish, long-necked head pop up for a second, then scoot forward in a long-legged scamper. The other hunters must have spotted birds as well for they were all hurrying. The pace quickened and I found myself starting to break into a lope. I glanced to my right. Dave was running beside me, his interest centered on the ground ahead.

"There one goes! Good shot, Ed!" Obviously, Zern had connected somewhere down the line.

The distance was narrowing. Suddenly a languid, ghostlike bird with long flapping wings lazily jumped up ahead. It was almost as if the effort were too much, but the bird kept going. I motioned Dave to take a shot.

His pump rang out with a concussion that reverberated over the flat. The bird flew on unperturbed as two other gunners threw shots after it. Now rail were jumping up or diving into the channel water along the whole line. Three more shotguns were heard. Curses and joyful shouts signaled hits or misses. Labs cavorted and dashed in rival retrieves. Men, panting and bedraggled, charged forward in a last burst of speed for the remaining few yards. As the first hunters stumbled to the waters edge, a ragged cheer broke out down the line to the left. The troops halted in somewhat broken fashion by the channel.

"Whew! Let's take 10," someone gasped.

"How goes it, Dave?" I asked.

"How could I miss that damn thing anyway?"

"There goes Pete into the drink!" Dave yipped and jumped in behind him. I couldn't make up my mind whether he was carried away with enthusiasm or was just plain scared of being left for last. In any event, he was paddling forward with vigor. The rest of the hunters were sliding into the channel with a mixture of groans and flip repartee. I slid down the bank and into the water. At least the mosquitoes couldn't get most of me now.

When the party reassembled Pete laid out the tactics of the next attack. We had had a good drive last year down the point of the small

71

peninsula we were currently crossing. Pete suggested that we swing
and drive it hard and fast straight to the ocean's edge.

The last few yards would be over a sand flat crisscrossed with tidal
rivulets and honeycombed with clams and other shells. We all agreed
and quickly swung into line. It would appear that a collective second
wind or a mild case of mass hysteria was pumping up everyone's
adrenalin. Old Dave was really chomping at the bit. Off we went.

Just before the sand flats at the shore line, there were a great many
clumps of sea grasses and reeds interspersed with water-filled depres-
sions left over from tide that was beginning to roll out. Occasionally
small fish or other sea creatures would be left marooned in these small
ponds. This little sidelight of life was brought home to me as I plunged

through a small pond and found that for some strange reason my right foot was considerably heavier on leaving the pond than it had been on entering. My mind being occupied with rail birds at the time, I ignored this excess weight until I found myself becoming increasingly hung-up on the passing grasses and reeds. Finally I glanced down to my foot impatiently and stopped cold—a huge blue crab was firmly attached to the rim of my right sneaker.

"Dave, help! I've got a crab on my foot!"

"Tough," my old friend said as he passed at a fast clip.

With a bit of careful maneuvering I took care of the crab myself. However, I was not to forget Dr. Call's callous behavior in the face of my adversity.

I quickened my pace and managed to catch up with the other hunters. Dave was intent on the territory ahead and in a moment I was, too. Pete started to jog a bit faster. A scattered babble of shouts was heard as we advanced with our shotguns now held at a running port arms. Occasionally a man was seen to leap a bush here, a pothole there. A bird seesawed away in the wind at the edge of my vision; I heard a muffled shot. Another bird got up. Then another. Shots were sounding to left and right. I suddenly saw a lazy phantom jump into the air ahead of me. In a moment it had cleared the grasses and was silhouetted against the water. I swung to a halt and threw my shotgun to my shoulder. I fired and the bird crumbled and fell to the sea to drift toward shore. A Labrador—Ed's Rocky—came in from the right and plunged into the waves. Old Rock, the father of my own Lab bitch, Chula, bore down on the hapless rail.

Birds were getting up all around me now. And then suddenly I found myself waist-deep in the surf, the water shoving, crashing, swirling all about me. Rocky was treading water beside me. Without fully realizing or counting, I had shot and he had retrieved I didn't know how many birds. I belted my game bag; it was practically full. I stopped and stood there for a moment. A shot rang out fairly close and I turned to see a bird fall between Dave and me. He was lowering his gun with a satisfied grin as Rocky churned away from me toward the downed rail floating on the crest of an incoming wave.

The waves were breaking over my backside as I turned back toward shore. The shooting was over now and the hunters were assembling at the middle of the point. There was silence—at least of man's noise. An occasional muffled bark, a whimper now and then from a dog sud-

73

denly shivering in the wind, the steady gentle crash of the surf. Water gushed from the many holes of my sneakers. My sweat socks hung down like old laundry caught in a storm.

"Well, that was certainly something," a quiet voice intruded. Dave was standing beside me checking his game bag. "Four birds. Man, that was real action just now."

"Worth it?"

"Sure. Especially when you were waltzing with that crab."

Our return swing back to the road and our caravan of cars took about half an hour on a more direct route. It was a filthy but happy bunch of rail-bird hunters that pulled onto the roadbed for the last time that afternoon. Dave had shot the last rail of the day in the final yards before the road and everyone was overjoyed that he didn't puncture one of the cars with bird shot. And on that happy note we decided to call it a day.

Later after changing clothes on the roadside by the cars—which, as one might guess, involved some rather dexterous posturing and ducking when marauding cars intruded into our area—the whole convoy converged on a pleasant watering spot we know in the town of Tuckerton. This place is known to sell such delights as steak sandwiches and, it must be admitted, a nobly barreled tap beer. In the spirit of the occasion, a number of rounds of draught were purchased. It was noted by all present that the good doctor was seen to buy a round himself. I commented on this to Dave.

"Heck, so what if we struggling residents are a little poor right now. . . . Consider the day, my boy! . . . What sport! What companionship! What beer! . . . Say, how about next year's rail-bird season? There must be some sort of medical convention or something going on next September?"

Big on Pigs

I leaned, panting for breath, against the gnarled remains of an old tree and called to Tony to hold up for a second The lean figure in chaps and faded fatigues loping through the cactus and brush ahead of me slowed to a halt. His face took on an expression of concern as he turned back to check my unexpected delay.

"You all right?" he asked.

"I think I'm going to dislocate my breakfast," I said weakly. "I'll be O.K. in a minute. Boy, I'm in great shape."

"Don't worry about it. The pig circled back on us again anyway. Hear the dogs?" he cocked an ear back toward the rear. "The other boys should be getting a crack now."

I managed a faint grin. "Great. Just our luck. We do all the work and they get the shot," I said.

"Oh, I reckon we'll get a chance or two before this morning's done."

As it turned out, this was a vast understatement. We were to see many more pigs—javelinas or peccaries to be completely correct—before the hunt was over.

I have a curious claim to fame, one that's not jealously contested by anyone I know. Some persons are great sheep hunters—Jack O'Connor, for example—others are great bear, deer, or lion slayers.

Me, I'm big on pigs. All kinds of pigs. Small, large, European, African, Asian, American, it makes no difference. For some strange reason, fate has provided me with more varieties of pig hunting than could be thought possible. I've been in Arizona for javelinas, Georgia for feral (razorback) hogs, North Carolina for European wild boars, Mozambique for red forest pigs and warthogs. And this Texas javelina hunt in February was the best pig hunt I ever had.

Lee Wulff, hunting and fishing consultant for the Columbia Broadcasting System and a top-flight outdoor cameraman in addition to being one of the world's finest fishermen, and I had come out to Texas to make a movie for Winchester on jackrabbits. Dick Wolters, who is illustrations editor of *Business Week*, had taken a week of his vacation to be our still photographer. Since Dick is almost as qualified in the outdoor field—he is the author of *Gun Dog*—as in photography, we were glad to have him. L. A. Wilke, at that time editor of the Texas *Game & Fish Magazine* and a free-lance writer, was our genial host.

L. A. proved to be an efficient guide and organizer. We rolled up our footage in record time and then headed over to Old Mexico to visit his old friend, Maj. Gen. Jesus Jaime Quinones in Ciudad Acuña across the river from Del Rio. General Quinones, now in his late 60's, is a product of the turbulent days of the Mexican revolution in the first decades of this century. He became the youngest general in the Mexican army, a member of the Mexican Olympic Equestrian team, and a world-famous polo player.

We had a pleasant day hunting blue quail on the General's Rancho San Roderigo, then decided to shake some of the dust out of our clothes and do a bit of harmless celebrating that night.

It was harmless enough, but prolonged, and it was a sad-eyed crew that assembled in the dawn's early light after a meager two hours of sleep.

We had arranged to meet August (Gus) Timmerman of Hondo, Texas, to take us javelina hunting. Gus is a conservation officer for the state's Parks and Wildlife Department, but sometimes he does a bit of guiding with his son, Tommy, who runs a fine pack of cat and hog hounds in that section of Texas and into Mexico.

There was little conversation during the hour's drive to Hondo. We stopped to bolt down a typical Texas breakfast of about 111 dozen eggs, a gallon or two of grits, a small hog of bacon, and a bathtub of coffee. As it turned out, this was a mistake, but at the time it seemed to be a good idea.

A pickup truck with a large dog kennel in the rear was parked by the crossroad when we pulled up to the appointed spot. Four men lounged about the truck. Since the air was a bit nippy, they wore jackets and chaps. We were to find the chaps had a more practical purpose than keeping out the cold. When we climbed out of our car, the hounds started to whine and yip.

"Well, boys, I see you're right on time," Gus said. We had met him the week before when we'd come through Hondo on our way down to Del Rio.

"Through no fault of theirs," L. A. mumbled.

The other Texans stood quietly in the background, sizing up the situation and the members of the party. While Gus was a big, barrel-chester man with a booming voice, they were all lean and hard.

76

"This is my boy Tommy," said Gus. "He just got back from the army. This is my son-in-law, Capt. C. W. Gregory. He's on leave from the Air Force. We call him Moe. Over there's Tony Zerr. He guides with Tommy." The Texans murmured quietly as we were introduced. "Well, let's get to it," Gus continued. "Those hogs is waitin' and the dogs are ready too. If you boys can pull body and soul together and climb back in the car and follow us a piece, we'll get to huntin'."

The truck turned onto a dirt road and we followed. This Texas hunt with dogs was going to be a new experience for me. Dogs are forbidden in Arizona, and though I had hunted European wild boars with dogs in the Great Smoky Mountains of North Carolina, that too was a different type of hunting. Since the country there is extremely rough and steep, the local guides seldom let a hunter accompany them as they follow the hounds once the dogs have hit a trail. Even if the hunter wanted to follow, he probably couldn't stand the pace, and there would always be the chance he'd get lost. Hence, dudes are put on strategically placed stands, firmly told to stay put, and the hog is run with the hope that he'll pass within range of one of the stands. It's largely a question of patience and luck, but I was to find that nobody stood still for very long on this Texas pig hunt.

We entered an increasingly rugged jungle of cactus, thornbush, and twisted, stunted trees. The ground cover, which extends above a man's head in most areas, is a mixture of every type of hostile, prickly, scratching plant the Southwest can produce. It looked like, and is, a great place for snakes, lizards, scorpions, and other such creatures. I began to have doubts. In a few minutes we pulled to a halt behind the truck, and the dogs let out a fierce racket as we unloaded. Gus whacked the side of the kennel as he walked past it toward us, and I thought he was going to stave it in. The dogs yipped and shut up.

"Don't have to look too far for pigs," he said. "They're all around us in that cover. You could never clean them out of country like this. That's why there's no season and no limit on the critters in this part of Texas. They're a pest, rootin' around and tearing everything up. But we don't slaughter 'em. Shouldn't shoot too much of anything, or for no good reason either."

Actually, javelinas are a lot more than pests, and Gus would be the first to admit it. As with many of our native animals, javelinas, or peccaries, are popularly supposed to be one thing when actually they're another. They are not true pigs despite all appearances. Javelinas are a distinct family of tropical, or desert, American animals known as

77

Tayassuidae. They are the New World's only native species of piglike animals, and they maintain a habitat extending from our Southwest through Mexico and Central America and deep into South America. The unrelated wild boars, on the other hand, have been successfully introduced in several places, notably New Hampshire, Tennessee, North Carolina, and California. European wild boars of the same type have also been successful emigrants to a number of South American countries.

Though there are many legends surrounding the javelina's supposed ferocity, this small animal is usually quite harmless. If a javelina is brought to bay by hounds, however, it can make good use of its razor-sharp tusks. Any pack of javelina hounds bears well-earned wound stripes. While a javelina's tusks are for defense, its small, cloven hoofs are used to root out food—plants, fruits, nuts, insects, lizards, and snakes. A well-chewed prickly pear cactus is often the first evidence that javelinas are in the neighborhood.

While relatively unknown to many American hunters, the javelina has many trophy uses. Its head and cape make an impressive mount, much more fierce looking in death than in life. Its hide is much desired for gloves. If prepared properly, the meat is tasty but a little tough. Since the javelina is a rangy little forager, its meat can use a little marinating. This was to be Lee's and Dick's first chance at hunting this fine little animal.

"What are the ground rules?" Lee asked.

Wulff is a tall, reserved man with a dry sense of humor and a marvelous sense of proportion. Though in his mid-50's, he has a physique that is the result of years in the outdoors. He can travel anywhere a young sprout of 25 can go, and sometimes farther.

"Well, we'll unload the dogs, and the boys will take you off in the bush," Gus replied. "I'll stay back here with L. A. and the vehicles so we can bring them around when you're ready. We can't drive into this stuff, but we can drive around it. I'll guarantee you ain't goin' to come out where you went in."

Gus and Tommy unloaded the half-a-dozen dogs, and, bursting with energy, they sprinted into the nearby brush. When Lee, Dick, and I followed, we found that each of us was in the personal charge of one of the Texans. Tony and I paired off. The dogs were nervously sniffing and skittering ahead of us. Soon they were loping from side to side, steadily increasing their range until I only occasionally caught a glimpse or heard a rustle as one went by. The Texans strode quietly

forward. We followed, picking our way carefully through and around a wide variety of cactus and thorn.

Suddenly, we heard a low, accusing wail and then an excited answering yip. Tommy held up his hand and we stopped, silent and listening. The hounds were ahead and to the right of us. Their first tentative yips soon gave way to a sustained chorus of baying.

"They got one goin'. You boys take off thataway, and we'll head up to the left in case they circle him. Let's go!"

Tony Zerr took off without a word or a glance back. Since I was the youngest, I guess he figured I could keep up. He was wrong.

Forgetting the others, I plunged after Tony as he slid silently and swiftly through the tangled brush ahead of him. I say slid, because no

79

tree bent, no branch rasped back over his body. He went through that cover like a greased javelina. I followed as best I could. It was no great problem for the first 100 yards or so, and then I realized the pace wasn't slackening. In fact, it didn't appear from the sound of the dogs or from Tony's steady pace that it was going to slow in the foreseeable future. My legs began to tighten, but the worst problem was my wind.

I began to lose a little of my coordination, and then a lot of it. I became increasingly clumsy. Where I had been almost childishly careful in placing every step at the beginning, I now found myself stumbling, kicking against rocks and fallen branches instead of side-stepping. My heart was pounding in my ears, and my chest ached from my tortured breathing.

Never again, no more cigarettes. I must have smoked two packs last night, and I'm sure paying for it now, I thought. My stomach turned over. Those eggs and grits weren't holding too well. I lurched to a stop.

As mentioned earlier, Tony pulled up too. The dogs had circled and were heading the javelina back toward the other hunters. After a few minutes we started back. He took it easy with me and kept the pace down for the first few minutes.

It didn't make any difference; the dogs were too far away now for us to catch up before the other hunters had a shot. We jogged along steadily until suddenly the dogs seemed much closer and a lot louder. The steady yipping, growling, and howling indicated they almost had the little pig at bay. We sprinted forward. I now had my second wind and felt fine. A shot—a loud, big-caliber report—cracked across the plain.

"That must be Lee. He's the only one with a centerfire rifle," I said.

Lee had a .243 Winchester Model 70. Tony nodded and kept on going.

As we ran forward, I caught a glimpse of Dick and Moe coming from the right. Ahead of us, the snarling of three irate, bloodthirsty hounds pinpointed the center of attention. Wheeling and making short, thrustlike charges in all directions, a small, dusky, bristly looking animal was making things lively for Lee and Tommy. The sight of reinforcements must have been too much for the pig. He suddenly made a beeline away from the dogs right for the open spot in the brush where Tommy Timmerman was standing.

"Yee-OAOW! He's trying to climb my leg!" wailed Tommy as he skeetered back on his tiptoes, his shots sounding like a string of firecrackers going off.

80

I have never heard faster shooting from a non-fully automatic weapon. When we got there, Tommy was standing over a dead javelina, a grin on his face and an empty .22 pistol in his hand. He had fired nine times in as many seconds, or less.

"Boy, that old hog sure wanted outa here in a hurry. He was so scared he darn near climbed my leg comin' through."

Tommy shook his head and turned the pig over with the toe of his boot. Blood oozed from just about nine holes in the pig's head and shoulders. The dogs, whining, panting and wagging, worried the carcass. Tommy pushed them away with his boot.

Lee had creased the back of the javelina when it first came to bay, and the .243 Winchester bullet had produced an instantaneous desire on the part of the animal to get out of the area. But the pig had broken bay only to be recornered a few feet farther on. We examined Lee's rifle and decided the scope was off. It had been too easy a shot to miss. Lee took the scope off and shoved it into his jacket.

"I think I'll stay with the iron sights from here on in. Not much point to a scope here anyway." He was interrupted by the sound of dogs baying and everyone turned toward the racket.

"By golly, they've got another pig goin'. Lee, you stay with your pig. We're going to get another." Tommy took off, and the rest of us eagerly charged after him.

We spread out in a wide skirmish line and tore through the brush abreast. The dogs were right in front of us and moving fast from the far left across the country. If we got forward fast enough, at least one of us would most likely get a shot as they drove the pig across our line. No one paid any attention to rock, bush, thorn, or cactus. We were racing, fully aware that we were going to see the pig any minute and anybody had a chance.

"There he goes!" someone shouted from my left. I slowed down and cast a wild eye ahead and to the left. At first I saw nothing, and then suddenly a little dark, grayish bundle appeared racing close to ground about 100 yards away. He was coming at an angle, a little from the rear and moving ahead of me from left to right. As he shortened the distance from me one way, he began to lengthen it in front of me.

I jerked to a stop, half aware of a chorus of shouts in the background, threw my Winchester slide-action .22 Magnum Rimfire rifle to my shoulder. The pig was about 70 yards from me and running as fast as his little legs could carry him. The dogs weren't far behind, and I guess he figured he was about to get his rear end made into hamburger. As he quartered away through the brush, I hopefully shot at his hind flank. I figured I had about as much chance of hitting him with the little 40-grain hollow-point .22 Magnum as I had of hitting a gnat. He kept right on going. The other men swept up and by me as the dogs came through fast to the spot where the javelina had disappeared into heavy brush. Disgusted, I stood there for a moment until, suddenly, the dogs began baying. The pig was cornered.

I ran forward to find the rest of the hunters excitedly circling a wildly mixed turmoil in the bushes. First a dog would dart in, then there would be one howling racket and a dog would come whimpering out with his tail between his legs. Then there would be more noise, dust swirling, dogs snorting, yipping, barking, whining, and yelping, and another dog would come flying out. All this took about 10 seconds before Tommy dashed in and grabbed a dog by the tail and slung him backward.

"This pig's hurt bad. Hurry up here, Jim, and finish him off before these dogs tear him to pieces or get hurt themselves."

The pig was lying down, belly to the ground. I shot behind the ear, and he merely stiffened for a second and collapsed. The dogs rushed in, and Tommy and the other Texans moved to pull them away. The javelina was a big boar with teeth to match. One of the dogs was licking a long slash that ran four inches down one flank.

"Lookee here. You hit him in the right rear hip, and man look at the hole it made comin' out up front."

A two-inch hole gaped on the left front shoulder where the bullet had exited as it had angled from the rear. That little 40-grain bullet had done a Magnum-size job. Later, when we dressed the javelina, we found that the bullet had coursed through from hip to shoulder and made havoc of most of what was in between.

As I bent down to dress the boar, a yelp rang out about 100 yards away. The other dogs needed no more incentive. In five seconds there wasn't a hound in sight, but the air was filled with the sound of a pack in full pursuit. They had another pig going. The next thing I knew, I was all by myself. Lee, Dick, and the Texans disappeared behind the dogs.

"Well," I said to myself, "you shot it, I guess you can dress and carry it."

When I'd finished, I slit the hind legs and inserted a carrying stick. I'd been working for about five minutes when I heard a shot. It was the big gun again; Lee had had another shot. I cocked my ear toward the sound of the hounds. Lee had made a kill and they were milling around, worrying the carcass.

And then I heard another baying pursuit. Another pig! The dogs were in full cry now, so they had probably sighted the javelina. We must have been in the middle of a javelina convention hall. I slung my pig over my shoulder and started after the dogs.

The sharp crack of a .22 punctuated the barking racket. Since Dick was carrying a Ruger Single-Six chambered for the .22 W.M.R., I guessed that he'd got a shot with it. There was no more shooting, and the dogs sounded once again as if they had a dead pig. The noise settled down to a slightly murmuring, collective growl.

As I swung through the brush with my pig, I half expected to hear the pack take off on another chase. There seemed to be no end of javelinas.

"Hey, wait!"

I turned to see Lee, also with a pig slung over his shoulder, making his way through the brush toward me. He had a good-size boar about the same as mine.

"Looks as if we've got a full house, and it sounds as if Dick nailed one with that peashooter of his," I said.

We walked through the brush separating us from the rest of the party. It appeared the dogs had either been called off or were simply bored with the surplus of pigs. Dick was standing over his javelina with a little pistol in one hand and a big grin spread across his face, at least the part of it that wasn't obscured by his 10-gallon hat or his handlebar mustache.

"There'll be no living with you now, I suppose. First head of big game, and with one shot yet," I said with mock concern.

"Don't let him kid you, Dick," commented Tony with a sly grin. "Ask him what he was doing back there on our first run. I'd say he was a might porely for a time, but he picked right up soon as the shootin' started."

"I give up," I said. "Boy, this is some place for pigs."

Biggest Bird Bonanza in the U.S.

"Get down! You're drawing fire!" Dave Call urged. We flung ourselves belly flat on the bottom of a small arroyo paralleling a dirt road. It was a natural trench and we were using it in the same fashion as GI's. Another shadowy flight of low-flying, phantom wings skimmed and darted through the early morning light above us. A cascade of shots pursued them. There was a faint rattling of shot about us. I looked down and noted a small leaden ball rolling gently to a halt beside my hand.

Suddenly a figure rose up over one of the surrounding mounds. A large cowboy hat shadowed an indistinct face. A long shotgun barrel hovered anxiously over our heads.

"Hey, fellows, whatcha doing down there on the ground? Did a bird fall in there?" The stranger gave us a funny look and disappeared.

A few seconds later another fusillade of shots boomed as he and others turned to more birds.

The birds were whitewing doves. Once again I was finding out that opening day for doves in Arizona is like no other hunting in the country. Small stores close and big factories have an epidemic of absenteeism. Practically everyone is out to bag a limit of his favorite game bird. But what makes the difference from other hunting is that Arizona has a limit on doves like no other state—37 birds a day.

When an Arizonian says "dove" he really means a mourning dove, because he is singularly lucky in having this other dove which is simply called a "whitewing" and is one and a half times as large. Whitewings fly like—but I'm getting ahead of my story. . . .

This bird is governed (as is the mourning dove) by federal migratory game-bird regulations under which open seasons exist in Arizona, California, Nevada, New Mexico and Texas. There is one important detail: in all other states *except Arizona* the whitewing bag is included in an aggregate limit with mourning doves and that total is 12. Outside of Mexico, Arizona remains the proverbial "mother lode" of whitewings for American hunters. A man hunting in Arizona can knock over his 12 mourning doves PLUS 25 whitewings a day. This makes, I believe, for the biggest single limit on one basic type of game bird in the U. S.—and, unlike some so-called limits, this one is a realistic possibility for any hunter.

Since whitewings are found over an area of some 30,000 square miles in the southern and southwestern parts of the state—and almost 75 percent of Arizona is in public lands open to hunting—there are plenty of birds and places for the average man to hunt them.

Strangely enough, few hunters outside of the Southwest know about the fabulous bonanza in this sun-baked, arid land. When I found that I would be lucky enough to be there for the September opening of the season recently, I got in touch with an old friend, Dave Call, who had just moved to Phoenix to set up medical practice. We arranged a hunt with a group of others that I had shot with in previous years when I was an Arizona resident. Wendall Swank, Fred Weiler and his son, Hunter, and Pete Brown would join us in the morning for the expedition to Gila Bend, some 80-odd miles to the west toward Yuma.

Wendall knew a large flock of whitewings had been spotted a few days before, but Phoenix had just witnessed some of the most spectacular stormy weather of its history. While much of the state's whitewing population usually leaves before the season's opening in a normal year, Wendall figured that many more may have been pushed down by the harsh heavy rains.

The road was lined with cars as we neared the huge maize field that we hoped would draw the birds like filings to a magnet in the early morning hours. Hunters were everywhere. For a state with one of the lowest population densities in the nation, the proportion of hunters must be high indeed.

I loaded my 20 gauge Model 21 with 7½'s. Early in the season, low-base 7½'s, 8's—or even 9's—are fine for low-flying whitewings and mourning doves. Mine was a good quail and dove gun, its improved and modified 26-inch barrels often proved from New Jersey to Georgia. I was anxious to try it out on dozens of whitewings that were already skitting through the sky like so many large bats.

"Man, there must be hundreds of them," Dave said.

"Thousands. Tens of thousands," Wendall remarked.

The whitewing has a tendency to come flying from its roost into fields in small flocks, often just skimming over the tops of rises and brush trees. The shots can be fast and very low . . . and dangerous, since whitewings then fly just about head high and the early morning light can camouflage a man in the desert brush at even a short distance.

We had walked down the ditch for 50 yards or so when the sound of shooting began to increase in both intensity and proximity. The season was on!

The road and its ditch on our side served as sort of boundary between the rough, untilled or improved desert on our side and the large cultivated fields—all crisscrossed with small irrigation channels—on the other side. Here was a perfect setup for whitewings and mourning doves. It had everything for the dove hunter—and enough people knew it to add still another factor to the situation: a whole lot of hunters.

We could make out shadowy figures moving around some 50 to 100 yards in front of us. Whitewings were getting up all over the brush-covered plain ahead of us. I could see and hear them by the thousands as they began to leap into the air from their roost trees. Flocks of five, 10 and 20 were swooping in toward the maize fields. It seemed impossible that any could survive to reach our ditch, but we were constantly amazed to see the great majority swoop over our heads. When we remembered our misses, it was a bit more understandable.

A wild-flying dove is a deceptive target at best; a maddeningly elusive escape artist at worst. This age-old fact of hunting life was once more brought home by the sudden flare of a flight of birds to my right. I swung on the lead bird and fired. As my second shot matched the empty results of the first, I heard Dave's pump gun bark out a couple of more misspent loads. The doves flew on—a bit faster, but unscathed.

"Here come some more!" Dave yelled. A pair of doves was sweeping in low and to the left from brush surrounding the field in front. *Lead,* I told myself. *Lead it more. Don't stop your swing. Now . . . and follow through. Damn!* I tossed a good shot after the first bad one. Still nothing tumbled from the sky. A year's layoff makes a difference in dove shooting and I needed some fast, intensive practice.

If a gunner has had a difficult time in bagging his limit in the early morning hours when the flights are making their hunger-driven rush to the breakfast table, he can settle back for more leisurely shooting about midmorning when the birds come back with full craws to roost in the desert trees for a siesta. The whitewing's habitat in Arizona can be divided into approximately three types. The most important is the broad saguaro-palo verde areas of the state; the second is the bottom-land thicket growth of the lower river valleys like the Salt, Santa Cruz,

86

Verde and Gila, where we were. The third is the foothill canyons of the higher mountains. The number of birds frequenting each area is directly dependent on the available feed, water and nest sites. In any event, a hunter can take a stand on the edge of the nesting—or roosting —sites bordering feed and water and he will get all the shooting he wants, both coming and going.

It was brightly lit now. It doesn't take long for the Arizona sun to search out even the most lurking nooks and crannies and fill them full of light. In a few more hours it would be as hot as anyone would want it. People would be taking their first swims of the morning in the pools of Phoenix. I pulled Dave's sleeve and motioned him back toward the way we had come and started down the road. We could see hunters everywhere now that the sun was out, crisscrossing the desert, strolling the road, hiding in ditches, watching by irrigation canals. The early morning booms and bursts of firing had settled down now to a steady, rhythmic pattern of firing.

A flurry of movement would catch the corner of my vision and instinctively I would swing my shotgun to my shoulder and to the right to catch a darting series of objects moving across my path from left to right across the ditch. Without thinking, I isolated one flying object, swung through, led a bit and fired. I was gratified to see that object fall. I continued my swing to catch up on another similar object. I fired but it didn't fall.

I ran down into the ditch, marking the spot where the first dove had fallen. Luckily I found it, crumpled in a soft ball, its white-slashed wings clearly betraying its presence in the brush. I turned back toward the road, my shotgun cradled in my arm, my hands automatically stripping the feathers from the still-warm body. I hadn't forgotten this lesson of my dove-hunting days of the past; it's no fun stripping a day's limit at one sitting.

A few short yards further down the road I came across Fred Weiler, his little 28 gauge double gently draped in the crook of one arm. Suddenly, but smoothly, he swung the gun up and over to my right. Two shots blasted out. Two doves were falling in the air.

In another moment Fred's Brittany had wagged its way up to deposit one bird in his hand and had taken off for the other. Fred added the bird to the cluster he already had dangling from game strings on his belt. Earlier he had pointed out that conventional rubber-coated game pockets were poor for carrying doves in Arizona's heat. A hunter

87

must cool his birds—and keep them cool—in desert heat or the meat will go bad. As I approached, he dropped another dove and slipped down into the ditch to retrieve it.

Dave Call joined me. We looked up to see a low-flying flight of whitewings skimming the treetops. Crouching beside a line of brush as they darted toward us, I held my breath waiting for someone's shots to flare them before they reached us. On they came. Probably 10 or 12 in the bunch. Good chance for a double here.

They were almost up to the arroyo when a flurry of shots rang out in front of us. The whitewings broke formation—three spun off to the right, a bunch in the middle climbed high to get out of range, a pair swooped low and directly into the guns, another few peeled off toward the left. It was a classic maneuver; the formation had broken off into buzzing, darting smaller groups and singles.

I watched the low-flying pair. They had their tactics down cold. They buzzed a few scant feet right over the heads of the gunners in the arroyo. Those gentlemen—in the process of hurriedly reloading— were so unnerved that they never got another shot off. On came the dove duet, up and over the near side of the arroyo's dunes, still only a few feet over the brush. I remained absolutely still, crouched on one knee, gun ready.

As they broke out over the brush in front of me, I stood up and they flared—too late—in almost the same instant. I swung the double, blocking one out in my swing in almost a No. 8 high house skeet shot, kept swinging as I pulled the trigger and, without breaking my rhythm, swung through and over my shoulder to pick up the second bird for a companion shot. I was acutely aware that I had seen the first bird fold as I swung through and was elated to see the second plummet to earth with equal dispatch. I ran forward to pick them up and as I knelt for the second, I caught sight of another single flitting in from the right. I swung the gun—click, click! Damn. I had forgotten to reload.

Before I had retrieved my second dove, I had dropped another and missed one. Luckily I found both my old and my new downed birds, but I spent some time on the older one. It's wise to mark your bird and go to it as soon as possible before shooting another. Doves are hard to locate in the best of conditions; almost impossible when the cover is thick and the hunter gets turned around. I had wasted valuable time. As I hurried back to the road to find Dave, I heard two shots ahead. When I reached him he was adding another dove to a small pile at his feet.

"You should have been here! A whole squadron came by. I nailed two then, a couple of singles later and another right now," he added happily.

"How many shells?"

"Spoilsport—did I ask *you* any personal questions?" His initial dove hunt was proving educational.

I well remember the first time I hunted whitewings when I moved to Arizona in 1956 shortly after my marriage. I was going to graduate school and a bunch of my Arizona classmates were full of the wondrous glories and unnerving flight characteristics of this dove. Having been brought up in Indiana and Ohio, I knew pretty much about pheasants, a fair bit about quail and had a nodding acquaintance with the occasional grouse. But doves—outside of those lazy, cooing creatures I had often observed perched on telephone wires—I hardly considered to be game.

When the early September dove season rolled around—barely a month after my arrival in the state—I was persuaded to haul out my old Winchester Model 12 pump gun and join the annual expedition. It didn't take me long to find out a couple of pertinent facts about the Arizona whitewing: it's fast, a worthy target and game bird for any hunter, and there is an unbelievable number of them. It was unlike any shooting I had ever witnessed, almost something out of the dim frontier days of bountiful game or the great flocks of modern Africa.

89

For the man used to a limit of two pheasants—and happy to get them a few times during the season—it was a hunter's paradise.

As the morning wears on during a typical September whitewing day, the flights grow fewer and smaller in number. Early in the morning, flight after flight—in numbers up to 30 or 40 at a time—will come winging over from the roosting trees to the grain fields. Then the flights will diminish to a dozen or so—with occasional triples, doubles and singles interspersed. Finally a lengthening pause between flights becomes apparent as the pattern changes. Steady flights of two to six birds dwindle to the occasional single. And then the number of singles —and even multiples up to half a dozen—begin to crisscross the sky. The hunter will soon discover that these new arrivals are slightly smaller and there is no white stripe on the wing. As the whitewing flight drops off, mourning dove activity has picked up.

After that opening-day shoot I had to return to Phoenix in mid-September on another business trip. Naturally I thought the whitewings would have long since made their annual migration to Mexico, especially in light of the harsh weather earlier in the month. I was happily surprised to find that there were still some around. A flock had been located a mere 20 or so miles from Phoenix. It turned out to be a completely different—and in many ways a much more pleasant shoot—than my earlier one.

While there were fewer birds in total, there were enough for everyone to get his limit with a little snappy shooting, and lots of shells. And there weren't so many birds in flight as to confuse the shooter. As with quail shooting, an eager dove hunter has a tendency to "covey shoot" when startled by the sudden, unexpected appearance of a large group of zooming birds. If there are only half a dozen in a flight, there are only that number from which to pick targets—not 20 or 30 potential customers. Getting one's limit may have taken a little longer, but this was a plus too, because it meant we could stretch our good time longer.

Lastly and most importantly, there wasn't a fraction of the shooters to contend with that engulfed us on our opening day hunt. I suppose the opening of Arizona's dove season is like opening day anywhere— all the armchair enthusiasts in town are out beating the fields, only to disappear to other pursuits a few days later.

On that mid-September hunt, our party had the field to ourselves. And in this case, "field" encompassed all the land the eye could see from mountain to mountain in this particular valley. There were 15 of us and we could spread out as far as we liked. I don't think a shot pellet landed anywhere within striking range of any of my stands.

We took stands by the edge of the desert's thick brush and waited for the birds to come over for their morning feed in the grain and maize fields stretched before us. A man could stand there in the shade, pick his shots, leisurely filling his limit in idle fashion and savoring the possibilities of each shot without worrying about being hit by an over-zealous gunner sneaking in from the rear or flank.

Later in the day, when the birds were returning, we had a long view of incoming birds and some opportunities for some fine shots. Some we made and some we missed. Since they had been gunned for a few weeks, most of our whitewings that day were flying quite a bit higher and were a lot more spooky than during our earlier shoot. They had become extremely wary of movement and color and veered off in frightened zips on very little provocation. The casual maneuverings and careless cover that we had adopted on opening day were definitely out of place for this latter shoot.

Arizona dove hunting provides a rare opportunity for practice al-most impossible for the average hunter to duplicate today. There is only one way for a man to become a good wing shot—to have a chance at a lot of birds, day after day. Only in this fashion can a shooter draw parallels between shots in a string so that he knows what he has done wrong, how he has corrected himself or not.

A dove is a humbling creature, doubly so when allied with other hunters. I remember a flight of three whitewings breaking over an irrigation ditch late one morning. As they swung toward my stand, the thought flashed through my mind that this was probably the last dribble of birds filtering through before the midday heat locked the flocks to the shade of their roosts. The whitewings climbed steadily and broke a bit high over the trees, but were still heading in my gen-eral direction and away from Dave some 60 yards' distant. I started to raise my gun in what I considered a superbly graceful and pro-fessional swing. I brought the double to shoulder and started my swing through on the birds that were veering ever closer to my stand. My birds. My double.

I caught up with the first and a shot rang out. The bird fell, but I hadn't pulled the trigger. I raised my head an inch or so from the stock even as I continued my swing. I was just in time to see the second dove fall as the accompanying shot rang out. The third bird made it to the brush unscratched. I turned to see Dave Call running forward for his doves. Glumly I followed.

Dave was standing in the middle of a dirt road. There was a thoughtful look on his face.

"How many shells do you think are shot for each bird downed? On an average, I mean?"

"Between five and seven. Someone once said that if the ammunition industry ever erects a statue to anything, it will probably be to the dove."

"Boy, from the sound of things," he cocked an ear toward a not-too-distant barrage, "this oughta be the spot to put it up. Come on, let's add our share to the percentage."

First Buck

Every year in late September or early October, the funny feeling finds its way into my body. I wake one day and the summer is over. There is a cool snap to the air, suddenly the leaves have turned and the wind is pulling them down. I find a new energy, long dormant with the summer heat, and a strange sort of nervous excitement lies just beneath the surface of my day-to-day outward demeanor. It's hunting season. As any man, from earliest pre-history until even these too modern years, I wander the fields and forests, tramping the ground in search of game. For me, it is the best of time, days to be spent with my dogs and, lately, my son.

My son was seventeen the first day of this month, November, 1978. He is about two inches taller than his liege, his hands are an inch longer and he wears a size 11½ shoe, wide and getting wider. I take a somewhat courteous approach in my corrective attitude these days than he previously enjoyed. I have also always held the opinion that firearms are like sex—an irresistible attraction to normal tads and one, that if not properly attended to at home, will certainly be experienced somewhere else, not necessarily in the best interest of all concerned. Consequently, my son has accompanied me on a number of what we tell his mother are necessary "survey" trips in the field.

He made his first Canadian fishing trip—with a motley group dubiously labeled "The Winchester Irregulars"—when he was nine. Since we had a small discussion prior to this first big expedition away from the nest, he remained reasonably quiet while the "gentlemen" were having refreshments, relating historic feats for the benefit of posterity and sharpening their skills at games of chance. He said "Yessir and no sir" at appropriate times, displayed passable table manners, fetched cooling fluids with a minimum of urging and kept his mouth shut upon his return home. He also caught a hellacious big bass and decided that he liked these sorts of trips better than going shopping with his sisters.

Shortly thereafter, young Jimmy found that virtue (and listening to the Old Fellow) occasionally pays off in more tangible reward than a pat on the noggin. His "Uncle" Harry Tennison launched the first Irregular's Texas deer hunt and invited both Rikhoffs the next December. Jimmy turned ten November 1, 1971 and, among other presents, there was an old cut-down .257 Roberts rifle Jack O'Connor had had made back in Arizona when he was just starting out as a gun writer. The rifle had a Sukalle barrel on a Mauser action and the woodwork, believe it or not, was by Griffin and Howe. Jack's wife Eleanor had used it for years in their early days in the Southwest and both of Jack's sons, Bradford and Jerry, had shot his first deer with it. Jack had taken a fancy to my wife Janet and, noting she was only 4'11", had decided that .257 Roberts was just the hunting rifle for her. She agreed and carried it with some honor on a long Scottish deer stalk a little later. With Jimmy coming of age for his first deer hunt, what more appropriate rifle to carry than the O'Connor gift?

A week or so before Christmas, Gene Hill, Ed Zern and the two of us drove to Newark Airport and what we hoped would be a fast flight to San Antonio, where the troops were mustering prior to heading for the Texas Hill Country. As luck would have it, it was Jimmy's first airplane trip and it almost decided him against flying forever and hunting too, if it took airplanes to get there. Without over-reliving horrible moments, let it suffice to say we were scheduled to leave at 1:00 p.m. one afternoon and finally arrived after several plane changes, at 4:30 a.m. the next morning. After three hours sleep, we loaded into a travel lodge and headed for deer country. It was a good break-in trip for a young hunter.

Our tyro hunter had good companions with whom to identify. In addition to the aforementioned, Grits Gresham, Joe Hudson, John Thompson, Guy Coheleach, Junior Hummel and Ben Wright were on hand to lend weighty advice and a bit of needling to keep him in line. After settling down in the bunk room and getting our gear organized, Harry took Jimmy and me out late in the afternoon so we could get the lay of the land.

As our pick-up crested a gently rolling hill, a young six-point buck popped up ahead of us and, after a cool scrutiny, leisurely took off over another adjoining ridge. Jimmy's eyes followed the buck's retreat with a great deal of interest and, I believe, a smidgeon of blood lust. There was an old abandoned loafing shed for cattle in the middle of what must have been an old pasture. The fences were broken down and the shed itself had about half its roof and sides missing. It was a perfect blind from which to cover the open fields surrounding us for about half-a-mile in most directions.

We left the truck some distance away in a patch of mesquite and settled down in our shed. We cautioned Jimmy to remain quiet and motionless. There was no wind and sound carried the proverbial country mile; the shed was sufficiently open that movement was easily discernible to wild eyes on the alert. Time passed, shadows lengthened in the fading sunlight, animal noises punctuated the stillness with increasing frequency and, then, a couple of does silently glided into view. Jimmy almost had a stroke.

We watched them for minutes that stretched into timelessness. No buck. A couple of other does, one with a yearling, joined the first group. We remained quiet and immobile. Our legs cramped and we stifled nervous coughs. Then Harry slowly reached over and nudged Jimmy, silently beckoning him to look over to the far left. The six-point buck had returned. He stood still and alert on the edge of the field. After several moments, he cocked one ear and then picked his way forward toward the does.

Jimmy slowly raised his head as the buck ambled closer. Harry whispered the obvious question. Did the boy want the buck? He did. Ever so carefully he raised the rifle and inched it through the broken boards. For an eternity of time, he peered through the 4-power 'scope. The barrel was weaving from side to side in about a three-inch arc. I looked at Harry. He was patiently holding his tongue and his breath. Finally, the boy allowed as how he couldn't see the deer. It looked like the deer could see us.

Finally the buck moved closer, but to one side, and was lost to Jimmy's view completely. There was no choice, the light was fading and we had to move out of the shed. The back wall was completely down so we crawled backward, scrunched down on our bellies until we were lying by the side rear section. Jimmy rose again, bringing the old O'Connor rifle up over a fallen timber. The gun still weaved. The buck was about 70 yards away and on the alert. We were fast losing light. Harry whispered: "The next time your 'scope passes through his shoulder, squeeze off a shot!" He was desperate. Jimmy fired seconds later. The buck leaped sidewise and took off. I jumped up with my Model 70 and was bringing it down on the buck when Harry's voice stopped me: "Don't shoot! He's going down!"

We were strangely silent as we walked to where the deer lay about 100 or so yards away. The buck was absolutely motionless and I could see the small hole just behind his shoulder. A well-placed shot and a stone-dead deer. I looked at Harry and he answered with a quiet smile of mixed pleasure and relief. We both looked down at the young hunter.

"Is he dead? Did I do it right?" he asked.

"Yep, nailed him right through the shoulder . . . A good shot . . . Well, you've got your first deer. How about that! Congratulations . . . Must have been dead while he ran . . . They often do that . . . ," Harry's and my exclamations, once released, tumbled out in mixed excitement. The boy shivered a bit and then, suddenly, he was crying. Harry and I stopped, dumbfounded, and then Harry reached out and enveloped the boy in his arms.

"Thank God you've done that! Thank Heavens you care! I'm so glad you feel like that. Don't you know, that makes his life mean something. . . . If you hadn't cared about killing him, it would have meant that he wasn't worth anything. I always feel the same way and so does your Dad. You don't have to be ashamed of crying. I'm so glad you did. . . . It means you cared," Harry's words rushed out and around the boy, who looked up at Harry and then to me.

"That's right, son, we all feel that way the first time and, to be honest, a little bit that way *every* time. You've got to face up to what you're doing. Nobody should ever take life cheaply or else none of it is worthwhile. I think if I ever stopped being a little sad after killing an animal, I'd give up hunting."

"Pardner, it's as natural as anything in the world—both the hunting and the sorrow mixed with the satisfaction of a good hunt," Harry said, releasing the boy, but keeping an arm around his shoulder. I bent down and broke off a sprig of sage.

"Well, it's not evergreen, but this is Texas and it'll have to do." I leaned over and dipped the leaves in the spreading patch of blood on the deer's shoulder. "They have a custom in Europe called blooding. They dip a piece of evergreen in the animal's blood and smear it across the hunter's face. Then they stand silent for a minute over the animal, with the evergeen laid over the wound. That's so everyone can think about what they have just done and about God's creatures, hunted and hunter, and how it's always been this way since man first crawled from a cave. The hunter doesn't wash the blood from his face for the rest of the day so he will remember." I raised my hand and gently brushed the sage across my son's cheek. His hand reached up and the fingers came away with a faint crimson staining the fingers. He was still silent but the tears had stopped. We stood by the fallen buck for a moment, heads a bit bowed, each with his own thoughts.

"You forgot," Jimmy said. He reached over, took the sage from my hand and placed it over the wound in the deer's shoulder. Harry smiled and I found that my tension slowly relaxed.

"It's getting dark," I looked up. "Now comes the other part of hunting." I rolled up my sleeves, took out my hunting knife and crouched down over the deer. Harry helped me roll him over on his back and I made the first cut down from his chest cavity, around his genitalia and anus, opening up his unpunctured stomach cavity. As with most Texas hill country deer, he was rather small-bodied and he was easy to dress.

"You really know what you're doing," Jimmy said, seemingly surprised that his father, whom he had always secretly suspected of dimwittedness, should know something so basic as cleaning out a deer.

"Everyone has to do at least one thing well," Harry chuckled, "and it took us years to teach him that!"

We loaded the deer and drove back to camp. Jimmy had made a full recovery of both his emotions and his mouth. He kept reliving the hunt, the shot, the deer's last run and how he had dropped "like he had been axed." I looked over his head and caught Harry's eye. His wry grimace said it all. That deer was getting bigger by the minute, the shot was stretching out longer and, at the crucial moment of truth, the light had faded—even more than we realized.

We had another deer hunter on our hands.

III
AFRICAN ADVENTURES

A Note on Part Three

I made my first trip to Africa in 1962 when I hunted Mozambique in June and July of that year. It was the answer to every dream a crazy gun aficionado and hunting enthusiast could ever imagine. I was thirty-one and full of it. Nothing seemed to phase me and, during that trip, a lot of people and circumstances tried. Among other things, I was stranded by myself in a native village between the Rovuma and Lugenda rivers up by the Tanzanian border—the area that later was devastated by guerrilla warfare.

Needless to say, I got out and returned home with the firm conviction that it would be years before I would ever get back to Africa. I was wrong. I was back in Kenya the following year—the week of Uhuru (or "freedom") in June of 1963. In the following years I was to return to Africa four more times. I was to hunt in Botswana and Kenya again, plus visits to Tanzania, South Africa and Rhodesia.

The first three stories are tales of hunts—for a sable in Mozambique, a record-book leopard in Kenya and a wounded lion in the same country. The last article is really an essay on the status and possible future of Kenya's—or, for that matter, all East Africa's—game. It was written about fifteen years ago and some of the data is obviously dated, but I think you will also find that much that was said and observed then holds true now.

I hope one day to return to Africa. I pray some vestige of the beloved, fascinating land I once knew is still there.

Long Stalk for a Sly Sable

The slow steady purr of the Land Rover was interrupted by a sharp, yet muffled, knuckle-rap on the cab's metal roof.

"Stop!" and then with more urgency, Luis Cardozu whispered, "Sable! About 20 of 'em, maybe 300 yards over there in the grass by that grove of trees. There's two bulls at least."

"One of them looks pretty good to me," I answered with excitement. "Should we try for him?"

Luis and the two trackers, Jofrice and Alfonso, held a hurried council. The natives silently lowered themselves from the truck. Luis motioned me to follow.

"This grass is too high to get a clean shot from here or I'd let you squeeze one off," Luis whispered again. "We've got to get closer."

Silently, we moved forward through the grass, Luis and Jofrice, the old man from the Gorongoza country, in the lead. I followed with Alfonso, the quietly dignified giant from the great coastal plains stretching to the Indian Ocean. The truck—with its silent crew of remaining natives—stood still and alien behind us.

Since the grass was head-high to everyone except the giant Alfonso, we could no longer see the sable, but could only hope that they remained unafraid and unmoving where we had last seen them. For a time, we were able to look back to the truck for a silent signal indicating the sable were still there, but soon that was lost from sight as well.

The grass spread across the plain in all directions. A dark fringe outlined distant forests bordering the great plain. Forest for refuge; the plain for food. It was a perfect combination for game—especially antelope. The country looked somewhat like the great plains west of Kansas. No jungle here. An occasional acacia tree—its wisplike foliage hanging like Spanish moss—or a bright yellowish-green fever tree marked the only interruption in the interminable grass. While the country bore resemblance to some of the American West, the similarity stopped with the land—and didn't extend very far into animal life.

America has one true plains animal—its native pronghorn, falsely dubbed antelope. Africa has literally scores of species. I have always loved plains hunting in its best sense: the long, careful stalk in sparse cover for a wary, always alert, devastatingly swift quarry in its own environment.

But my plains hunting has been necessarily limited by seasons and availability. Since I moved to the East from Arizona some five years ago, I have managed but one long hunt to Montana in 1960.

Then Joe Simoes entered the picture. An old friend, Joe is the owner of Simoes Safaris in Beira, Mozambique. During his last visit to New York, in early 1962, we had lunch together. And we indulged our favorite pastime—the comparison of the virtues of American hunting versus the African variety.

It never entered my head that I might someday enjoy an African hunt, anymore than I might stroll out to purchase a spare yacht or two for a weekend sail. Hence, I argued hard and vigorously in defense of American game and hunting, as only a man can who realizes that he has to love it best—for it's the only hunting he will ever enjoy. Finally, after a particularly spirited skirmish over our respective plains hunting, Joe turned to me and made a startling challenge.

"You know, Jim, safaris don't have to be all that expensive." He gave me a long look and suddenly smiled. "If you really want to experience the greatest hunting in the world, you can—with a little planning and sacrifice. I have a cancellation in June. Come on over."

At first it seemed an impossible plan, but then I began to think: why not—it will probably be the only chance I'll ever have to go to Africa. The world and game situation were not that noticeably bright and the future was dubious at best. But Mozambique was an island of tranquility in a continent of unrest and ferment. Its game supply was one of the best in Africa. Transportation, once so costly in both dollars and—more importantly for the man of limited vacation—time, had been simplified by the jet age and economy fares. Alitalia could pick me up in New York in the evening; have me in London the following morning; Rome at noon; Salisbury, Southern Rhodesia, the following day. Salisbury was only about an hour and a half's air time from Beira, Mozambique.

I went home to pack my bag and my .264 magnum Winchester Westerner. I had already tested the rifle on pronghorn during my Montana hunt, but it had been in enforced retirement for the past year. When I arrived in Beira in June, Joe had put me in the capable hands of his cousin, Luis, and two of his best trackers, Jofrice and Alfonso, all of whom had been alerted to show me the best Mozambique had to offer. They had asked what I wanted most—lion, leopard, elephant or buffalo?

"Antelope," said I. "Kudu, nyala, but above all, the sable."

Now, 10 days since my arrival in Beira, we were in the main Simoes camp in the central concession, 250 kilometers northwest of Beira in the Sena River country. We had seen game every day—scores of waterbuck, zebra, reedbuck, warthog, small bushbuck and the diminutive oribi, large eland and curious kongoni, secretive duikar and belligerent buffalo.

We had been lucky; we had seen leopard and heard lion. I had already taken a number of good trophies—one reedbuck we were sure would make the records and a warthog held the same possibility in its huge tusks and elongated skull, all whitening in the African sun at that moment. And I had taken a leopard and a buffalo—two of Africa's "Big Five"—plus a number of other trophies. Now, everything in me was pointed to one objective—the taking of trophy heads of nyala, kudu and sable. The sable was number one on the list.

Suddenly—with a return to reality—I realized the sun had burnt off the morning mist and damp coldness. The grass still left beads of fine, powdered moisture on my old New England canvas-faced brush pants, but the air was already warming up to the strong heat of midday Africa. It was 10 o'clock. I was uncomfortably aware of the sweater I wore under my bush shirt.

We continued through the brush, silent and careful in the choice of each step. Luis quietly slapped the back of his leg ahead of me. I looked down. A small warthog hole, half hidden in the grass, waited to twist my ankle. I sidestepped it, slapping my leg for Alfonso, who, of course, had already seen the hole.

Twenty minutes passed. We reached a small knoll—and carefully worked our way up the far side away from the sable. Luis motioned us down on our knees and Jofrice crawled forward, parting the grass ahead with skillful fingers. He seemed to insert himself—as into some sort of green envelope—through the grass rather than actually crawl. A minimum of grass stalks were broken with each movement. There was no noise, little motion. We crept behind him, keeping 10 or so feet to the rear and well below the skyline. With extreme care Jofrice slowly raised his head, and parting a blade or two of grass with one dextrous finger, fixed a searching, darting eye on the glade some 200 yards ahead. He made no sound, no movement, no sign.

104

A moment passed. Another moment added to still more seemed to stretch for an eternity. Jofrice remained unmoving, almost a part of the land. *Carved out of native ebony and just as hard and valuable,* I thought. Luis remained equally motionless.

The plainsman, Alfonso of little words and strong feats, lay on his side behind us. His eyes seemed unseeing as they gazed glassily through and passed us, fixed on something known only to his own mind. That mind seemed in another world, but I knew—even from only 10 days of hunting with him—that he was intently involved with our immediate problem. Alfonso, who could outrun certain small antelope on his native plains, lived for hunting. When the time came, his curious, introverted absorption would produce some softly, shyly tendered bit of advice that would contribute mightily to our success.

Jofrice glided backward and downward with a sublime economy of movement. He shook his head and with a fast eloquent gesture of his hand made it painfully clear that sable were gone. With a carelessness that told us the large antelope were out of sight and sound, he and Luis rose up on their haunches and gazed out over the knoll toward and beyond the trees below. I joined them. Alfonso remained as before. It was not yet his time to participate and he wasted no movements or energy.

"They've moved out," Luis said. "Now, what we don't know is how they moved out. Under a full head of steam, or simply grazing down the valley." Luis had gone to school in South Africa and had picked up a full range of English slang and colloquialisms.

"How about moving down to that grove, using it to cover us, and getting a look-see from there?" I suggested.

"Better than that," Luis said, getting up, "Jofrice and Alfonso can probably pick up their trail there."

"Let's get going," I suggested. "It's starting to warm up and those sable will be heading for some big woods before too long—or so you told me a couple of days ago," I added.

"You're starting to learn—so you remember what I told you for a change," Luis laughed and picked up his hat. He and Jofrice started down the slope toward the grove. As they moved out, I removed my sweater and handed it to Alfonso who tied it by the arms around his waist before we followed.

We entered the small patchy woods below us and Jofrice and Alfonso cast about sniffing like two old veteran bird dogs hot on the scent.

105

They moved slowly about in ever-increasing circles. Occasionally they stopped, closely examined a leaf or blade of grass. In a few moments they held a conference, reached a quick decision, referred their opinion to Luis, who obviously concurred, and then led us out of the grove into the surrounding grassy plain. Even I could follow the trail then. Although the sable seemed unalarmed, they had moved at a steady gait, perhaps a bit faster than normal grazing would allow. They were quite out of sight and sound. As we worked our way through the all-encompassing grass, the heat asserted itself with increasing discomfort. I looked at the sun. It was almost overhead.

Jofrice stopped. Luis motioned me to halt. Suddenly a head popped up in front of us. The animal stood fascinated and stupidly transfixed in her attention. She looked—and acted—like a Montana muley.

"Kongoni," Jofrice grinned. We started moving through the grass again. The Kongoni twitched a nervous ear, cocked its head, then jumped away in the curious goatlike gait peculiar to the species. We waited for a frozen minute to see if she would spook any hidden sable. She proceeded in her strange bounding fashion until she crested a small grassy hill and was lost to sight. Nothing joined her in flight. With a relaxed sigh, I followed Luis as he and Jofrice again picked up the trail. Alfonso followed, eyes and ears alert for sounds and sights unknown to my senses.

A half hour passed and became an hour. At each half hour we would stop and rest five minutes under a solitary tree—if one were available —in silence dictated more by heat than necessity. My shirt was soaked with sweat in half-moons stretching back under my armpits to join a dampened splotch spread across my back. I took off my bush hat. My ankles itched. They were covered with bites and scratches. *What in God's name am I doing here?* I thought.

Boy, what I wouldn't give for a great big drink of something cold. With real ice. Frosted sides on the glass. And inside? Now let's see, that's the most important ingredient—no, the ice is—but what should be in the glass? How about a Cuba libre? Sort of sissy drink in some circles, but you have to admit that it can be the most refreshing damn drink in captivity. Let's see, I could use a really big glass—about a 12-ouncer—with some of those raw, jagged chunks of old-fashioned ice chopped off a 25-pound block, then a jigger or two of very fine white rum—a "silver label" at the least—and a quarter of fresh lime. Then top it all off with a full ration of chilled Coke or Pepsi. Hot damn! Or rather, cold damn is more like it.

106

"Come on, Jimmy," a hand gently squeezed my arm. We got up and with silent consent resumed the ordered file of our march.

I wish we had brought some water with us. The truck isn't all that far so there's no danger, but I wish that we had brought the water, warm or not. Suddenly a thought slipped into my mind. This stalk is taking longer than they intended! They didn't think it would take this long. Probably guessed we'd pop that bull when we topped that first rise. They hadn't counted on this anymore than I had. I glanced at Alfonso striding quietly behind me. No, that one knew, I'll bet. And I'll double or nothing he knows we're nowhere near them now. He looks like he couldn't care less.

"Where's the sable, Alfonso—are they gone?" I asked.

"It's all right, boss—a little more time and we see them. Don't worry."

"Thanks."

Alfonso nodded. I didn't flatter myself, but I knew he liked me. He liked me for a very basic reason; he knew I liked and respected him and I had shot sufficiently well in his opinion that my estimation meant something. It was that simple. We got along. If Alfonso said things were going to be all right, that was enough for me. Suddenly I felt very strongly that we were going to find the sable and I was going to let the hay out of that big bull.

I forgot the sun, the bites and the scratches, the nagging thought of half-gallon frozen Cuban libres in air-conditioned bars in Beira, Rome, Princeton, Columbus, Ohio and Glendale, Arizona. It was 1 o'clock. If we didn't catch them soon, they'd be too deep in the woods for us to ever get close enough for a shot without spooking every animal for miles around. No need to worry though, Alfonso knew.

But we kept walking and the time kept ticking by in a relentless march. One-thirty. Two o'clock. Two more breaks and nothing was said. I looked at Luis. I wondered if he was beginning to think how he could begin to feel me out about breaking it off and going back to the truck. The situation is really international I thought. Every year in every place where men come to go out with other men to hunt game the same thing happens again and again. The time comes when the guide begins to add things up in his mind and he realizes that the point of return has been reached.

Then comes the diplomacy; the measure of the expert guide who knows how to measure his client. Now, can he turn to him and say simply "let's go back—it's a bust?" Or must he keep going on until the client is so tired and miserable—and bored, maybe mad—that he doesn't give a damn about the hunt anymore but only wants to get back to camp as soon as possible? Then the client either sulks a bit or, if he's halfway decent, sheepishly comes around with hopes and plans for the next day.

"Well, Jimmy, it looks like we've had it," Luis stopped and, pushing his hat back to wipe away the sweat, turned to Jofrice, who with a solemn nod gave his assent.

"They're traveling bastards today, aren't they," I offered cigarettes around. "What say, Luis, shall we head back?" I'd do my part and make it easy.

"Well, it's almost 3 and they're sure to be holed up in the deep shade by now—probably over there in that forest to the northwest," he gestured to the darkened edge of the plain a few miles ahead. "The way this wind is shifting they probably got a whiff of us somewhere along the line and kept moving. That's probably why they never stopped to graze a little more."

"You're the doctor."

"I hate to stop now, damn it. We've almost shot the day. Look, it's too late to go back to camp for lunch. Let's head back to the Land Rover. If we move out sharply, we should get back in time to skirt that big patch of woods bordering the plain on the other side on our way back. Maybe we'll see something before dusk." He was trying to salvage something out of the day. His professional pride was a little out of joint.

I bent down to tie a lace and, straightening up to sling my rifle, I saw Alfonso. He was standing to one side of the beaten-down path we had made through the grass. His lips were pursed and his cheek muscles taut. His eyes were distant and almost clouded over. He was listening for something. No, he was smelling! I saw his wide nostrils twitch. Jofrice, who was urinating to one side, turned to watch Alfonso. Luis paused and appraised Alfonso with a careful scrutiny.

"Hold on, Jimmy," Luis murmured. "We may be on to something after all. Alfonso, what it is? Good luck?"

"Water, boss—sable." He lapsed into a native dialect with Jofrice, who, after a moment's argument, shrugged his shoulders and gave what appeared a reluctant agreement. Luis walked over to Alfonso and held a rapid, almost unintelligible exchange.

It turned out that we were standing in a drainage area. Covered with high grass now, it was a runoff stream in the rainy season.

"When the rains stop and the grasses grow, the stream disappears here," Luis explained. "But a lagoon remains in that woods up ahead where this trough ends in a big dip. Alfonso says there is always a little water there—even in drought."

"A water hole for game, I take it," I said.

"Yes, and for us a particularly good one. Alfonso says that the sable are there right now, holed up, and taking on water at the lagoon just inside the woods instead of going deep into the forest for a siesta. They'll probably come out again at dusk or later."

"What will we do—it might be too dark by then for a shot, let alone getting back to the truck?" I asked.

"Alfonso says we should head for the woods about there." Luis pointed to a jutting peninsula of trees that was closest to our party. "We can come up on the sable by the lagoon."

Luis started striding toward the woods. Alfonso quietly and swiftly moved up ahead of Jofrice and then Luis. He had taken over with Luis' full consent. This was the business he had been trained for and he had learned his lessons exceedingly well. In a short time we were in the first trees on the edge of the forest. Alfonso changed his course abruptly and, threading phantomlike through the brush and trees, carried us on an angled path that brought us a little deeper in the forest with each step while carrying us closer to the lagoon at the same time. The sun was well in the West and the shadows deepened in increasing darkness in the forest.

A few birds, awakened to the dusk and our intrusion, shrilled a scolding warning and curiously quieted in a few moments. The forest then remained hushed, seemingly barren of life.

Alfonso's movements became more deliberate and—if possible—more silent. He began to pick each step with extreme, almost gingerly care, pausing every few yards, then feet, to listen and smell. Finally, he stopped dead. We, who had almost unconsciously attempted to duplicate his pattern of tracking in our own fashion, stopped as well. He stood, tall and immobile, but slightly bent as his head cocked to one side, nostrils flared.

Now, for the first time, Alfonso brought his eyesight into play and we knew that we were very close. His eyes methodically searched the impenetrable fastness of the woods, vines, brambles and bush about him. He suddenly froze all movement—even of his eyes. We knew he saw—perhaps only sensed—the immediate presence of game. We saw nothing and remained rigid.

He waited another moment or two and then slowly stooped until one hand touched the ground. He carefully ripped a clump of dried grass from the earth and crumbled it in his strong fingers. He brought the

powdered fragments within sight of his straining eye and slowly released them. They gently floated downward in haphazard seesaw drifting until, ever so slightly, they began to glide a bit to the rear. A little
wind coming from the right direction. A small smile played about
Alfonso's lips. He straightened and motioned Luis and me forward.
Jofrice hung in the background. With a silent, almost imperceptible
movement, Alfonso raised his hand and pointed.

"Sable," he said simply.

They were spread around the near edge of the perimeter of the
lagoon. Perhaps two dozen sable antelope—the most beautiful animal
in the world to many, and certainly to me at that moment. All of the
animals, both male and female—except calves—had horns, but the females' horns were relatively small. Perhaps they went a foot or so at
most. The cows were a chestnut red running to a dark brown. A young
bull, its tail automatically switching flies, moved among a group of four

or five cows on one side of the lagoon. I followed Alfonso's nod and found the big bull. He stood to one side as an anointed leader should. The white markings about his face stood out in startling contrast to the magnificent glossy black of his coat. His huge horns curved scimitarlike back over his body in two large graceful curves. They looked as if they should just make the records.

"Now," Alfonso whispered.

I swept the lagoon with my 4x scope, taking in animal after animal, until the crosshairs rested on the shoulders of the bull. He stood—facing to my right—in the tall grass, but his shoulder joint was clearly in view where the grass broke to either side. I pushed the safety off.

The rifle cracked sharply through the forest. For a second the herd stood transfixed, but its leader had already dropped in a crumble. As the remaining sable bolted, some crashing through the brush, others splashing across the lagoon, the big bull staggered to its feet and lunged into the bush. For a moment he was lost from sight. We dashed forward, oblivious to the cutting edge of briar and thorn as it lashed our plunging legs.

"There!" Luis grabbed my arm and pointed in the bush.

The sable's head was silhouetted above the brush line against the background of the forest. I shot again. His neck dropped forward in a swift, climactic swing and he lay still. He was lost to sight in the undergrowth, but we knew it was all over.

We all stood, unmoving and unspeaking. We could hear the last clomp of hoofs and rasp of thorn brush as the sable finished their escape. And then, very suddenly, there was the complete absence of sound. Utter and total silence. I ejected the spent cartridge, jacked in another and slipped on the safety. A hand touched my shoulder.

"Very good. You shoot and kill. First shot kill too."

Alfonso was indeed my good friend.

"It's a damn good one," Luis said quietly. "Let's go check his horns. You may just make the records. I'd say that shot was just about 150 yards. Not bad—for a forest shot!" he laughed and Alfonso grinned, a rare occurrence on any day.

We walked forward through the grass and by the lagoon to the sable. It was a magnificent animal of some 400 pounds. Luis took out his tape measure while I examined the two wounds. One 140-grain bullet had gone directly in at the shoulder, making a small slitlike opening where it entered and leaving no exit. It must have broken up inside the lung cavity. My second shot made an identical entrance in the neck, but had exited on the far side with a hole about the size of a quarter. Both wounds were fatal.

"Well, this is it, Luis. I don't think I'll ever take another head of game that means as much as this one. It's the most beautiful animal I've ever seen. I've got to admit it—we haven't anything like this back home. Heck, it makes our elk look drab in comparison!" I was babbling like a 4-year-old with a new prize.

"I do believe you're pleased at that," Luis laughed. "Let's see now. No, just a shade under 39 inches, has to hit 40 to be in the records. But they're magnificent horns. Look how thick they are around the base."

"And that hide. Talk about ebony black! I've never seen a blacker hide on anything—and I don't see any scars on it anywhere," I said.

"That's rare in a mature bull. Usually they've picked up a few tokens of combat." Luis was carefully examining the bull's coat.

"I could go home now—if I had to—and be completely satisfied. Tonight's the night we crack that bottle of brandy. Boy, I can just see that head in my hallway now! And that devil Alfonso," I turned to thank the plainsman, but he was gone.

"He's gone back for the truck," Luis anticipated my question. "There's a lot of meat here and the boys will eat hearty tonight."

"I just wanted to thank him for the great tracking job he did," I said.

"Track, hell," Luis snorted, "that lean old hunter didn't track these sable. He *sensed* they were here—and don't ask me with what sense!"

My hunt was to last for another 10 days and I was to take a total of some 20 animals of various species. I was to spend six days of vigorous, often discouraging, hunting before I finally bagged a good representative head of the rare nyala, the forest phantom.

Through misunderstanding and downright stupidity on my part, combined with a little bad luck, I would turn down an easy 100-yard broadside shot at a magnificent kudu bull with horns of at least 55 inches. (I would see no more kudu that trip and the memory of what easily might have been still haunts me. But perhaps that is the way it should be; we should always leave one to come back for.)

I would have many more experiences. But the sable—the ebony black bull with the huge, curving horns—holds a special place not only in my memories of Africa but in all my hunting experiences in any land, in any time.

Full House on Leopards

"Careful, Jim, it's a steep drop," John warned. "Look out for the edge. It's overgrown with foliage. Here, I'll hold your ankles and you can snake up to the edge for a look." John Kingsley-Heath carefully eased back from the edge of the karonja, or deep ravine, where he had kneeled to peer over.

I squirmed forward and inched my way toward what appeared to be the edge. A spurt of fear shot through me. The edge was actually a foot or so closer than I had thought, but it was disguised by heavy grass bending over the end of the bank, which was badly undercut.

"Easy . . . easy. That's right, hold it there: Feel the edge?" John's voice guided my fingers, and his hands firmly gripped my ankles. I parted the grass and peered downward.

"Whew-w-w!" I whistled. The karonja fell away and in from my bank in a sheer drop of literally hundreds of feet. I could make out scattered boulders protruding from the side of the opposite bank. There was a tangle of vines and other lush foliage crisscrossing the whole complex ravine from top to bottom and side to side.

"Something, huh?" John chuckled. "We've got lots of this sort of thing up here in places like Hell's Gate. Most clients don't get to see them though. Too much trouble to get back in, and too tricky a spot for a wounded leopard."

"I don't know much about leopards," I commented, "but I'd bet my last drink of water that this is prime leopard country."

"Right," replied John. "And we're going to build a blind right over there in that tree." He gestured with his head back and below our observation point. "Come on, we've got work to do if we want to string up all three baits by nightfall."

It was the first week in June, 1963, and Scott Healy and I had come to Africa for a three-week safari. We both work for Winchester and, as with many men in the sporting firearms business, our work blended in with lifelong hobbies. Scott, who lives in Connecticut and has hunted all over the United States and Colombia, was on his first African safari. I live in the Hunterdon hills of New Jersey and my hunting experience

113

had included the United States, Canada, Korea, and Mozambique. Scott and I had boarded an Alitalia jet in New York and were in Nairobi some 26 hours later.

We had booked our safari with Ker, Downey & Selby, Ltd., a Nairobi safari firm that operates in Tanganyika, Kenya, and now Bechuanaland. Harry Selby and John had visited, surveyed, and hunted the new Bechuanaland country to the south. In fact, John was still down in Bechuanaland when we arrived. As a consequence, Scott and I went out with Dave Ommanney on our safari rather than with John. John and I had many mutual friends in America, however, and had corresponded for some time. John, who was badly mauled by a lion in 1961, has also accompanied Jack O'Connor, OUTDOOR LIFE's shooting editor, on many of his East African safaris. John, incidentally, described his terrible mauling in "A Lion Mangled Me," featured in the March, 1963, issue of OUTDOOR LIFE. John and I wanted to hunt together, even if only for a few days. When he came back to Nairobi, he joined us in the Narok District of Masailand. John could only stay four days, but he wanted to make the most of it.

Dave Ommanney is a young Englishman of marvelous temperament and rare hunting ability. In the days prior to John's arrival, and even afterward, Dave showed us much game and helped us take some excellent trophies. Scott and I took practically every head of game we wanted.

Scott, Dave, and I left with the usual complement of native bearers, trackers, cooks, and other safari personnel. Dave's men were mostly Wakamba, a tribe well-known for its hunting abilities. Our start was inauspicious to say the least. Kenya's rainy season had not abated and, although we had had a day or two of sunshine, it started to rain again as soon as we left town. It turned the plains into mud. We had to change camp three times until we found a suitable site. The rain finally stopped on the fourth day—the same day John and his men arrived from Nairobi.

While we had good luck hunting, in spite of the rain, we hadn't had any success with cats—lions or leopards. The rains, of course, hadn't helped matters and, though we had found one spot where lions and leopards had been, we had no luck with our baits. Since we couldn't bait for lions in Masailand, we had to depend on luck, and it wasn't holding up too well in the lion department. Scott and I had both taken good Grant's gazelles. Scott also collected a fine impala and I shot an eland, so we were quite happy with the results of the first few days.

114

·

When we returned for lunch with our eland, John was waiting in camp and anxious to get hunting. It was decided that we would first concentrate on nailing a leopard. Dave and Scott would form one team, John and I another. Each team would head out that afternoon and put up baits in likely spots. Next morning we would check out the baits and, if we had two being worked on, we would each take one for a stake-out that evening. It didn't make any difference which team had the leopard working. The main thing was to get two cats feeding on at least two baits. Scott had taken a zebra that morning and that would make two baits for his team. We also had a half a Grant's, half a kongoni, and I was to shoot an impala that afternoon on our way out. If possible, John and I would put up three baits that afternoon. It was going to be hard to finish the job before dark.

We had hardly left camp when Kiebe, John's senior gunbearer and tracker, spotted an impala gazing at us from the edge of a patch of wood. With a bit of luck and a good rest on a stump, I shot it with my .264 Winchester Magnum. I breathed a sigh of relief that I had not goofed my first animal in company of Mr. Kingsley-Heath.

"Jolly good shot," John commented in a matter-of-fact tone that indicated he certainly expected nothing less. "Now let's get to work and get ourselves a leopard."

The impala was loaded into the back of the hunting car and John headed toward the dark, crevice-lined hills that guarded the far approach to the main plain where we were camped. The country was flat and rolling, occasionally punctuated with a higher, lusher grass that indicated a boggish swamp, or perhaps a stand of acacia or fever trees that sheltered a water hole and sometimes an abandoned Masai village.

Game of all types, sizes, and shapes was evident on the plains. Kongoni, huge elands, zebras, Thomson's gazelles, impalas, Grant's gazelles—the plains were full of them. They stood watching until we approached too close, then they would bound away 40 yards or so before stopping to watch again.

John was silent as we rolled along. As we began to climb from the plains, the going got rougher. Tangled bush and fallen trees hindered our progress. There was no trail, of course, and we had to keep a sharp eye out for grass-covered rocks and hidden ditches. Soon it was impossible to find a path through the trees and bushes, and John began to make one as he knocked over small trees with the front of the hunting car.

115

He pulled to a halt on a ridge and glassed the country below. We could make out the darkened slash that marked a karonja. John motioned for me to follow him as he jumped from the car and made his way down the slope toward the karonja. It was this ravine that appeared to me to be prime leopard country. John selected a tree that had a big fork about 10 feet from the ground. This was to be our bait tree. He figured there was a good, clear field of fire from a blind site about 50 yards to the left.

After much maneuvering, we finally got the car down onto the slope between the tree and the blind. We hauled half a kongoni up the tree and tied it on one of the forked limbs about five feet from the crotch. John has a special way of hanging his baits. If it is a whole animal, he has all four legs tied together and the animal is suspended head and

116

back down by the legs. If it is half an animal, it is suspended by its remaining two feet. The bait is covered with branches and foliage. This accomplishes two purposes. It shields the carcass from vultures, and, more important, makes it possible for the hunter to glass the bait from a distance and tell whether or not a leopard has been feeding on it. If the covering branches are gone, you're in business.

After the bait was properly hung, John began to drive the car back and forth between the blind and bait to break down the intervening bushes. Meanwhile, the gunbearers and I made the blind. It was a brush blind, closed on three sides and with a hacked out, smooth earth floor. A small hole was made in the front at eye level and a forked rest stick lined up for sighting a rifle. The whole process took about 1½ hours.

"Right," John said. "I think that will do it. It's a fine set-up, but we're going to have to hurry if we want to finish before dark."

We were lucky. We found two more good sites, though neither quite as ideally suited as the first. With a minimum of discussion and maximum effort, we managed to finish the last blind as the sun set. All three baits were relatively close to each other, within the sound of a gunshot, but not so close as to draw the same leopard. We headed for camp. We had done our part, now it was up to the leopard.

It was almost 8 p.m. when we finally pulled into camp and found Dave and Scott were waiting for us. They had also put up three baits. If things went according to plan, we thought the chances good that we would have at least one, possibly two, leopards working in a day or so. That is, as soon as the baits were ripe enough to stimulate a little interest.

Next morning our two teams made a beeline for the respective baits. We didn't expect anything so soon, but the attraction was irresistible. We planned to meet back at camp at noon and compare notes. Since we knew where we were going this time, we made a straight line for Hell's Gate, then up to our karonja blind. John stopped the car on the same slope we had glassed from the night before.

"Well, now," John said. "Look at that." He handed me his glasses. "We're in business. The branches are all torn away and something has taken a hunk out of that hindquarter. A big leopard, I'd say."

I was so excited I could hardly find the bait in my field of vision. Then I saw the kongoni. With the protective branches removed, it stood out like a newly butchered quarter of beef. Without another word, John turned the car around and headed toward our second bait.

117

Even I needed no coaching this time. The impala hung naked and unadorned from the tree limb. Every last branch lay in a heap on the ground below. Again, there was a reddish blotch, about eight inches in diameter, to mark where a cat had been feeding on one of the hindquarters. Two baits and two leopards—and on the first morning!

"I must say I'm pleased," John said with a slow grin. "I believe we'll have ourselves an exciting evening after all. Shall we check the last blind just for the record?"

The third blind lay under a tall cliff honeycombed with smallish holes and crisscrossed with layers of ledges and rock shelfs. It was a rather high cliff, 100 yards or so. It was also an ideal place for a leopard to use as a scanning post before going to the bait, which, in this instance, was the Grant's gazelle I'd shot two days before. It was the only complete animal we had strung up.

We followed a ridge across from the cliff. The bait and blind were in a small hollow between. We could get a clear line of view from our ridge and both of us silently scanned the layout below. John turned to Kiebe and spoke to him in Swahili for a few moments.

"I'm not sure," John finally said, "but I think we've got another leopard on this bait. I can't quite see from here, so I'm going to pull up to that tree where we can get a better look at the Grant's rear." He did so.

"A full house!" John whispered excitedly. "Sh-h-h! The leopard could be up in those ledges watching the whole business. It's a little late in the morning, but in country like this, it's a possibility."

John started the car, gently slipped it into gear, and quietly rolled forward about 50 yards. He came to a halt behind a tree that screened us without completely blocking our view. It took about two seconds to confirm John's suspicions. The branches had been pulled away from the rear of the Grant's. Though the hole was small compared with the marks on the other baits, there was definite evidence that a cat had been feeding. Without a word, but with a smile and an affirmative nod, John backed out and away. We drove for a full five minutes before he spoke.

"It's hard to say how big a cat is on that last one," he said. "I'm fairly sure it's a leopard and not one of the smaller cats, but I can't say how big. It could be a small one, but it might be a larger one that didn't find the bait until almost dawn, then scared off, maybe by us."

"But what a batting average," I said. "Three cats the first morning after we hung three baits. Boy, you're batting 1.000."

"I beg your pardon," John said. "Is that good?"

118

"Never mind, it's too complicated to explain to a soccer player, but, yes, it's good, it's the best." Wait till Scott hears about this.

We were back in camp 20 minutes before Dave and Scott showed up. They had stopped to shoot some camp meat on the way. Nothing was feeding on any of their baits. It appeared all the eager leopards were on our side of the plains. When we told Scott we had three leopards working, he cast an extremely suspicious eye. Finally, after much protestation of innocence and good intent, we convinced him we really did have three leopards on the bait and one of them was his.

John and Dave pointed out that it was imperative that we be in our blinds no later than 4:30 that afternoon, preferably earlier. John and I would leave camp about 3:30. Dave and Scott would leave a few minutes earlier as they were going into their blind for the first time. Then we sat down to lunch and the important discussion of who would take what bait and the tactics involved in the approach to each blind. John finally decided the matter, as it was obviously his decision.

"You chaps take the karonja blind," he said. "It's the farthest and the one that's been worked on the most. There's a big cat on that kongoni and I'm sure he'll be back tonight. Jim and I will take the impala bait. It's been well eaten, too, and we should be in luck."

Later, as we crossed the plains toward our blind, John casually took up the subject of our choice of blinds. "Jim, I rather think that Scott and Dave are going to get a really big leopard, probably much bigger than ours. It won't make much difference, will it?"

"Are you kidding? A leopard's a leopard. I'll be happy to get any leopard." I meant it. I had hungered for a leopard so long that the idea of finally getting one was the only thing I could think about.

We pulled up a ridge and followed our tracks until we reached a grove of trees about 100 feet from where we had glassed the impala that morning. John stopped the car and explained that we wouldn't drive up to glass the bait as the leopard might be in the tree. Instead, we would get out farther down the trail and make our way around and down the slope to the blind. John started off with his Westley-Richards .470 Nitro Express double, I followed with my Winchester Model 70, chambered for the .264 Winchester Magnum, and Kiebe brought up the rear. The other two gunbearers stayed with the vehicle.

John quietly made his way down a narrow game path that led to the foot of the slope. We had just passed around a jutting boulder overhanging our path when John suddenly crouched and motioned us back. Moving swiftly, we flattened ourselves on the side of the boulder. I

119

didn't know what was happening, but I knew it was something important. I tried to stifle the sound of my breathing. My heart sounded like hammers pounding in my ears, throat, and chest.

"There's a huge cat in the tree," John whispered. "I just caught a glimpse as we rounded the corner. Don't think he saw me. Be quiet now." He slowly peered around the boulder and stopped, his gaze riveted on the scene below. He quietly slid back.

"Lion." I caught a strange inflection in his single word and guessed immediately what was wrong. Female lions were on the protected list.

"Lady lion?" I asked. John nodded and motioned for me to crawl forward for a look. I looked down the slope past our blind, still some 25 yards ahead of us, to the bait tree. As I looked, a huge, tawny cat jumped down from the tree. She was the biggest lioness I had ever seen and the first one outside of a game park or zoo. She sat there like a big tabby and scratched her ear. She looked about for a moment or two, then effortlessly leaped back into the tree. She stood over the bait, methodically tearing flesh from the impala's hindquarters as her huge tail swayed from side to side.

A pressure on my shoulder and a backward jerk of his head signaled John's intention to pull out. We quietly eased our way back to the car and jumped in. John slipped the brake and rolled back down his tracks, making a rear turn before starting the engine. In less than 10 seconds, we were heading back toward the last blind.

"We've got to hurry," John explained. "We have just enough time to get into the other blind. No time for fancy approaches. I'm going to swing right by the rear of the blind. You be ready to roll out as I go by. Cradle your rifle and keep rolling toward the blind as you fall. The ground is beaten down there and you shouldn't get messed up. I'll swing back and park the car. Kiebe and I will crawl up to the blind, but you may be in business before we get there. Be careful and don't start anything until we get there. That leopard might be in the tree right now."

I nodded. I was so excited I couldn't talk. I knew there was a leopard in the tree. I had seen the lioness and, after that, I was prepared for anything.

John swung by the blind. I rolled out in my best paratrooper fashion, crawled into the blind expecting to meet a leopard fang on the way, and settled down for one of the longest periods of my life, or so it seemed.

In a few moments, John and Kiebe joined me. I was tense with excitement, every nerve in my body was straining toward the bait tree some 40 yards away, where I knew my leopard had to come. Kiebe stretched out beside the blind in a little hollow and went to sleep. This irritated me no end. Didn't he know we were about to be accosted by a big leopard? John pulled out a notebook and began to make out a report on Bechuanaland.

Fifteen minutes later, we heard a distant shot, then another. John looked up from his notebook and smiled. Scott had connected. Kiebe scratched his nose, pulled his hat back over his eyes, and went back to sleep. My legs began to cramp, but I was afraid to move. John said no movement.

Half an hour passed and I had given up all ideas of immediate conquest. An hour went by and I started to daydream. It was 4:45 when we entered the blind. At 6 p.m. I despaired of ever seeing a leopard from this blind. Luck was just against me.

By 6:30 I was counting the minutes until dusk when we could pull out of this place for a tall, cool drink back at the camp. After all, Scott had taken a leopard. We would have ample reason for celebration. Tomorrow was another day and maybe we'd nail one then. I looked at my watch. It was 6:45. I felt a hand on my arm.

"Quiet," John whispered. "There's a big leopard under the tree. Be careful. Gently now. No fast movements. Ease your gun up."

I had my rifle resting, barrel in the fork, butt on the ground in front of me. I moved it slowly up to my shoulder. The telescopic sight came to my eye. I gently eased my position until the fading light filled my scope and the tree came into view. I slowly dropped the sight down the tree trunk. There, sitting majestically in all its feline grace, was a large, yellow cat. A giant head, immobile on its intent concentration of the surroundings, crowned its powerful shoulders. The great cat appeared fascinated by the blind. It looked as if it was peering right down the scope and into my eye. It knew I was there and what I was going to do. I was frozen.

"Get ready. Take your time. Take him in the chest," John whispered.

With a graceful, almost lazy movement, the leopard suddenly sprang into the fork of the tree. I turned and sat once more. The crotch of the tree framed the animal against the fading light. I held my breath. The crosshairs finally settled on the leopard's chest. I squeezed the trigger and the sound of a rifle shot reverberated through the hills.

121

I have a fleeting memory of the leopard hurtling backward from the tree, as if someone had yanked him with a strong wire. The shot finished its echo and there was a moment of complete silence. Then there was a low growl, two more, then silence again. Nothing moved. Finally, I heard John expel his breath in a quiet, controlled fashion and he carefully stood up. Kiebe also rose and, finally, I did, too. It was suddenly quite dark.

Picking his way with extreme care, John eased around the blind. Kiebe, with equal caution, moved around the other side. I followed John until we all stopped a few feet in front of the blind.

"I don't like those three growls," John said. "One's a sort of death rattle. Three could be bad. Where did you hit him?" His voice was serious and low. I pointed to my chest. We were standing abreast, our guns pointed to the low brush behind the tree. Even though we had beaten it down yesterday, there was still enough cover for a wounded leopard to hide in, belly against the ground.

John motioned and we crept forward, each putting a carefully placed foot down, stopping and listening, then moving again. It took a good five minutes for us to reach the bait tree. No sound nor movement betrayed any sign of life in the brush. A faint stream of light from the moon was now making its way overhead. We inched forward another foot or so, then John straightened up, but he was still careful to keep his gun covered on something in the grass about 20 feet ahead. Kiebe threw a rock and hit the animal on the flank. No movement. He threw another. Still no movement. We went forward.

The leopard was beyond caring about tossed rocks. He was dead. My 140-grain Powder Point .264 Winchester Magnum bullet had hit him squarely in the chest and had put his heart and lungs permanently out of business.

"Well, Jim," John said quietly, "you've got yourself a beauty. He's the biggest leopard I've seen for quite some time. You can be proud of this one. I think he'll make the record book."

John pulled the leopard's tail out straight as the gunbearers drove up. There was much excitement, clapping of shoulders, shaking of hands, and wild shouts. I found out just how big the leopard was when we loaded it into the back of the car.

The lights of the camp sent a gentle glow through the trees as we approached. As we drove up, we found Scott and Dave sitting in front of a burning log with their nightly sundowners firmly grasped in their hands. A leopard was stretched in magnificent splendor before them.

122

Its front paws were stretched out to flank its head, which was supported by a forked stick. It was an impressive sight. Home was never like this.

"Well, what do you think of that!" Scott said. He pointed to the female cat stretched out before us. "Darndest thing you ever saw. We barely got into the blind and TWO leopards came to the bait. TWO! This one here and a smaller male."

"Scott decided to take the female as she was considerably larger," added Dave. "Did you hear our shots? Well, he hit her to one side first and she came out of the tree like a bolt of lightning and headed up that slope to the right at about 50 miles an hour. Old Scotty swung on her as if he had a shotgun and bowled her over with one shot through the shoulders. Fine shot. How did you chaps do? Didn't hear any shots."

"Oh, we've got a little camp meat in the back of the car," John remarked casually. "Don't suppose you're interested though."

"Oh, what is it?" Scott asked politely. Dave shot a fast look at John and me as we began to stroll toward the car.

"I think we've been had, Scott," Dave said. "Kingsley-Heath is grinning like some sort of Cheshire cat and Rikhoff's fit to burst. Come on, let's get it over with and really start celebrating."

We did. We measured my leopard and found he pegged out to seven feet three inches—well in the records. He weighed 146 pounds. A certificate of record from Rowland Ward is currently resting in a place of honor.

Scott and I took more heads after our great leopard hunt, but that evening ranks as one of the highlights of our safari. I took a lion a few days later and both of us shot fine buffaloes the last week of the trip. Scott collected his buffalo with a Winchester Model 70, chambered for the .458 Winchester Magnum. I nailed mine with a .375 H. & H. Magnum bullet, also out of a Model 70 Winchester. We took our buffaloes under the shadow of Mt. Kilimanjaro, a fitting climax to a successful safari.

123

Lions Are Deadliest Just Before They Die

On the fourth night of our safari in Kenya's Masailand we sat with our two leopards propped up in front of the fire and celebrated. We shared a comaraderie that can only come when everything has gone for the best. My professional hunter, John Kingsley-Heath, and I had strung up three fresh baits the day before. My partner, Scott Healy, and his hunter, Dave Ommanney, had hung another two. This evening Scotty and I both had knocked over leopards, which must be some sort of record for speed and efficiency in leopard hunting.

We had the best of everything and that happens rarely in anyone's life. We knew it and we were making the most of it. Tomorrow would be another day—perhaps the same as today or, by some fantastic chance, better, but more likely a little drab in comparison to the achievements of this fine day.

Then, as we sat with our drinks late into the night, we heard a distant cough. Silence fell upon the group as if by some signal. A grunting rumble rolled in from the night. It was a sound I had heard only once before, in Mozambique. Scotty, even though he had never heard the sound before, knew exactly what it was.

"Yes, that's a lion—a big, hungry, male lion," Scotty said. "It's over there on that hill where the Masai boy said it would be." It was that simple. We got up from the fire, the excitement of our leopards swept away by the insistence of that impatient, grunting demand.

We had a lion in our district and it was only a mile away. Everything had changed. We now had a lion in our own backyard, and it was up to us to figure how to take the animal.

In our beds that night we listened to the lion over on its hill. The animal was either very hungry, very passionate or very disgruntled because it kept up its steady grunting-coughing routine for as long as I could keep my eyes open. I went to sleep with its roar in my ears and its picture in my mind. The picture was sharply defined. The lion was big, with a heavy black mane. It was stone dead and I, gun in hand, stood over it in a Teddy Roosevelt stance.

At breakfast the next morning our leopards were almost forgotten. The talk was of lions. John Kingsley-Heath spoke in the quiet, final

124

tone that I had grown to respect. "Listen, chaps," he said. "we should not pass up that poached giraffe that Scotty and Dave spotted over on the private farm outside the preserve." A lion had been working on one of the hindquarters. Scotty and Dave agreed that they would check the carcass.

"Jim and I will head for the lion's hill," John said, nodding toward me. "It probably killed last night on the plain and is sleeping its gluttony off not very far from the remains."

Breakfast was a hurried affair. We had other things on our minds. With Scott and Dave off in one direction, John and I loaded up the other Land Rover and made a straight line for the round hill where the lion had spent its noisy night. It was a short trip and in a very few minutes we were loading our rifles for a sneak up a path we had noted the day before.

I had brought only one rifle to Africa with me—my favorite Winchester Model 70 in .264 Winchester Magnum. But Kenya's law requires that a .375 or larger must be used on lion, so John had loaned me a well-stocked and slightly worn Model 70 in .375 H&H Magnum.

As I loaded the big rifle with 300-grain Silvertip ammunition I hoped that I would shoot well—or miss cleanly. A wounded lion is no nicked whitetail deer. Many consider a wounded lion to be the most dangerous animal on earth and the record would seem to bear this out. More hunters have been killed by wounded lions than by any other species in Africa. The year before a wounded lion had killed an American hunter in Angola shortly after he had made the mistake of shooting the big cat with a small .300 Magnum bullet.

John loaded his .470 double-gun, handed it to Kiebe, his senior gunbearer, and with an inquisitive glance at me, started walking up the hill. He had the lion figured for an area immediately on the crest. We would follow our winding path from the base of the hill, proceed around it toward the opposite side and would hope to come up on the animal before it either winded or heard us. From that moment on, its actions would decide what form the script would take. I slung the .375 over my shoulder and followed John. I kept thinking, *This is really it—I am finally going after a lion and anything can happen.*

I had spent a lot of time speculating on exactly what could happen. First, the lion could be gone and that would take care of the matter right away. Or, the animal could be there and I could kill it with one shot—and that would be fine for everybody, with the obvious exception of dead simba. Next, I could miss completely and the lion could take off in the other direction; we could consider this a draw—we don't get the lion, but then the lion doesn't get any of us. Lastly, I could wound the lion. I didn't like to think about this at all, but it kept intruding into my thoughts. It was not a happy picture.

But none of these possibilities turned out. We crept along the trail for about 15 or 20 minutes. We were steadily climbing and the going was rough in spots, so that I began to find myself a little winded. Suddenly, as we neared the top and were coming around a corner, John stopped short and called me urgently. But all I had seen was a flash of yellow hurtling with unbelievable speed into the brush. I didn't even get the rifle to my shoulder.

On the way back to camp John outlined a plan. While he thought we had ruined our chances with our lion that morning, he felt that we should at least make a drive through the heavy cover the lion had disappeared into on the slope of the hill. There was a chance the lion had remained hidden there rather than cross the open plain for another patch of cover somewhere in the surrounding country. We would equip the camp personnel with pots and tin cans and send them across the cover. Scotty and I would be on stands.

Scott and Dave were having lunch when we drove up. They had had bad luck too. They had heard the lion coming to the dead giraffe. But the animal must have winded them before coming into the open. In any event, it had suspected all was not quite right and had never shown itself. They were still full of hope for the evening or following morning. In the meantime, they were enthusiastic about John's plans for the afternoon lion drive.

In a short time our mixed band of hunters was back at the hill. After a bit of planning and assignment of responsibilities. Scotty and I were taken to our stands by Dave. I was left by a tree about midway up the hill with instructions to climb it, get comfortable on a good-sized limb, keep quiet and wait.

Dave and Scotty took off and I felt very much alone. I got up the tree in very short order, but my position dismayed me somewhat. While there was quite a bit of space between the ground and my limb in front, there was very little between my sagging posterior and the sharply rising ground behind me.

John had taken the drivers to the opposite side of the brush. After another 10 minutes or so I suddenly heard the first tentative banging and rattling of pots and cans, and some of the most unenthusiastic shouting I've ever heard. The Africans, understandably, were not very keen about their job. The noise continued and then I made out the

126

first figure carefully wending its way forward through the brush on the opposite flank of our hill. Soon a few more men drifted into view. Nothing seemed to be stirred by their noise-making. If there were any lions in the vicinity, they were lying mighty low.

Then I heard a slight noise. Perhaps it was the rattle of a small rock as it rolled downhill. I saw or heard nothing for the next few moments but I knew that something was making its stealthy, quiet way toward my tree ahead of the beaters on the other side. I gripped my rifle and my limb tightly, checked my safety, placed it on half-safe, tentatively raised the Model 70 to my shoulder.

Another noise. And then I noted a movement in the brush a scant 20 yards directly in front of my perch. I brought the rifle up as the silent figure glided out of the brush and walked directly under my tree—and I almost fell off the limb as the hyena lost itself in the brush behind me. It was the only animal the beaters put out that day.

We were now a discouraged crew. On the way back to camp John gently pointed out that our lion-hunting days were probably over. We had had our chance, which is all any man can ask for, and now we would go back to hunting plains game in a nice leisurely fashion. Meanwhile, Scotty and Dave would go back to their giraffe carcass to wait out their lion. They had a good chance since that particular beast had not been rustled up as much as mine.

Dave and Scotty got up in the middle of the night and were off for their lion site long before dawn. John and I luxuriated in our cots until the decadent hour of 6 a.m., had a long lazy breakfast and decided to make an easy hunt on the plains in the early morning air about 7 a.m. In short order we were casually rolling along in the Land Rover with Kiebe and Mohammed as companions. There was an early morning haze drifting up from the plain.

There was a grove of acacia and fever trees shielding a small water hole to the right of our intended path some 300 or 400 yards away. We were plotting a course between yesterday's lion hill and that water hole when John suddenly pulled to a halt. He remained silent as he continued to stare ahead. I looked forward and suddenly something— I know not what to this day—made me uneasy. I was aware that something was somehow wrong, but I could not put my finger on it. At the same time Kiebe murmured something in Swahili to John, who grunted what seemed to be an affirmative.

"Listen to those jackals over at the water hole," I remarked, "sounds like they're really feasting."

"Yes, yes, look a minute, Jim." John's quiet tones had an undercurrent of expectant excitement. "See those kongoni! They should be staring at the water hole or us, but they're not . . . they're looking up at the hill. Let's see . . . Hell's Bells, there are two lions!" He shoved the Land Rover into low, spun the steering wheel, drove in a wide circle. We were heading back behind the hill.

In no time flat John had the Rover revved up into second and then third. We were soon bouncing along the plain at a good 35 miles an hour, which is a lot faster than anyone should. I crawled back into the rear seat and got our big-bore rifles ready. Then—as we jostled and bounced along our way—I stuck my head and shoulders through the porthole in the top of the cab so I could keep the lions in sight. John wanted to know if they moved or showed any alarm at our movement.

Once we rounded the hill the lions were out of sight. Without a word, everyone but Mohammed jumped from the vehicle. With John in the lead, we took off at a fast pace for the top of the hill. I stayed right on John's heels.

"Look, you'll have about half a minute at best for your shot when we pop over that hill. The lion will be in that thick brush in a flash when it gets wind of us," John whispered as he lengthened his stride.

I nodded, a thousand thoughts and questions going through my head. And then we were at the top of the hill and John crouched down as he eased his body over the crest. I was a second behind him, but only a second. I looked down and there they were. I threw my rifle to my shoulder as the lioness popped her head up and the male jumped to its feet.

"Shoot—shoot quick! They've seen us!" There was a flash of yellow that sped through my telescopic sight. I swung the Model 70 like a shotgun and pulled the trigger as my sight swept through the lion's running shoulder. The crack of the rifle blurred my vision in the sight and I raised my head for a second just in time to see the lion spin its back quarters a bit. I hurriedly worked another cartridge into the chamber and tossed another bullet behind the lion as it disappeared into the brush, the lioness hard on its heels. The whole thing was over in less than 10 seconds.

"Oh, hell . . . you've missed. Well, that ties it, you'll never get another chance like that!" Kingsley-Heath said in quiet despair. "Two great chances . . . I guess lions just aren't your meat."

"No, no!" Kiebe was gesturing violently and with firm conviction. He had raised his left arm and repeatedly pointed with his right forefinger to the rib area directly below the armpit.

"Shot? Are you sure?" John turned to me, "Jim, Kiebe says that you hit. Did you? I didn't hear the bullet hit or see anything."

"I think I hit him the first time . . . his hind end seemed to spin around. It happened so fast I can't be sure, but I think so." Kiebe had run to where the lions had been sitting and was shouting and wildly gesturing. We ran forward. There was blood and bits of flesh on the ground.

"Oh, my lord, you've shot him in the ass," John sighed as if someone had just passed a hanging sentence with little hope of reprieve. He stood there shaking his head, silent for a moment or two, listening carefully for another minute and then turning to speak in a long, low conversation in Swahili with Kiebe who had lost quite a bit of his previous enthusiasm. After a moment, he turned to me, gave me a careful glance, seemed to make up his mind about something, and motioned me to check my rifle and closely follow him. Kiebe brought up the rear.

We walked very slowly and quietly forward for a few paces and then stopped. John and Kiebe said nothing and I—in the blackest despair—kept my mouth shut. Both of my companions seemed to be straining for some sixth sense that would keen their natural five to some sort of hint of what was ahead. Silence. No bird sang. No animal chattered. The wind was still. We went forward a few more paces. We were entering the first scattered bits of brush and bush that thickened a few yards ahead and concealed anything that might be lurking in the shadows.

We stopped, listened and then continued a bit farther. Again and again we stopped. Still nothing. Only an occasional bit of flesh on a bush or a crimson drop on the grass forced the reality of the situation onto us. We could not forget or pretend that it had never happened. And then John motioned us back.

We slowly walked backward, our faces and guns pointed forward into the hidden danger ahead. In a few more minutes we were back in the open and down the slope. Mohammed was waiting for us by the tree that had sheltered the lions for their sunbath another world before. He had brought the Land Rover up, expecting to load a lion. Instead he had found a mess—the classical case of the wounded lion in heavy brush with possible death for some.

When we got back to the vehicle, John sighed heavily, propped his rifle against the fender and lit a cigarette. I stood silent and ashamed. Ashamed that I had put these decent, hardworking, honorable people in such a rotten mess. I knew that John had been badly mauled by a

129

client's wounded lion in 1961 and had very nearly died. Kiebe saved his life but had been chewed up a bit as well. Both of them had a finely engraved memory of wounded lions.

Kiebe suddenly barked a short Swahili sentence and pointed downhill and across the plain below us. We followed his finger to the slowly moving Land Rover patiently making its way on a parallel path some miles distant. A lazy ribbon of dust rose behind the car for some distance We ran forward shouting and waving our shirts. When it seemed that they would continue on without seeing us, the Rover suddenly veered in our direction and picked up speed. It was Scotty and Dave, of course, and in five minutes they pulled up beside us.

"What goes, chaps, got a lion or something?" Dave said with a grin.

"Yes, a wounded lion—over there in that brush," John said.

"Goodbye," Dave said. But they got out of the car. Dave's grin was gone. He had been bitten by a wounded leopard a couple of years before. As I hurriedly briefed Scotty on one side, Dave and John held a conference with their senior gunbearers. In a few moments they came over and told us to load up our rifles and take a stand on the top of the Land Rovers. We would be able to command the area below a small bluff they intended to climb for a view of the brush they thought hid the lion. They took a long swing around through the open, went over the rim of the ridge and approached the knoll from behind. We watched from below as they hunkered down to scan the brush below them.

They sat and sat and sat. Then they conferred and sat some more. And so it went for a good 20 minutes. Finally a decision was reached. The whole party got up and proceeded down on the opposite side— through the brush—from which they had climbed originally. In another 10 minutes they were back.

"We got a surprise," John said. "We thought he was down in that brush under that little knob. But when we took a long swing around and down through the brush on our way back, we cut his blood trail leading out over to that heavy brush farther along the side of the hill. We've got to follow him up right away before he runs across a native."

The two pros got out their double rifles—both .470s. Scott limbered up his .458 Model 70. Kiebe, Katheka and I all had .375 H&H Model 70 rifles. John outlined the ground rules. The name of the game was kill the lion as fast and as completely as possible. If you saw the lion, start shooting . . . you might not get many seconds to make up your mind. Dave led the way and John backed him up. Scotty covered the high ground. I covered the low ground below our path. Kiebe and Katheka covered our rear.

We would stalk a few yards and stop to listen. When we did, everyone would face outward to form the classic "British square." Safeties off. In no time at all we had picked up a patch of blood where the lion had lain down after its first escape. Spots here and there showed its retreat on a steady line to the left around the hill.

We went forward a few yards and stopped as before. Every sense was tense, expecting the worst. Curiously, I felt a strange excitement. We continued a few more yards and stopped, then a few more punctuated by another hesitation. And then suddenly John, who was immediately in front of me and slightly above to the left, raised his rifle and fired. All heads and rifles turned toward the spot where he had aimed. Nothing moved.

"I missed him," John said. "I just saw the top of his mane and took an estimate where his head was and shot. Couldn't take a chance. I saw him take off." He moved forward and held something up. His .470 bullet had clipped a bit of mane.

A shout from Kiebe drew our attention behind us. We turned to see Kiebe bending down over a dark patch 20 feet directly behind where Scott and I had stood.

When we ran down, we found a patch of darkening, already clotting blood.

"John, you shot at another lion!" Dave gasped and turned his rifle toward a bloody path leading away from the gore. "He must have laid doggo here through the whole thing . . . boy, we're lucky he didn't take somebody when we all turned at John's shot. Two lions . . . just what we needed!"

"Let's get to it," John said. "He can't be far ahead and from the look of that blood he's hurt worse than we thought." Without another word, the white hunters started down the path of broken grass and occasional blood spore.

We had just got our party sorted out and in their customary position on the trail—with each guarding an approach to the group—when there was a low growl. Dave came skittering back toward me and a flash of yellow spurted out of the brush as two quick shots split the air. The lion turned and was gone again.

"Missed him, I think, but maybe not," Dave said. "Can't tell, but he won't be turned again. Come on, Jim, he's your lion. Scotty, keep your safety off too." He checked his partner with a glance and they were off. We hadn't gone 20 yards when that same growl filled my ears, heart, bowels and every inch of my frame. I forced my feet forward just as I saw Dave raise his rifle again. The lion was coming out of the grass. Dave shot. The lion jumped, the bullet tearing into its back.

"Get him, Jim!" I shot. The bullet bit into the upper shoulder, breaking the animal down. The lion savagely bit at the wound as I shot another time. The bullet hit the paw and entered the head. The animal raised its head, but the mane obscured a good shot. I shot again, tearing into its spine. The lion was turning and twisting, trying to get back at us. I shot again and the lion collapsed. I had finally found the brain. The lion quivered, shuddered in a last convulsion and relaxed into death. We watched the still form for a few tentative moments. Kiebe tossed a rock, then another. He poked a long stick at the lion's eyelid.

"He's dead," John said. "He ought to be—with all those holes in him."

"You said shoot till he didn't move and I shot," I answered.

"I'm not complaining, I'm not complaining!" John's face opened in a wide, happy grin. "Well, I must say I'm glad this ended this way." Kiebe was examining the lion's chest and muttering to himself.

"What's that?" John asked. "Jim hit him in the ribs with the first shot after all?" Kiebe was acting very smug. His estimation of my original shot was right. My shot had entered directly below and behind the shoulder. But due to my elevated position on the top of the hill,

132

the bullet had angled down to come out of the bottom of the lion's body instead of coursing through the lungs to the other side and out.

"I take back all those things I've said and the many more I've thought," John said. "That was either the best or the luckiest damn shot you've ever made in your life!"

"Lucky, I didn't even know I'd hit him for sure, but I'm glad I didn't make a botch of it with a shot in his rear."

"That would have been a dead lion in a couple more hours," Dave added.

The mention of time brought me back to reality. We had not been thinking about hours and minutes. I looked at my watch. It was 11 o'clock. I had shot the lion about 7:30. This had been a hair-raising way to spend a sunny morning in Africa.

Kenya's Game

Some 55 years ago Teddy Roosevelt shot a lion on the outskirts of the then frontier town of Nairobi. If today's traveler bothers to glance out of the window as his jet lands at Nairobi's modern airport, he might still see lions roaming with considerable freedom a few scant yards from burgeoning developments. The lions, of course, are protected pampered pets of the Nairobi National Park, but they are undoubtedly wild and their way of life—based on a steady diet of readily available antelope—remains unchanged from Teddy's more romantic day. Whether or not the great tradition of African game shall remain in any form is the question in the minds of a singularly mixed bunch of interested parties.

Although there are those who steadfastly oppose all change of the status quo—be it African lion or colonial government—most African observers are reconciled to the world's oldest fact of life: Things are in a constant state of change. While that change may not necessarily be classed as "Progress," it is a sure bet that Africa's wildlife generally —and Kenya's specifically—will never be the same again. The argument —and it is often violently partisan—lies in what role game will have in the new world of *uhuru* and *harambee*. It may well be that "independence" and "work together" hold little promise for an itinerant impala intent on new graze.

African game has always held a fascination for the peoples of Europe and America. The almost prehistoric qualities of many of the great beasts combined with the utter magnitude of the herds themselves has served as an almost mystic passport to another world, a world strange, forbidding yet fascinating, to the over-civilized pedestrian man of the West. Africa has always been a forbidden garden and the white man has indulged many a surreptitious passion in the continent's black heartland.

Not the least of these indulgences has been the European and later the American—devotion to Africa's game. This almost monomaniac interest has ranged from the plain, undisguised blood lust exhibited by the worst trophy and market killers to the equally extreme over-protection of an Albert Schweitzer.

Trophy hunter, market slaughterer, safari manager, park ranger, professional game ecologist, conservationists (both dedicated and dilettante), agricultural specialist, emerging statemen of similarly emerging African politics, old recalcitrant settlers, and newly assertive tribesmen: The list is legion. All have a vested interest in what position game will have in the "New Kenya." All have very definite ideas on how that position will be first determined and second implemented. It is not too great a surprise that most of these opinions are in wide contradiction. A review of positions is indicated.

There are three basic land uses in Kenya: (1) areas where man's interests are paramount (2) those where game interests take precedent, and (3) those areas where neither game nor man are the prime consideration. Needless to say, the areas devoted to man's interests are already well-defined and will continue to expand in the future. The pressure for more farm land by the impoverished tribes will be almost impossible to withstand regardless of logic opposing it in many areas. Man, in the last analysis, must always come before animal— even when it is to man's ultimate detriment.

When we speak of "game areas," we mean those lands under control of the trustees of the National Parks, those game reserves under control of African District Councils and, lastly, controlled area blocks where only photography is permitted. These areas are vastly important not only to the future of game specifically, but Kenya generally. The National Parks and controlled game reserves can provide the sanctuary needed to preserve the many endangered species and, by this unselfish act, guarantee the selfish goal of tourist promotion. All of these lands will be under pressure to contract by shortening and rationalizing existing boundaries. Some preserves will simply disappear.

Those great areas of land which at present are devoted neither to man nor beast provide the most interesting and most important question mark in Kenya's future. Since man has not recognized their value yet—or at least put a premium on it—by coveting it for himself or dedicating it as a game preserve, these "open" lands are largely classified as "hunting blocks" and the game is managed by the game department.

These areas are all defined and boundried at present. Since they are usually open to hunting, they are managed by the game department in order to provide the best proper harvest compatible with local conditions. Two goals are considered: the economic harvest of surplus game animals and the provision of income for Kenya on both a national (licenses) and local (trophy fees) level. While there would be

135

no overt acknowledgement of the fact, unfortunately, man's needs are often favored over the game as a result of tribal pressure.

Since the future of game in areas devoted to man's interest is hopeless and game parks are beneficial only to those species able to adjust to an unbalance of nature, the best hope for long term prospects is in the so-called "hunting blocks"—provided man is given no major advantage and controlled professional hunting is encouraged. There are sound reasons for this statement and I will cover them later.

Unfortunately, there is little unity of purpose among those most concerned with Kenya's game, but the future is far from dismal. The old market hunter and safari slaughterer are practically creatures of the past. The modern trophy hunter is often a conservationist more determined to preserve game than most of the "bleeding heart" animal lovers who rarely put any money where their mouths have been quivering. Needless to say, the professional game management people—whether they be scientist or merely dedicated game rangers—are solidly on the side of the angels. So are the conservationists. It's just a question who and what the angels are. There is a division of opinion concerning how game is to be preserved and where hunting fits into the picture.

Many of the old settlers wiped out the game on their farms in the belief it was competing with their cattle. Since a great deal of the game already had been removed from farmland and the white settler's influence is diminishing anyway, their position will have little influence on the future of game in Kenya. What is more important is the attitude of the people who will be taking over many of the larger farms and moving into previously uncultivated areas and putting it into small farms. The land and meat-hungry African has little love for the game as such. It is hard for a starving African to appreciate the esthetic beauty of an animal he wants to eat—or which he feels is stealing his crops.

The effect of agriculture—and land distribution as a result of the new government's reforms—on game can be devastating unless properly implemented. In areas devoted solely to man's interest, game will simply be eradicated by what we would call "clean" farming on the tight sectionalized farms of high-density settlement schemes. A large ranch or a mixed plantation growing cash crops such as coffee or pyrethum, is not very much affected by game damage. When such farms are purchased and split up for small holdings, game causes severe damage and loss to the African farmers involved. The game goes.

The problems of mass land distribution are new; the age old evils of over-grazing are traditional with the African tribesman. The problem of over-grazing—and subsequent soil erosion—is made doubly difficult by the fact that the African continues to count his wealth in his number of cattle regardless of quality. It is much the same sort of trap our own Navaho Indians pursued with their sheep and with much the same results. The solution—according to the Kenyan Government—lies in education rather than legislation, but one wonders if the game or the land can afford to wait.

Poaching is one of the great problems facing any government attempting to manage and preserve game in any African country. The native African does not naturally "love" game, but rather regards it either as a pest that complicates his life or as a meat market that will never close or empty. There is no reason why he should regard it as anything more.

In the past, the shooting was usually reserved for the European, and the African was severely punished—if caught—when he presumed to kill any animal that he might regard as a trespasser or his just due from the land. The esthetic beauty of photographing or preserving animals in a park for their own sake simply escapes the average tribesman. Hence, he is little affected by the argument that game should be preserved for wealthy foreigners to shoot or for little old ladies from Minnesota who want to snap pictures for the folks at home. Why should he be? What does he get out of it?

But the leaders of Kenya—Prime Minister Jomo Kenyatta, Lawrence Sagini, the Minister for Natural Resources, and R. Achieng Oneko, the Minister for Information, Broadcast and Tourism—are dedicated to the knowledge that game is a vital asset to the economy of the country and must not be squandered. The new government is determined to conserve wildlife and other natural resources and, frankly, they make no bones about their reasons.

Mr. Sagini has said that "the destruction of East Africa's wildlife would mean the destruction of one of the mainstays of the economy of Kenya—for in there lies a vast income potential for which we have no alternative and which is our own unique heritage." Forget the heritage: One realistic conservation statement based upon old-fashioned appreciation for money is worth a hundred altruistic sentiments.

The new government's attitude appears to be based on a full comprehension of the problems facing the country's game. Recently, F. D. Homan, Permanent Secretary for Natural Resources, wrote me the following evaluation:

137

The government is determined to conserve its wildlife and attract visitors. However, we can only allow a limited number of hunters per annum if game populations are to be maintained and therefore the expansion of tourism must be for visitors who come to view and photograph wildlife. We can quite easily obtain the maximum number of hunters permissable and therefore do not need to go in for cheap or government sponsored safari schemes.

In other words, Kenya apparently has no intention of going into the inexpensive mass safari business as epitomized by first the Uganda and now the Tanganyika Wildlife Development Companies that provide an all-inclusive safari for some $2,700, including roundtrip Alitalia airfare from New York and all licenses. These schemes, which have been the subject of wide argument by hunters, safari companies and conservationists all over the world, have been successfully operating for the past several years, first in Uganda and later in Tanganyika. Since they pose a threat to the traditional safari companies, they have been perhaps the most explosive element injected into the African wildlife picture. Regarding Kenya, its game future and the old line safari companies, Ernest Juer, the organizer and first general manager of the new development projects, had this to say in a signed statement:

Kenya could well institute schemes for getting not only the licenses fees but also profits from hunting operations back where they should be, to the owners of the land and its game, and not into the pockets of 'game mining companies.' Kenya could well restrict, as have the other territories, the bags taken to sportsmanlike proportions, thus spread the available game over many more clients and get more value from it, in terms of total income. Kenya's safari industry may eventually have to live on Kenya's resources in game, instead of milking those of its neighbors. It could do this by instituting schemes similar to those already successfully operating in Uganda and Tanganyika.

The big safari companies could not agree less to such proposals and take violent exception to some of Mr. Juer's other remarks. John Kingsley-Heath, one of East Africa's most famous hunters and a director of Ker, Downey & Selby, Ltd., possibly Africa's most well-known safari firm, made this rebuttal:

It is inevitable that Kenya's Nairobi, as the main communication center in East Africa, shall perhaps see more of the tourist than the

138

other two territories as this is where most East African tours commence. Traditionally the center of the safari business, Nairobi is becoming more so due to the increased facilities offered to jet aircraft and good hotel accommodations.

The game policy of Kenya has always been a little in advance of other territories, particularly at present where the African District Councils receive profits from the sale of game licenses in their area and the fees charged when hunters enter their tribal reserves. The greatest cooperation and trust exists between the Professional Hunter's Association, the Kenya Game Department and the National Parks. Hunters are always represented at game conferences. The Professional Hunter's Association takes an active part through its members on the National Park Board of Trustees in preserving game. Often the first move to protect a species is innovated by the Association who are perhaps the people in fact most in contact with the game situation throughout the whole territory.

Hunting therefore is controlled not only by the Game Department, but also by the hunters themselves whose first interest is that their livelihood should prosper. Without careful control in cooperation with the authorities, it never would. The tourist industry relies to considerable extent on its publicity of the attractions of the countries of East Africa or film companies making a location in East Africa. Large safari outfitters have both the experience and staff with which to take care of this. Safari business is therefore an integral part of the tourist trade and not necessarily entirely devoted to hunting.

Secretary Homan appears to agree with Mr. Kingsley-Heath not only regarding the future of cheap or government-sponsored safaris, but also in regard to the value of letting some of that safari money sift down to the local level:

Poaching is, of course, one of our main difficulties. We feel that a long term answer to this problem must lie in encouraging local people who live in game areas to realize that wild life is a valuable asset. We have under consideration a plan to allow local authorities a very much greater share of the revenue from licensing and from the sale of trophies from animals shot on control. This would enable them to set up their own schemes to pay compensation for damage to person and property and, since they will obtain financial benefit from game, it is hoped that they will themselves stop the menace of poaching.

139

Money then is the key. Any conservation scheme that ignores the vast hungering needs of the native peoples of Kenya is based upon an unrealistic—and doomed—foundation. Kenya's game is far from lost, but its continued preservation is dependent upon a few harsh facts of life. One, all the hand-wringing protestestions and representations made by professional conservationists will not accomplish the salvation of one species without some evidence offered that those animals can pay their way. Secondly, any conservation scheme that tries to ignore—or, worse, attempts to exclude—the necessary reality of hunting is very likely doomed from the start. Hunting is the only means by which sufficient money can be injected into the country's economy to make any appreciable effect upon the local native people concerned.

Purist conservationists who reject hunting are long on sentiment and mighty short on bucks. A short examination of the history of game management in this richest—and most soft-hearted—of countries will reveal that the costs of preserving American game are carried by the hunter. When the sweet little old ladies of both sexes whimper in joy over the sight of a wild animal, that pleasure was quite likely paid for by some bloody-handed hunter down the road.

As far as Kenya is concerned, the African Wildlife Leadership Foundation—the leading American group concerned with Africa's game and a very fine organization—is proud of the fact that it has put approximately $200,000 "to work to save the African game" in one three-year period. This is very admirable, but it is a drop in the bucket compared to the over $1,500,000 hunters spent in Kenya alone in 1960. I do not downgrade the efforts of sincere conservation organizations; I only wish to place them in proper prospective. They simply do not have the means to preserve African game without the revenue provided by hunting licenses, fees, and other expenses.

Game is the only practical crop for much of East Africa. And it is a money crop. Areas which would never provide a dollar or pound sterling from farming or industry can and do bring countless thousands from both photographic and hunting safaris. The excess animals of any crop—domestic or wild—must be harvested or they are forever wasted. Which is the greater sin—to waste or to harvest as efficiently as possible?

Yes, "harvest" means killing, but isn't death a part of life—especially in Africa? The whole game ecology of East Africa is based upon the give and take of one species to another. If man is to intrude into this arrangement and game is to somehow survive, a working relationship —that does not disturb the basic system—must be worked out.

If one takes the game away from East Africa, what will be left? There are no historic cities of ancient days, no pagan temples, no medieval castles, no glorious battlefields, no great museums, nor art galleries. Africa has its land—its mountains, its magnificent lakes, and its game. If that is lost, so goes the tourist—and his dollar.

While the 1964 Army riots and the increasing influence of both Russia and Red China in East Africa—plus the recent expulsion of British residents—do nothing to bolster the outside world's confidence in the political future of the area, the conservation-economic problems remain constant regardless of the vagaries of men and parties. Kenya and all East Africa still need the tourist's all-mighty dollar and pound sterling to help close the desperate gap between income and expenditures. Game remains the key to tourism regardless of what faction runs the country.

Those who are concerned with Africa and its unique game can only hope that the story told by old hunter Sid Downey on a network television show on Africa's "Irreplacables" will somehow become an anachronism in the new Africa. Mr. Downey told of a conversation between a Kenya game ranger and an African hunter as they stood on a hilltop and discussed the game herds on the plain below:

"Isn't that beautiful?" asked the ranger.

"Yes," said the tribesman. "I'd like to kill them."

"Why?"

"Because they are good to eat."

"Then what of the lions and other creatures?"

"I would kill them too."

141

"Why?"

"Because they are not good to eat."

It is significant that the Swahili word—"nyama"—for animal and meat is the same.

IV

FISHING, HORSES AND FUN

A Note on Part Four

This is the section that breaks away from the hunting theme and strikes off into tangental areas. If you're a hunter-shooter, don't be too quick to flip on to the next section as you just might miss something that might bring the odd chuckle or two.

The first two stories are fishing tales—but they are a wee bit different from the run-of-the-mill "lunker" scripts usually associated with the outdoor magazines. The first tells the story of a salt water fishing trip out of Kinsale, Ireland; the second ponders that age-old problem—how does a sportsman maintain himself in proper style under his wife's budget-oriented gimlet eye.

Years ago I was the Eastern editor of *Horse & Rider* magazine and had a lot of fun writing a column entitled "Wranglin' East." My editor, Ray Rich, was a benevolent sort who allowed me the same sort of freedom—some would say "license"—that George Martin now indulges me in *The American Rifleman*. The result, I think, was also a lot of fun and, whether you are infatuated with horses or not, I hope you will find some of the five columns included of more than passing interest. If you have ever placed a bet on a bangtail, you will find much with which to identify in my adventure as an "owner" of race horses.

As for "Scars," the last article in this section, well, *everyone* has a scar or two that conjures up memories, both good and bad, so I'll let that piece speak for itself.

More Down There Than the Lusitania

On May 7, 1915, the passenger ship *Lusitania* was torpedoed and sunk off Old Head of Kinsale, Ireland, by a German U-boat with a loss of 1,195 lives including 114 American citizens. Now, almost 50 years later, a few other Americans are finding a new deep sea fishing bonanza over the wreck of the ill-fated liner.

I first heard of Kinsale and its fishing last summer while studying a calendar of coming events in Ireland. Intrigued by the cryptic notation that there was an "Open Deep Sea Angling Competition" at Kinsale, County Cork, on Aug. 8, I made inquiries of the Irish Tourist Board, Irish Airlines, and American anglers who had visited Ireland. There seemed to be one stumbling block. While Ireland is justly famed for its excellent trout and salmon fishing, its deep sea fishing was and is largely unknown. But there is evidence that it may well be the best sea angling area in Europe.

After the Dublin Horse Show I drove to Kinsale in time for this mysterious "deep sea angling competition," I had reservations at the Trident, a modern hotel built and managed by the J. Arthur Rank organization, headquarters for the contest. While most Irish hotels or inns outside of Dublin are what might be termed "old-fashioned," the Trident is ultra-modern in both decor and convenience.

The competition is run by the hotel's tackle shop, the domain of a most charming and formidable lady, Mrs. Peggy Green, who viewed me with a dubious eye. She had been forewarned that an "American journalist" was coming. As soon as I told her that I merely wanted to photograph and accompany one of her boats and didn't want to commandeer her fleet, or even fish for that matter, she warmed and set up my participation as an observer with her finest captain, one Willy ("The Shark") O'Connell. His was a mixed party of visiting English and local Irish anglers, a combination guaranteed to provide good copy if not outright hostilities.

When I presented myself at the dock at 8:30 a.m., I found two Englishmen firmly entrenched in Willy's boat, but no Willy. The other boats—the Angling Center owns four and charters two—were already

146

motoring over to the municipal dock to check out with the angling competition officials prior to leaving the harbour. Just then Willy, a long, lean man with a cap perched jauntily over abundant locks, glided around the corner. His steps were placed as those of a man who had been mightily involved with good Irish conversation and spirits the night before.

Without a word he threw his gear in the boat, winked to one and all and prepared to cast off. I jumped in the boat. The two Englishmen, brothers, both mustached like guards officers, nodded a greeting to Willy. He grunted and steered the boat to the municipal pier where a dozen anglers in all sorts of rain gear waited.

A Mixed Crew

There was a great commotion on our arrival. Five Irishmen jumped in our boat, which fished only five. The Englishmen didn't budge. Finally, one of the Irish fishermen, a middle-aged man with balding head trimmed with white, peered over his glasses with an accusing eye. "I'm Tom Cronin, Master Angler of the Kinsale Deep Sea Club and fishing captain for the day."

"I'm Harry Glover and this is my brother, Douglas. We drew Willy's boat at Mrs. Green's," the Englishman stood his ground.

The Master Angler silently considered this for a moment or two, then shrugged his shoulders and jerked his thumb to two of his companions. With a look of disgust, they climbed out of the boat. After the officials checked our party's names and affiliations, Willy cast off our line and we pulled away from the dock.

I sat with the two English brothers and soon found that on many counts they were ardent sportsmen. Harry Glover, a principal in the school of art in Barnsley, Yorkshire, England, and a director of the local art gallery, was also an international judge of dogs. Douglas, his brother, a resident of Dublin, was an avid shooter and fisherman. He also had won his class in the 1963 International Circuit Rally for automobiles. We had bounced along with the five anglers busy preparing light tackle for mackerel when Willy slowed the engine and told them to toss their lines overboard. We were very close to the spot where the wreckage of the torpedoed *Lusitania* lay. While they concentrated on their fishing, Willy went over to a foul-smelling bait box and dumped some aged fish carcasses into a barrel. He sat himself down on the mid-seat and started pummeling the mess with a club.

147

Mackerel for the Rubby-Dubby

"Making chum, huh, Willy?" I asked him.

"Chum, lad? Naw, I be making rubby-dubby for the sharkeens," he replied. Rubby-dubby was made of bran, chopped fish and pig's blood, a lovely combination.

There was a shout and Harry Glover pulled in a mackerel. His brother congratulated him and the three Irish fishermen pointedly ignored the initial catch. A few moments later Harry landed another. The Master Angler bent over his pole with grim determination. Harry caught another mackerel and then another. There was feverish activity among the Irish, much changing of lures, shortening and lengthening of line depth, jigging and bobbing of poles. Harry hauled in another mackerel.

"It's a good thing you have a Yorkshireman fishing!" he beamed.

The Master Angler choked and hunched his shoulders. His companions avoided both their leader and the two brothers. I smiled with what I hoped was a placating manner to all. Willy churned the rubby-dubby.

Fortunately, one of the Irish anglers, Dick Healy from Cork, then caught a mackerel, followed by another caught by his friend, David Ridgway. In a short time, mackerel were flying all over the boat as ardent anglers whipped their rods, flinging flopping fish into the bait box. Willy smiled happily. We had guaranteed both his bait and his future supply of rubby-dubby.

We were now ready for serious, competitive fishing. The order of the day was sharks for our boat. After all, when you were fishing with "The Shark" it hardly seemed appropriate to dally with less ferocious creatures. Willy dumped his chum—I mean rubby-dubby—over for a chum line and our anglers, having switched from light to heavier tackle, threw out mackerel-baited hooks in the water. So far, it was a striking parallel to many days off Montauk.

I was gratified to see that Irish captains are just like their American counterparts. A good deal of time was spent on the radio, bitterly complaining that a "slack day it was indeed." Slack is Gaelic, I think, for lousy. Later, when we had action, I noticed that they depreciated their good luck to each other the same way.

I spent the time interviewing my companions. I was particularly interested in their "Master Angler" business. Tom Cronin was happy to

educate me. The master angler of each club in Ireland is determined by the number of points accumulated on various "specimen" fish through the year. Obviously, the member that has the most points is the master for the following year. The Irish Federation of Sea Anglers has evolved an elaborate system of scoring practically all species of fish likely to be caught in their waters. A "specimen" fish is what we would term a good representative trophy, but not in the records. They have a record system as well for those fish that are in the top category of measurement.

Their angling competitions are based upon points granted on both the number and total weight of the fish caught by fair means during the time limits of the contest. David Ridgway had been runner-up at the Kinsale competition for the past two years. He had had the heaviest catch the previous year, but had been beaten by three points because his opponent had caught many more individual fish. Tom Cronin had represented the Kinsale Club at the Wicklow National Competition which is limited to the master angler of each deep sea club in Ireland.

149

Time for Sharkeens

I was half-dozing after a fine lunch and a pint of ale when a shout, "Gad, there's one, Harry!" startled me from my reverie just in time to see Harry Glover's pole bending heavily. Obviously, it was no mackerel on the other end. As a matter of fact, it was one heck of a big sharkeen, estimated at well over 150 lb. This first shark dove and cut Harry's line above the tracer after a 15 minute tug-of-war. There were murmured expressions of regret.

The Master Angler looked on with an air of supreme sadness. "Oh, did you lose him now? What a pity!" he mournfully intoned with the phantom flicker of a twinkle behind his glasses.

A few minutes later David Ridgway had a shark on that soon found itself, all 50 lb., flopping about the deck as Willy belabored it with his club. The home team had boated the first real catch of the day. The Master Angler beamed and his smiling countenance even embraced those ancient enemies, the English. In victory, he was magnanimous.

We went through another "slack" period and then Harry quickly hooked and landed a small 30 lb. blue shark. First blood for the English team. "Well, he's not so bad," the Master Angler innocently observed. "He's sort of like an ugly woman—if he's the only one you've got, you've got to like him, I suppose."

Willy smartly whacked Harry's entry with his club and we sat down to wait for future developments. It was about thirty minutes before a small sharkeen played about with three of the baits, but never took one. Willy made motions that it was getting to be about "that time"— the universal time fishing captains the world over dearly love, namely time to go home. Harry, who was now toying with some light tackle, to relieve the slack, took a "specimen" gar fish that had been feeding in the chum stream. It was the last action of the day and we headed for home.

Luck of the Irish

It had been a most enjoyable and interesting day from many standpoints. When we arrived back at the Kinsale docks in time to check in before the 7:00 p.m. deadline, we found a large crowd waiting for the incoming boats. A couple were already checked and docked, others were following closely behind us. As luck would have it, a Mr. L. Keenan of Mellow, County Cork, was champion with a 110 lb. shark. England's Harry Glover would have undoubtedly won if he had landed

150

his first shark of the day. Perhaps, in the interests of Anglo-Irish harmony, it is just as well that his Irish shark remained in Irish waters.

The Kinsale Angling Center was started by Mrs. Peggy Green's brother, one Garry Culhane, who must surely be a fine lad if only half the tales told about him are true. Mr. Culhane had spent some 30 years in Vancouver, Canada, where he studied deep sea fishing on the west coast of North America. When he returned to Kinsale in 1958, he was soon preaching ideas considered nothing short of mad by the local inhabitants. He wanted to sport fish for sharks.

As far as Kinsale was concerned, there were no sharks to be caught and, if there were, why would anyone want to catch them? Culhane's answer was that Americans, English, and Continental Europeans would be eager to widen their sporting opportunities. Since all three categories of potential customers outlined were considered equally mad-by Kinsale's population, it was begrudged that perhaps the idea had some small merit after all.

The English and French Love Kinsale

Culhane developed his center so rapidly and well that he soon had a thriving clientele among foreigners, especially English and French angling tourists. As Mrs. Green now points out, "The French and English are very keen" (the ultimate accolade among English and Irish sports) "but there have been relatively few Americans who have visited Kinsale. It's just off the tourist track," she sadly added. "They all make a bee-line for the Blarney Stone and Galway Bay as soon as they land at Shannon." While this is true, it is interesting to note that the first mako shark caught out of Kinsale was taken last year by a young American teacher, Rosalind Murphy, of Indianapolis, who was visiting cousins in Kinsale.

No one really knew what Kinsale had as a fishing potential when Culhane started his center and the surface has only been touched as far as Mrs. Green is concerned. Her brother sold out to J. Arthur Rank two years ago and Mrs. Green stayed on to run the Angling Center in conjunction with the new hotel. While they had only six boats available last August, they expect the increasing demand for angling will add to that number for the 1966 season. English and French customers, the backbone of their clientele, acknowledge Kinsale to be the best fishing center in Europe.

Kinsale's sport fishing runs from May to October, a long season for Northern Europe, but Ireland is blessed with Gulf Stream-influenced

151

weather that gives the country a temperature that hardly ever varies to extreme. The Gulf Stream moves closer in September and October and the best fishing would be then, except that this is the season for gales that sometimes mar otherwise perfect fishing conditions. Kinsale is doubly fortunate in that it has a good harbor that shelters it from prevailing winds, which are west to southwest outside the harbor. The Center's boats had been cancelled only once since May when I was there in August.

Erin Go Rubby-Dubby

Shark fishing begins in the middle of June, but Kinsale boats don't seriously fish for them until July. When I visited last August, the biggest shark to date was 205 lb., the biggest fish landed, a 212 lb. skate. In all, they have sport-landed some 28 species of fish, and Mrs. Green feels that there are many more waiting for the proper knowledge, boats, tackle and skill.

Perhaps the most exciting possibilities concern tuna and broadbill. A fleet of Norwegian trawlers brought tuna and broadbill in from outside Kinsale in 1962. One boat had ten swordfish. Likewise, Spanish trawlers have brought tuna into Bantry, southwest of Kinsale. The possibilities for deep sea fishing around Kinsale are intriguing.

What might happen if an American team with the necessary equipment, boats, and knowledge were to explore and evaluate the waters off Kinsale? In not too many years American sportsmen might be going to Ireland for more than its superb fresh water trout and salmon fishing, and American angling tourists could be hurrying to a spot on Cork's coast before they rush to the Blarney Stone or Galway Bay.

Fishing, Money and/or Wives

There has long been a widespread suspicion among a large segment of wives that a great proportion of the annual family income is squandered in the local sporting goods emporium. This income might better be expended for what is loosely referred to as the "common good," which—in actuality—means simply money spent according to a tightly organized budget.

After years of study, I have come to the conclusion that there is little room for fishing tackle in most of these budgets. In the face of such a formidable feminine program it takes a highly skilled and devious male to maintain the necessary standards of sporting gear as dictated by the advertisements of the manufacturers and his own peculiar desires.

The continued prosperity of the numerous manufacturers and purveyors of sporting goods testify to the success of this resourceful brand of husband. Contrary to—and in spite of—ill-conceived budgetary schemes, not all fishing and hunting equipment is purchased by either pre-puberty youths or unspeakable bachelorhood.

However, as all good generals know, a secondary line of retreat should be prepared in case of disaster. Since disaster in this case means a freezing of the local funds, our alternate action should revolve around various and time-considered plans to utilize our meagre bucks as far as possible.

Regardless of wistful hopes and the social pressure of our wealthier fishing compatriots, not all men can afford imported English tackle, custom bamboo rods, or their luxurious accessories. In fact—if facts were ever any criteria by which to judge sporting matters—it is probable that most fish are caught by a rather nondescript array of mismatched equipment finished off with that ignominious bait, man's best friend, the noble worm. Be that as it may, millions of dollars are still happily shoved across countless counters for a fantastic conglomeration of varied equipment and, on more than one memorable occasion, junk.

I know, as my closets have their share.

A compromise is needed. Something that will fill our craving for decent equipment, but will not cause a family revolution over our financial management. As the subtitle of this article indicates, somebody somewhere showed up on the banks of a trout stream with all the necessary paraphernalia of the cult for under twenty bucks.

Since trout fishing is sometimes regarded as one of the more expensive forms of the sport, it follows that if a man can get under way for a relatively small outlay of cash and still catch trout, he can do it with any other type of fishing also.

It so happens that I had occasion to purchase a workable outfit for a friend shortly prior to the opening of last season's trout adventure. The sum spent (less tax): $19.81.

Shortly before opening day I received a phone call from Mr. Dan Noyes, then residing in smug complacence among the many fishing and hunting advantages of New Mexico. In tones of bewildered shock he informed me that he had been transferred to New York City and was seriously considering piling all of his sporting equipment in one huge bier, applying kerosene and match, and then committing suttee by leaping into the flames.

Struck by the urgency of his situation, I quickly assured him that all was not lost. If worse came to worse, I would allow him to hold my small daughter's hand while she illegally angled in Central Park.

In a less frivolous vein, I hastened to add that there was fishing and hunting to be had a few hours from Manhattan if one had only the courage to brave the rush hour on Friday afternoon. Promising to postpone his proposed fiery exit until further on-the-scene observation, he bid me prepare his initial onslaught upon New York's wildlife resources. I immediately made reservations at a certain spot in close proximity to the Schoharie, a stream of wide and justified fame among trout fishermen.

It would seem that we would only have to wait a few days and the problem of solving Dan's adjustment would be begun. However, circumstances and a certain transportation system conspired against us and Dan found that to his horror his twenty-odd boxes, crates, parcels, bundles, etc., of fishing gear were sidetracked to Eel Ear, Texas, or some other such inaccessible place.

After a short tussle, I managed to calm Dan sufficiently to convince him that all was not lost. I knew of a place. We would purchase him a new rig at a modest cost. Muttering to himself, he allowed me to lead him away to a certain establishment that specializes in bargains; i.e., good equipment at a considerable savings.

There I proceeded to make a fast series of purchases before my friend's incredulous eyes. First we set him up with a rod, reel, line, and

154

accessory tackle. For six bucks we bought an eight-foot, medium action, glass Horrocks-Ibbotson "Lucky Strike" fly rod. Two-sixty-five paid for a Pfueger "Progress" single-action reel.

Another $2.15 went for a "H-I" level fly line with a tin of line dressing thrown in. Two knotless tapered nylon "Berkley" leaders of 2X and seven-and-a-half foot length cost $.50. Two eyelets were twenty-four cents. (I figured Dan was too distraught to be further frustrated by having to tie any more knots than necessary.)

Since it was early season and the only fishing was with bait or streamers—and I drew the line at worms—I forced him to buy a conservative selection of three streamers at a special price of $1.89. To top this rather functional outfit, I also threw in a fifteen-cent bobber as a snide little reminder that he would have to forget his troubles and keep his eye on the job.

We next turned to the problem of waders. Frankly, this was the one thing I was afraid would upset our fish cart. Fortunately, the genial manager of the shop was currently trying to unload a bunch of obsolete plastic waders before new models came in.

Hence, we were able to buy a pair of chest-high stocking foot waders for $5.75. This, combined with a pair of old sneakers, made a reasonably dry wading costume. As a finishing touch, we bought a landing net for $.89. In a few days Dan was waddling happily through four foot snow drifts to flail the water with his new tackle on opening day.

Now the outfit described above probably wouldn't excite any fit of jealousy on the part of the more devoted members of the dry fly set, but it will do the job. It is all good sound equipment. It's not the most expensive, but also not the cheap junk (usually concocted in Oriental sweatshops) that is often foisted off on the unsuspecting beginner or the pennypinching old hand who should know better. When you compare this outfit and its cost with what could be spent before entering a stream and casting a line, it is a little staggering to the imagination in its contrast.

It is possible to spend more than $200.00 for a custom bamboo rod; there is a series of fly reels that run around a hundred dollars, depending on size and type; lines run up to thirty; waders anywhere up to $50.00. Then the extras enter: vest, fly boxes, leader pouches, streamer wallets, just the right old hat, miscellaneous gadgets—some necessary, others less so.

If a fellow really fishes in style, he waltzes out in a special shirt, trousers, and, maybe, even underwear. Naturally, he carries a handmade creel and possibly a wading staff also. When he is finished, his appearance is very likely to resemble nothing so much as a down payment on a house to the cynical eyes of his spouse.

This sort of thing combined with his bass fishing costume, waterfowling rig and apparel, deer hunting outfit, upland game shooting togs, surf-casting and salt-water tackle, and the other miscellaneous necessities important to his existence, may well bring an agonizing reappraisal of his sporting life when his wife begins to add item by item. There are a few courses left open for the smart man.

In the first place, he could quit everything and wither away in despondency. This is sometimes done due to force of circumstances, but never willingly and certainly isn't recommended. Secondly, if one is lucky, most of the equipment has already been bought before marriage and the annual compulsive additional purchases can be successfully hidden in the garage. However, if you are one of those million unfortunates like me, you never had enough cash to buy most of your own stuff when you were young and used your old man's hand-me-downs. After you got married, you weren't young anymore and had lots of other things to buy like food and rent.

Sooner or later, though, the old mind—after the initial staggering responsibilities of marriage and parenthood have become dulled—turns back to thoughts of fish, game, and other things. Before you know it, you find your feet casually—but purposely—wandering into the neighborhood sporting goods store. When you walk out, more than likely your arms will be full of various assorted packages. This gain in gross tonnage will be more than offset by a substantial lightening of your wallet—which will also be immediately discernible to your wife.

This is the crisis. It is often here (and not at the pub or in the other woman's arms) that the modern American family flounders. Success or failure; defeat or victory; happiness or misery; trout or tinned sardines. All hinge on the outcome of this first trip back from the sporting goods store. If your packages include imported English fly reels and other such sundries, you are stacking the deck against future happiness.

I'm not saying that we give these things up forever, but all things must be worked up to gradually. If you start out with the best of everything, you may find that all your time will be devoted to fishing as your wife will be back home with mother. Start out slowly—and cheaply. Appeal to her sense of a "good bargain." Leave a few pamphlets casually open on the table. Sooner or later she will pick one up. The pamphlets will be ones that describe the more luxurious types of fishing gear. She will be struck with the enormity of what COULD have happened.

Being a realist, she will be prepared to compromise on the relatively cheap amount you have spent and consider herself lucky. This is the first wedge. From here on in she will be fighting a losing battle. The beachhead has been won; it is only a matter of time until you do purchase that English fly reel you originally coveted. Careful planning and superior tactics have won the day. You have your fishing and your marriage. If you are one of those who would prefer to leave out the latter, be less subtle in your maneuvers and you will either end up single or deceased, depending upon the latent nature of your spouse.

There is one other choice left open. It is the most devious and can often backfire disastrously. It is simply the process of kindling an interest in your sport in your wife. Some people might regard this as cutting off one's nose to spite one's face. They state very vehemently that this is ruining the whole idea; you are bringing your wife into your "other" life and fishing will never be the same.

This is not exactly true. These horrified individuals are not really fishermen, but escapists and cowards. They do not fish to catch fish, but to get away from the house and their keeper. True fishermen can be identified by their fanatical compulsion to infect others with their curious disease. This even includes their wives.

157

In fact, some men skillfully ferret out their potential mate's attitude on important fishing matters before making a step anywhere near an altar. This is perfectly justifiable, of course, but it is also wise to find out whether the possible wife can cook, sew, clean house, etc. If she is as dedicated to fishing as you, you will have to hire a maid and such because your wife will be too busy to take time out from tieing flies and varnishing her rods.

In a short time, the added load of paying for a maid, combined with the double purchase of fishing tackle for your wife and yourself, will precipitate a crisis all of its own. It is called bankruptcy and is an even more irrevocable step than divorce. Both, however, are to be avoided if at all possible.

The best policy is to stimulate just enough interest in your wife to sustain your own selfish ends. Hypocritical stream types will maintain they initiated their wives in the glories of fishing purely for the spiritual satisfaction they received from a good deed. This is not true and brave men will admit it among themselves. It is really self-preservation and is about as old an instinct as we have outside of one other pretty important one that got us married in the first place.

I guess the degree of fishing interest most desirable in one's mate is the frame of mind that readily accepts the idea of spending the whole vacation fishing or hunting rather than back home visiting mother, Aunt Nellies, and high-school girl friends. When you reach this plateau, you may rest easy; the battle and the war have both been won.

There is only one thing that will spoil your happiness and that is the ironic female revenge reserved solely for selfish sportsmen. The day dawns when the fisherman's sport turns to ashes in his mouth. The realization comes that his wife consistently catches more and, worse, larger fish than he. Frankly, there is only one answer to this: start having children immediately before your fishing confidence is forever shattered. Admittedly, this is a rather drastic remedy, but the conditions warrant it.

Unfortunately, it is only a temporary remedy at best, but you will be forewarned and by the time your wife gets back in circulation in a few years or so, you will have an edge. Keep it. She will have forgotten the old productive trout pools. Don't tell her about the new ones. If she remembers the old pools and they are still good, divert the stream before she comes back on her first trip. Cut the strength of her dry fly dope. If things get particularly tight, put leader sink on her dry flies before you go out.

158

It will take every effort, but maintain that edge. If need be, file the barbs off her flies. Be careful; be alert, be unscrupulous, but maintain your advantage. If she ever surpasses you again, you are lost. You are in that dangerous in-between stage. She is through having children, but much too young to have grandchildren to take her interest away from fishing.

There would seem to be a moral or two somewhere around here, but I'm not sure just what or where. I suppose it would be something about money, or women, or fishing, or a combination thereof. In any event, I'm sure we've been discussing important matters. After all, fishing and women are probably the two most important things in the world (after hunting season). The trouble arises when either the world forgets this or we forget which of the two is really the most important. Of course, I know, but I'm too smart to put it in print and commit myself either way.

City Mice and Country Cousins

If any animal can make it onto our property, he's guaranteed safe harbor until dotage and the Grim Reaper swings. We can have the meanest cat, most worthless dog, stubborn pony—or even an itinerant ingrate turtle. They're all safe and they've all got it made.

Somedays, as I pull my aching body out of bed at dawn preparatory to making my daily two-hour journey into New York, I entertain fleeting fantasies of canine homicide, as I stumble over a supine Labrador or English setter lazily sprawled across my bed. More often than not, a resentful half-lidded eye balefully is cast in my direction.

The secret of all this job security resides in the small, grubby hands and eternally optimistic hearts of the younger members of any family. Once the small set first casts their collective eyes on any furred, feathered or finned creature that stumbles by—or is lugged home by a retarded parent—there is no way that animal can be dislodged short of a family crisis, possibly leading to runaways and even divorce. It is a terrible thing for a sporting parent to live with. After all, how much livestock can one afford or even want?

If a new bird dog's nose seems oriented to little else than the food pan, put aside any thought of losing him in the woods. If a pony comes on trial and turns into a biting monster, learn to live with it. In any case, they're all there to stay and either you can buy more acreage for more animals or simply resign yourself to what you've got, regardless of quality.

All of this bittersweet philosophy was brought rather poignantly to surface the other day, which happened to be my thirty-eighth birthday, which is pretty bittersweet too, come to think of it. My friend, Bill Read, gifted me with a fighting cock and hen. As my wife succinctly pointed out at the time, this is just what we needed.

Now our place is open on three sides, bordered by woods or fields, but the fourth unfortunately contains the budding buildings of a fledgling development, nice houses and all that, but still—well—people. Some of them are even city sorts. This means that they have some strange ideas about the country—like it should really be like the city!

160

Have you ever noticed how odd it is that certain urban types deeply bemoan the horrors of city life and scrimp and save for years to buy their pastoral paradise far removed from the evils of Gotham? Once firmly ensconced on their half or third of an acre—usually dubbed Mon Repose or some such twaddle—the new squire usually adopts a feudal possessiveness second only to Simon Legree.

Sadly enough, this pride in ownership manifests itself in a fervent attempt to superimpose city-styled rules of conduct upon the previously relatively unregulated country life. The first thing that horrifies the transplanted city dweller is the terrible concept of unleashed dogs. In no time flat, a campaign to save the world from rabies and worse fates is launched and it is only a matter of time before the little old ladies of both sexes have had new dog leash ordinances promulgated or have resurrected old ones and made the poor embarrassed local peace officer enforce them.

In short order, there is rumbling and mumbling about horses—they attract flies, you know—in the neighborhood. Fortunately, there is a farm on three sides of me and they haven't figured how to get rid of fifty or so cows without ponying up over a hundred grand to take over a farm that has been in operation for over two hundred years. So the horses and ponies are saved for awhile. Then one day some idling matron, dawdling over her sixth cup of coffee and seventh gossip session of the morning, looks out her window and sees the local farmer walking through one of his fields with a shotgun in his hands. In moments, the poor local policeman—still embarrassed—is called on the carpet to answer the hysterical charges of a pack of females possessed with the idea they and their children are all going to be slaughtered by a horde of blood-lusting hunters with high-powered rifles.

161

There is another fight in the town council and, temporarily at least, we are saved by the precedent of the farm, but how long can we depend on this buffer against the determined onslaught of militant mothers acting in the name of Western civilization?

You may well ask what all this has to do with the gift of a fighting cock and hen. Well, have you ever heard a fighting cock let loose on his lungs at dawn? It is something calculated to stir the blood of even the most timid male animal and to send a delicious shiver of anticipation down the spine of any female creature. That crow is primeval. It is beautiful in its basic simplicity of purpose. It is also quite loud and somewhat different to ears more accustomed to the clink of an early morning milkman's bottles.

As one might guess, a cock's crow—a fighting cock's trumpet especially—has a certain effect on a neighborhood the first time it splits the morning hours. Among other things, a cock's crow seems to make telephones ring within fifteen minutes of the first triumphant screech. I have had a chance to evaluate and it seems to me there is a distinct scientific equation that can be developed around the factors of time of first crow as related to distance of closest house before first the phone call rings in my bedroom. Then one may further chart the course of the morning by establishing a graph with a curve plotted on other houses, according to their relative distance in any direction from our barn. You see, it appears that noise—country noise, that is—in the morning rates fairly high among those things to be utterly obliterated by transplanted city folk. Crosstown buses, delivery trucks and backfires cause not a stir, but let a dog bark, a cock crow or a horse whinny before eight o'clock and we are endangering the emotional stability of the neighborhood.

What does a man do when confronted on one side with misty-eyed tots clutching their pets to their bosoms and an outraged citizenry, determined to ban these self-same creatures, on the other? He fights, of course. And that, dear friends and readers, is what it is all about: our interests in animals generally and horses specifically. We are living in an age that unfortunately is becoming a crowded one indeed and the prospects do not hold much hope that things are going to get much better. People who enjoy animals and—perhaps, more importantly—enjoy their kids owning and loving animals have got to band together to protect their interests.

We are in the minority and, if we are to save something of traditional America, we had best look to our future or there will be few

162

horses and fighting cocks for our children's children—and even less space for them to be kept.

Maybe even dogs and cats will have a pretty rough time.

Saddle Sore Memories

I have been somewhat depressed the last few months by this magazine's running series on Jefferson Spivey's cross-continental horseback epic. As a guy who once enjoyed a certain small renown as the "Winchester Pony Express Rider," who rode 156 miles from St. Francis, Kansas, to Denver, Colorado, as part of the rifle company's centennial celebration, I now feel a little bit like the budding pilot who finished his solo run in a Piper Cub and found that the astronauts had landed on the moon.

But enough of such callow feelings. As the World War II vet once said, "Let me tell you about my war!"

Spivey's remarkable achievement has rekindled some warm memories of my much less impressive cross-country ride of three years ago. In a small fashion, I can identify with some of the problems and more memorable events that Spivey and his faithful companion, MrSol, encountered on their journey. Riding cross-country in the modern West is no easy thing—modern highways, barbed wire ("Mormon lace" to oldtime cattlemen) and other impedimenta of mid-Twentieth Century American life do not make the way easy for an enterprising horseman. There are compensations, however, and it's the people that one meets along the way that make the trip as always.

The country of West Kansas and Eastern Colorado seldom is featured in any brochures handed out by state tourist boards to lure unsuspecting out-of-state vacationers to the beauties of their respective states. It is a flat, dry, dusty and windblown land of few scenic virtues or outstanding landmarks. It sort of reminds one of the country illustrated in the "Grapes of Wrath" and the stories of the Oklahoma dustbowl—especially in early spring before the grass has come up and the land is still winter barren.

I rode through such towns as Anton, Cope, Joes, Byers and even spent the night of Friday the thirteenth camped in a bedroll outside of Last Chance, Colorado, which, I thought at the time, was spitting fair in the eye of fate.

I was riding three quarter horses in rotation—a great gelding named King; Cindy, a two-year-old mare, and a magnificent stud horse, Joe

Neill, who could carry you twenty miles in short order without raising a bead of sweat.

All of the horses were owned by Lou Flower, an outstanding quarter horseman who was then manager of the Salida, Colorado, Chamber of Commerce and now holds the same position in Wickenberg, Arizona. Lou and Fritz Rundell, a companion wrangler from Salida, trucked the spare horses along Route 36 from St. Francis and established relay stops for food and horse changes along the way. They also made evening camp and cooked some of the best food I've ever eaten. We were strong on steak and beans, as I recall.

While King was a fine, dependable, marvelously moving horse, my favorite was the stallion, Joe Neill. I never had ridden a stud before for any distance and the first experience that first afternoon out of St. Francis was memorable in more ways than one.

I had started the morning on King and had a great ride. I used the old cavalry system. Walk, trot, canter a distance, then dismount and walk on foot a mile or so, leading the horse. This kept the horse fit and me from getting stiff or cramped. As midday approached, I switched to Cindy, the pretty little filly I rode with a hackamore, for an hour before lunch.

After eating by the road, I had my first encounter with the formidable Joe Neill. I swung aboard and started to say something cute to Lou and Fritz, but was off in the proverbial cloud of dust before I could open my mouth. Later Lou told me that Joe's tail was twisting like a twirled baton all the way down the road—and the twirls were punctuated with playful little bucks for the first hundred yards, upon which, I believe, we set a new quarter horse record.

Joe had a neck as thick as his head and all that compressed, pent-up power was stretched out with ears flat, nostrils expanded and eyes bulged. In no short time, I realized that hauling about on the reins seemed to make little impression on old Joe. We long since had lost sight of Lou and Fritz and were eating up territory in gluttonish fashion. I didn't want to stop Joe's runaway flight in the classic fashion by sharply turning him around in ever decreasing circles, because I was bounded by a barbed wire fence on one side and the asphalt pavement on the other. Meanwhile, I just made time—lots of it, very fast.

Finally in desperation, I pleaded, "Aw, come on, Joe, Whoa!" And he did, like on a dime. I damn near kept going, but managed to hang in the saddle and on his neck.

After that, riding Joe Neill was like something to be remembered with more than casual sentimentality and nostalgia. Each night we

165

would make camp along the way, not too distant from the road, as we had to leave the horse trailers and the cars near by. Usually, Lou and Fritz had things set up and a long, tall one, well iced and waiting for the old soldier, when he hauled his weary bones out of the saddle after the day's long ride. One would think no one could be more isolated. Not a house could be seen and it seemed that few cars used Route 36. I'd look around and wonder where all the people were and how it appeared that no one in the world knew we were there. It could have been 1880.

Then, quietly and silently, the old battered pick-ups would loom up on the horizon and slowly rumble over the country-side until they came to stop a short distance from our camp. More often than not, a lean and leathery man, sometimes with a gangly kid or two, would sidle up to the fire, kick the dirt and hazard a "howdy." We would howdy back, offer some beans—which they would always refuse.

"You the feller making that ride from Kansas?" Yup. "Hmm, you really with that rifle company, Winchester?" Yup. "Well, how come you guys stopped making the good ol' Model 12 . . . best pump gun ever made!" And then it would start. Sometimes the back-and-forth yarn-spinning about guns, horses and game would go on past midnight and once until two o'clock in the morning. Other trucks would roll into the camping area and farmers, ranchers, wranglers and assorted types would join in the discussion. The Denver papers were carrying a running story each day on my progress and somehow the word spread by the prairie telegraph about where I was and how I was doing. So, each night they came and some even followed along after their chores and joined us each night.

A couple of fellows—after meeting us one night—would join up on horseback further down the trail and ride along for a mile or so.

I remember one fellow waiting by his ranch road as I came along. He just nodded and fell in alongside, as I went by. We rode on in quiet, understanding silence, first at a jog, then a gentle lope for a mile or so. As we slowed to a walk before entering a small crossroads, he turned off and, as he rode away, he mumbled his only words, "Thought you just might like some company for awhile."

I suppose Jeff Spivey has a multitude of similar memories and, as the years go by, the grass will get sweeter, the horses finer and the people more grand. I know how lonely that solitary ride can be and I decided I'd ride along in memory for a small stretch, because I thought he just might like some company for awhile, too.

166

Saddle Up!

Outside of the helicopter, the horse has to be the best way for a man to see country. In certain cases—in deep, narrow-cut, brush-covered valleys, for instance—the man on horseback will cover his territory better than even the ubiquitous whirlybird.

In these days of the superhighway and the high altitude jet, man too often is whisked by, or over, the beauty of his environment and has lost something his more pedestrian and equestrian forebears enjoyed. A man on horseback can go places and cover more territory than anyone on foot, in a vehicle or even a snowmobile.

I believe the first honest-to-gosh trail ride I ever enjoyed was more than twenty-five years ago back in Cedar Rapids, Iowa. My father, a man who enjoyed rod, gun and horse, held an executive position with the old Universal Crusher Company and organized a company trail ride and picnic as an employee relations project. It was widely successful and became an annual affair. Cedar Rapids has a heavy Czech and Bohemian population and these marvelous people soon became some of our most ardent cowboys. As I recall, we all would meet outside of town at one of the local livery emporiums where the owner would have collected a fantastic array of mounts for the one hundred or more riding enthusiasts assembled.

If the horses were varied—and they ranged from swaybacked ex-army mounts to wild-eyed half-broken Western imports—the riders were not to be believed. Every sort of costume imaginable was in evidence—elaborate cowboy suits with fringed jackets, silk shirts and ten-gallon hats set off the wide mustaches of proud Bohemian gents of more than ample girth. Others affected a more traditional English-style garb. Best of all, a few daring souls combined the best—or the worst, depending on one's viewpoint—of both forms of riding attire to make very startling sartorial appearances indeed.

A few of the horses were a bit taken aback.

In any event, each one was loaded aboard his respective horse and, grunting and groaning, yippy-upping and wahooing, the whole menage straggled off toward a pre-determined camping spot some miles distant

167

where, hopefully, kegs of beer and heaps of food awaited. It looked like the retreat from Gettysburg.

Needless to say, there was quite a bit of skylarking and—pardon me —horseplay indulged. Certain desperadoes—notedly one referred to as the Bohemian Kid—were great on galloping back and forth along the line regardless of the safety of others, but quite intent on making a lasting impression on one of the flaxon-haired Katrines or Maria Therezas giggling in the column. There were always stragglers. On the way out, they were the timid or the unlucky—they either lacked intestinal fortitude, trust or understanding of the mysterious ways of the equine mind and nervous system. In some cases, they simply had lazy or worthless horses and no amount of cajoling, threats or actual physical inducement could get the animals concerned to move one step faster than they had set as their optimum pace.

When the lame, the halt and the near-blind straggled into the campsite and deposited their moaning charges, the majority of the riders already had established a firm beachhead on the company-supplied beer supply and a few surreptitious bottles of stronger potions were making inroads. Someone always had a harmonica or a fiddle and soon the whole group was singing or stamping out surging gypsy-style airs.

It was very heady stuff indeed and I made a mental note to further explore the possibilities inherent in such a wonderful, gay people when I was old enough to enjoy some of the pastimes I was observing.

Later on the wild, stomping music made a curious transition to saddened, tearful laments as the stronger fluids took their inevitable toll. The campfire, the moon and the gentle wind coursing through the pines on that warm July evening all combined to make a romantic atmosphere. It was noted there was little galloping or charging about on the slow ride back to the stable.

There were still stragglers, however, but they straggled two by two. Strangely, the main body was composed of those that were the laggards earlier and the more daring riders—led, of course, by an oddly quiet Bohemian Kid—were the ones who seemed to lag the farthest behind.

Yessir, trail rides are great socializing events and I enjoy them as much now as I did those first adventures on the Iowa plains. Our Delaware Valley Horseman's Association in New Jersey holds periodic expeditions that often culminate in parties highly reminiscent of some of the festivities outside of Cedar Rapids years ago. Trail rides can be great family adventures and practically everyone—regardless of riding skill—can participate on an almost equal basis.

Western and Eastern styles of horsemanship mix as well on a trail ride as anywhere and there is a tangible benefit in the two groups of horsemen getting together occasionally to discuss mutual interests and problems. After all, the horseman needs to organize on a geographic and political basis, if he is to defend his interests in the scramble going on for recreational facilities and open space during this population boom and suburban sprawl we are witnessing in many sections of the country.

New Jersey's Conservation Department has taken the horseman into consideration in its recreational planning and there are plans for bridal paths along the shores of the two large reservoirs at Round Valley and Spruce Run in Hunterdon County. Facilities for riding already exist in other state lands and hunting areas. There is a great trail ride that covers practically the length of the state in the summer and numerous smaller ones in various localities scattered throughout New Jersey's horse country. Obviously the trail ride is no new thing to Westerners or even Midwesterners and Southerners. The West is the home of the trail ride and the most famous ones—Sheriff's Posses, Los Caballeros and others—are nationally known and attended by people from all over the United States.

Some of them last several days and a few a week or more. These big trail rides are highly organized affairs with a great deal of planning and logistics involved. Usually they are well run with good mounts, sleeping gear and sanitation facilities, pleasant campsites and plenty of good food and liquid refreshment.

If one is interested in increasing horse enthusiasm and activity in a particular part of the country, I can think of no better way to generate interest and new recruits to the equestrian world than organizing a good old-fashioned trail ride with all the traditional trimmings, including a buckboard for the wounded, the saddle sore and those who over-indulge by the campfire.

Here Comes De Judge!

One of those strange, seemingly senseless slogans that become a short-lived craze is currently raging across the nation. Midwifed by Rowan & Martin, everyone from doddering dowagers to toddling tots appear to be obsessed with "Here come de Judge!" After spending a twelve-hour day—in ninety-degree weather well flavored with dust and manure —dedicated to four small ones earnestly in pursuit of ribbons and glory at a horse show, I now realize that what everyone really means is, "Heaven help de Judge!"

I simply cannot understand America's seeming indecision in domestic crisis, the lament for our callowness in the face of adversity and all the other dry rots we supposedly embrace in the eyes of world opinion. After witnessing the fierce predation of our sturdy American mother and father in defense—nay, offense—of little Willy as he enters the lists of his local "walk, trot and canter" class, it fair boggles the imagination that we stand accused of a weakness in national resolve.

If a mere fraction of the fervor shown at the mildest adverse horse show decision were displayed at Geneva or other international tilting grounds, we would have the highest rate of diplomatic success displayed, since Russia shut out her allies ten to nothing at Yalta in 1945.

Unfortunately this manifestation of national backbone must have its sad side and it appears that the negative aspects of parental concern at the show ring far outweigh any possible good that might accrue from the determined example set. Let's face it: horse shows seem to bring out the Hyde in many an otherwise meek and considerate Dr. Jekyll. All too often, a frustrated mother bent on furthering Willy's chances for a berth on some future Olympic team resembles nothing so much as an overly protective mama piranha diligently tutoring her brood in the proper use of their choppers on living flesh.

While judges—many of whom lead a dual life as escape artists second only to the late Clyde Barrow—have a trying time indeed, coping with the maternal instinct, a great number have maintained health and sanity by developing adequate defense mechanisms and protective armor guaranteed to shunt off all but the most kamikaze of matrons.

171

The real tragedy resides with those in whose name all of these acts of aggression are committed—little Willy and his brothers and sisters. No one possibly can measure the damage inflicted upon young character by the exposure received during a season or two on the horse show circuit, big time or local.

Unfortunately, many horse shows—like so much of organized human sports endeavor—often have little to do with sport and the concepts of sportsmanship. In some instances shows really become a professional's business bailiwick—a place to exhibit and ballyhoo his products to potential new customers. The show ring is a dueling ground between rival trainers—and parents—who merchandise their young charges much in the same manner the Romans utilized fledgling gladiators. Quality often is subordinated to quantity—the quantity of cash available.

No one can blame the professional—least of all me, who, I suppose, is one also in certain fields—because he is only filling a need provided and nurtured by society and the people who demand what he has to offer. The horse show isn't the only sports competition to be blamed thusly. Field trails, auto racing, much ocean racing, skiing and golf—all have their "practical" sides. Money may not talk, but it sure communicates.

While it is discouraging to buck the professional and his wealthy backer, this can be avoided by limiting one's horse show activity to participation in carefully chosen events in the bigger shows or, better yet, to smaller shows whose prestige and loot are less likely to attract the attention of the top stables. The recent trend of the larger shows to restrict or eliminate pony classes and hold down registration in the other divisions to first grade horses (with a certain rating established in smaller shows) has done a lot to separate the amateur from the semi-professional rider and professional trainer. This is as it should be: nothing can be more frustrating and boring than watching a class in a big show bogged down with mediocre entries.

The main problem in this horse show thing still lies with the riders themselves generally and young riders specifically. Constant recent exposure to horse shows supposedly dedicated to young entry has firmed up an old suspicion that the real reason behind these affairs is the ego or wish-fulfillment of a group of adults.

I've seen supposed grown-up, responsible citizens reach the heights of almost incoherent rage—unfortunately, if not tragically, complemented by tearful fear on the part of the children involved—because

172

little Willy or Sally hasn't lived up to what Mom and Pop expects in equestrian expertise.

The fact that Mom and Pop didn't know a horse from a jackass before they embraced the horse world has minor relevance in their scheme of things. Somehow I can't help but feel that many a potentially life-long good horseman or horsewoman is forever lost because of the unpleasant associations built around their first experiences with riding and showing.

While it is fashionable to blame the old folks for all of society's ills these days, it would be somewhat less than fair to equate all horse show sin with the unrestrained neurosis of a few nutty parents. Obviously such behavior—while unpleasant to witness—is the exception rather than the rule in the horse world. Children encourage a great deal of competition among themselves and most of this is a good healthy sign of growing up in a competitive world. When a parent or other adult applies pressure way beyond the requirements of the situation, however, it is another proposition entirely.

Any time a sport becomes more work than fun—a nerve racking ordeal rather than a pleasant relaxation—an angry confrontation rather than an enjoyable association—then it is time to find a new pastime. Everyone—including judges, riders and mounts—will be a lot happier. Even parents.

The Loser's Circle

As one approaches the prosperous portals of Peter Kriendler's expensive New York beanery, the renowned *21 Club* of fact and fiction, both timid tourist and jaded jetsetter are somewhat awed by the stony stares emanating from a long line of miniature jockeys guarding the steps leading to a second floor balcony forbidden to all but an occasional janitor.

These statues sport a variety of jockey silks representing the racing colors of the famous clients of the restaurant, who carry a certain fame in other quarters like Saratoga, Lexington, the Jockey Club and even on occasion, Aqueduct. Needless to say, one has not truly arrived on the racing scene until final recognition has been bestowed by whomever handles the paint jobs on Pete's jockeys.

It was with considerable Machiavellian foresight then that I pondered my first venture into the racing world as an owner earlier this year. The social ramifications of both success or failure went far beyond the mere loss of a buck or two filched from the family budget. After all, being a owner of a real, genuine thoroughbred—registered, mind you—race horse elevated a guy just a bit above the riff raff who frequent the two-dollar window.

My good friend—I almost said used-to-be good friend, but the final verdict is not yet available—William J. Read III, Master of Foxhounds, horseman par excellance, boon companion and sometime bon vivant, approached me with what is euphemistically referred to as a "proposition." After much contemplation, he and three other gentlemen had decided to organize the Amwell Valley Stables as a syndicate of five owners, four of whom would provide a certain modest sum to bankroll the operation, while the fifth would carry his share by providing the training and handling of the horseflesh. There was one position left among the financial four and—after careful consideration—they had decided that they could think of no one better qualified in both judgment and temperament than me to fill that slot.

The strategy was to purchase a couple of horses that were sort of sliding down from the fringes of the big tracks, train them up and

174

condition them on farms in the Amwell Valley for the coming season, then spring them on the unsuspecting second-string tracks along the Eastern seaboard. Hopefully, we would upgrade our racing stock, until we had a horse ready for bigger things—like the Belmont—in a few years. Our trainer had an enviable track record (no pun intended) and was one of New Jersey's leading trainers for 1968. We shall call him Kenny, for that is his name. He is a good friend, an excellent trainer and he is not responsible for what later happened.

In no time flat Bill called to say we had two horses—a promising young horse named In the Money (a good omen, we all agreed) and an older chestnut gelding, Iadom, who actually won $3,737 in 1967 and $4,540 in 1966. What had he done in 1968, some insecure, suspicious type questioned? Rested up. Why? Tired, I guess. Oh. Hm-m. How old did you say he was? Oh, aged. Like how aged? Mebbe eight or nine. Nine. Well, yeah, nine, I guess. Hm-m. Is he sound? Oh, sure. Hm-m. I wonder why he didn't race last year. Don't be a cynic . . . he's beautiful and he's all ours.

Since New Jersey's weather became increasingly sloppy and sodden in February and early March, Kenny decided to take some of his horses and Iadom down to Dover Downs in Delaware, where the ground was in decent shape for galloping and the horses could be conditioned for racing later in the spring on that track. It appears there were others who had the same flash of inspiration. In short order all of the stalls at Dover Downs were filled, but—while the track was almost crowded during training and exercising—there was a mysterious lack of entries for the afternoon and evening races after the season opened on March 8. The management pondered this curious phenomenon, but not for long.

As I stood brooding in my office, I received a hurried phone call from Bill Read. It appears the Dover Downs establishment had handed down an ultimatum to the trainers and owners squatting in their stalls —either race or 'haul horse. Our horse, the renowned Iadom, was entered that very night and could I meet him in Newark at 4 p.m.?

We both were struck by the modern and quite lavish layout of the Dover Downs track. This was no leaking-roof, run-down second-rate, broken-down, gypsy track, but a facility worthy of top horses, riders and owners. Our chests expanded a bit with justifiable pride, as we casually picked up our owner's credentials and found the way to the stables, also quite modern and efficiently laid out. Inside our stall, we encountered a different atmosphere. It was difficult to evaluate, but

175

I think it was a mixture of fear, resignation, chagrin, gloomy despair and a touch of wry humor. Kenny and his Irish trainer were busy putting a race clip on Iadom, who looked just fine and a little bored by the whole affair. After all, he had been through this routine a number of times before. Quite a number of times. Gussy, who had found the horse for us, was not in evidence at this point.

"Seen Gussy?" Kenny asked. No. Uh-huh. "Seen the Dover Morning Telegraph?" Of course not.

"I thought so," Kenny said cryptically. What does that mean?

"Gussy's very upset," Kenny remarked to no one in particular, while applying the clippers with studied determination.

"Gussys upset about what?" Bill asked with a hint of suspicion. Kenny snapped off the clippers and walked back down the aisle to a tack and feed room in front. Silently, we followed and he handed us a paper turned to the racing page outlining the evening's entries and their records. Wordlessly, he pointed to the race captioned "9th Dover Downs." We followed his stubby finger down to the fourth horse listed. Its name was Iadom. We followed the finger across the record in fatal fascination. "Refused to break" stood out from the surrounding numbers like a ragged picket fence in the middle of a windswept prairie. In fact, it stood out twice.

I made a fast survey of the rest of the entries in the race. Then I looked at all the entries for all the races for the evening—all nine of them—and I was struck with the singular fact that only our horse was so described.

I thought it vaguely strange when Bill asked what it all meant, but my mind was too full of other things to consider it long.

"It means," Kenny said with a touch of fatalism, "that he did not leave the gate." Didn't leave the gate! "Nope. Didn't run. Twice." But all that money in 1966 and 1967? "I guess he got tired."

So that's what he was doing last year—resting, somebody muttered.

"Yeah, he did pretty good in those days, won a few and made some nice dough, but then his owners put him out to pasture after he refused to break the second time in '67. Probably wanted him to forget the humiliation," the Irishman gloomed.

"But he'll probably win if we can just get him out of the gate," Kenny added hopefully.

"Has anybody got a long stick with a nail in the end of it?" somebody suggested.

"Don't be funny at a time like this. We gotta have faith. I'd rather have a long stick with a—."

176

"Shut up."

We found Gussy standing in front of Iadom. Gussy had a pensive frown on his face. His demeanor was not one to inspire confidence in the outcome of the ninth race. Iadom looked bored.

"Gussy, I told 'em," Kenny said and picked up the clippers.

"Oh, hell," Gussy said with a resigned sigh. He turned to us and his countenance reminded me of a man who has just learned his best friend has run off with his wife in duet on Man O' War and Seabiscuit, newly purchased at bargain prices in their prime. Gussy loves all horses, but especially race horses, and his fame as a knowledgeable horseman is neither exaggerated nor unjustified. He is, quite simply, one of the best and this situation was near Grecian in its epic tragedy for him.

"I want to take the horse back," he said. "I will pay for everything." It was his finest hour.

"No, you will not," Bill said. "He is a good horse—sound and has made money. He was a bargain and he was inexpensive because he had been resting. Everything will be all right and it isn't your fault anyway. We knew what we were doing. Let's get to the track—the second race is being announced."

It was his finest hour, too. I felt proud to be involved with such noble associates in what indeed must be the sport of kings. Kenny just shook his head and went back to clipping Iadom, who had showed little interest in this moving exchange.

It was a beautiful track. Spacious grandstands and lavish clubhouse restaurant. We began to chance a bet or two—modest I might add—on the races. Iadom was not up until the last race, so we had sufficient time to familiarize ourselves with the track.

The excitement among the other bettors and owners was considerable, as betting fever slowly escalated during the evening's program. Our group was somewhat less enthusiastic, but even Gussy perked up when the horses for the last race paraded out on the track with their lead ponies.

Iadom looked just fine. Secretly I was a little relieved that we had not yet had time to purchase our silks and the jockey was up in Kenny's green and white colors with the distinctive "KK" and white diamonds. Better he than we, I thought, and mentally condemned myself for such smallness of character. As the horses paraded by, we gave a small cheer and a big silent prayer. I thought it passing strange that Iadom sort of strolled behind his lead pony, while the other horses were jigging nervously about, almost dragging their lead ponies forward.

177

How controlled he is, I hazarded to Bill. Gussy gave us a funny look and quickly turned his eyes away.

The ninth was 3½-furlong claiming race with a purse of $1,400. We weren't too worried about Iadom being claimed. His odds were fifteen-to-one on the morning line and climbing. Iadom was a nine-year-old in a field of seven, the other six all under seven with most four or five. He had no trouble getting into the gate once he was able to make it out. The tension before the bell was almost unbearable. No one spoke. Somehow the people around us sensed this was no time for frivolity.

"They're off!!!" They broke in a bunch, close-packed like a bursting covey of quail. As the old foxhunter said about a close-running pack of hounds, hot on a viewed fox, you could have almost put a blanket— a big blanket, of course,—over them.

"I see him . . . I see him . . . Me, too . . . In the middle . . . Oh, Lord, theres a head bobbing up and down in the gate! Someone didn't get off!"

It was terrible. No one watched the end of the race. Well, no one except Jimmy Stewart (who had come down with Gussy) and myself, who had secretly placed five bucks on the nose of the favorite, one Rowdydow, who walked home a couple of lengths ahead of the pack without raising a sweat. We also had placed a similar amount across the board on Iadom, more as an act of faith than confidence. We were viewed with some disdain when we picked up our winnings, but we just about managed to break even on that race, so I couldn't see what all the muttering of Benedict Arnold was about.

As we glumly walked back to the stable, I expected to find that the jockey had committed hari-kari somewhere between the paddock and the stall.

"Well, at least they won't have to cool him out," someone ventured. "Let's go back and beat him up."

"Who, the jockey?"

"No, that blank-blank so-called race horse!"

"You can't beat up on a horse."

"Wanna bet. I'd sure like to give it as try."

"What do we do now?" Bill asked, ignoring the fight challenge.

"What do you mean?" Kenny said disgustedly. "Hell, he's banned on every track in the country now. Three times and you're out. We couldn't get him in at the Cedar Rapids South Side Men's Festival now."

"We could change his name. What does Iadom stand for anyway?

"I think its Serbian for Mr. Standfast."

At the stable, we found the Irish trainer carefully inspecting Iadom, who—I swear—practically yawned in our faces.

"What are you looking for? Bed sores?" Kenny demanded.

"Well," the Irishman said defensively, "at least no one was hurt."

"What do you mean hurt? When the bell rang, his legs locked like a statue in Central Park."

"Where's the jockey?"

"I don't know. He just got off the horse and walked away. He didn't even go back to change his clothes in the locker room. I don't think he wants to talk about it with the other jockeys."

"I think I'll go home," Bill said in a sort of daze.

"He's still sound. Mebbe we can make a hunter out of him. Does he know how to jump, Gussy?"

"He will when I get done with him," Gussy said with a grim tone that even made Iadom look up with a worried alertness.

So now Iadom,—now known as Mr. Standfast—is well on the way to becoming a hunter. I expect that we will see him, well groomed and turned out as only a gentlemen's hunter should be, on the opening day of next year's foxhunting season. I am sure he will be jumping in fine, measured fashion, taking excellent care of his splendidly garbed master. Perhaps this is what he was always destined for anyway—the

179

well-bred, pampered life of the gentleman's mount. I think somehow that was what he was trying to tell us that last time he entered the gate. He expected better things in his autumn years. After all, there is many a fine twenty-year-old hunter going strong and well over jumps on a good run after a fox, but who ever heard of a nine-year-old race horse winning the Derby?

And what of the Amwell Valley Stable? We are preparing a second campaign even now. We have good words from Bill concerning our second horse, who, you may recall, is fittingly called In the Money. The horse is going well and we are taking him up to Green Mountain, Vermont. There may be a happier sequel to this story. In the meantime I have sent a telegram to Peter Kriendler at his eating emporium. It reads: Dear Pete. Don't throw away Calumet Farms Jockey. Stop. Slight delay in Amwell Valley strategy. Stop. Not prepared to occupy step yet. Stop. Hold space in line tho'. Stop. (signed) Your equine friend, In The Money.

Scars

A man's scars are like a log book telling him where he's been and what happened. Have you ever sat back and catalogued your scars—some so small almost forgotten; others too large in size and wincing memory? I bet you'd be surprised both by the number and also that you did remember so much about their infliction once you recognized their fading marks. We're told that Ernest Hemingway was so accident prone that an examination of his shaved head presented an incredible number of scars that literally bore testament to fifty years of vital participation in some of the fastest moving events of modern history. All of us who have a few years can produce the same sort of track record, although admittedly much more modest.

The frailty of man was brought to mind the other day as I sat contemplating my 48th birthday, celebrated this May 8, 1979. It was no consolation that Harry Truman was born on that day or that the Second World War ended in Europe on May 8, 1945. Such fame rarely transfers merely by association. I'm still 48, my middle is a bit thicker, my hair a trifle thinner, my breath a wee shorter—and I'm no richer and very little wiser than at 47. While musing over my fate, my attention wandered to my right hand, which was reaching for my glasses. The scars on the top part triggered a vague daydream. Where and how did I get them? How many more did I have spaced out, quilt-stitched, if you will, on this near half-century old epidermis?

It seemed logical to start from the bottom and work up, the head being a bit more dignified than my second toe, right foot, which boasts a barely discernible scar collected the Summer of '57. That was the year I had to move, kicking and screaming, from Arizona to take my first gainful full-time employment in New York as something called a "foreign trade specialist." (I never quite knew what that was but, after my employer decided to send me to Cuba as the comany's representative *after* Castro took over, I absorbed the hint and looked for employment elsewhere.) Anyway I hated my job and spent a lot of time that summer visiting friends on the straight part of Fire Island. A wave tossed me heels over head one day and scraped the skin from my toe.

No big deal, but the lowest scar on my anatomy, hence some recognition.

Moving up to my right shin, we come upon a fairly good-sized entry that took about ten stitches to close and, boy, did that one hurt! I'll never forget when I collected that memento. The late Larry Koller, perhaps one of the most qualified outdoor writers (both fishing and hunting) we've ever seen, had gotten me into his beloved trout club on the Neversink River in New York's Catskills. I made my first trip up there and, while it was raining, stayed in the cabin with Larry while he cooked on an old woodburning stove. Larry loved to cook and he was a master gourmet chef. He had had a heart attack a few months back and the doctor had told him to lay off the sauce and the smokes. Larry said to hell with that and, of course, was smoking away and having his third refreshment of the day while he philosophized about fishing, cooking and his life.

A little later I decided to go fishing and while clumbering around that tumble-rock stream, slipped between two big boulders and went right through my waders, pants, long johns and a good section of skin and flesh. Somehow I got back to the cabin and was loaded into a car to go to the hospital in Liberty, where a bored week-end emergency room doctor squeezed me in among all the other dumb accident-prone tourists. The next time I went back to the club it was to help spread Larry's ashes on his favorite pool. Larry had been trying to tell me something that last day and I think I finally realized what it was. I never went back.

Shifting to my right knee, we find a whole cluster of little, miscellaneous scars, the sort most kids and suspended adolescents seem to collect from skinned knees, bike accidents, ski falls, barbed wire, car doors and the like. I've also got an indentation on each side below my knee from where a pin was put through my leg for traction after an auto accident in 1947 that produced a broken femur, but that's a bore and hardly worth more than a sentence.

My right hand has quite a galaxy of assorted mementos. (Why is it that most of my scars are on my right side? Is it because I am right-handed or just fate? How about you? Does any doctor have any statistics on this)? First, there's a four-stitch slice under the knuckle of my middle finger, garnered from the top of a can of edible goodies I was secretly trying to open in the dark while incarcerated in Culver Military Academy, circa 1946. Complementing that embroidery-work is a respectable mark at the base of the thumb, neatly executed with my first Cub Scout knife about 1942.

The top of my right hand has three beauties. One is a skin-flap from going through a plate-glass door of which more later. Secondly, there is an inch-long cut that truly does bring back fond memories. I got that trying to push Bud Webster's jeep out of a ditch coming out of his cabin, which was Buffalo Bill's old hunting shack, outside of Cody, Wyoming, in 1968. We were up there helping to plan the annual July Fourth Parade and the dedication of the new wing of the Buffalo Bill Historical Center, which had been largely financed by the royalties of the Buffalo Bill Winchester rifle. Lastly, I've got the latest entry: another inch-long slash, resulting from trying to untangle my setter from barbed wire during 1976's hunting season. There are also a lot of little, itsy-bitsy spots on the fingers of both hands from burns, punctures and cuts that elude the memory.

Ah, now the head! It's a wonder I don't look like a comic-book version of Frankenstein's Monster, but nature is wonderful in its healing ways, helped out a bit on occasion with a bit of cosmetic surgery. Perhaps the earliest scar on my whole battered body was inflicted with some vengeance by my older sister, Jean Marie, with a Buck Rogers ray pistol applied vigorously to my forehead about 1938. This assault was perpetrated merely because I had some moments previous pushed her rocker off the front porch. (Yes, in answer to nitpickers, she *was* in the rocker).

It didn't help matters any when I walked into an airplane wing and opened up the same tissue on my forehead while trying to get out of Mozambique on July 4, 1962, as fast and with as little formality as possible. I had been stranded alone between the Rovuma and Lugenda rivers for a week. By the time Mary Pat and Louis Stumberg found me, I was rapidly turning into "whiteman-gone-to-seed-in-the-tropics."

We finally all piled in a small Cessna. How we ever got off the ground, I'll never know, so the scars could have been much worse, like permanent. And all I ever shot on that part of my trip was one small impala to eat with some bread and wine I had bummed from a Portuguese army patrol, plus one marauding baboon who fancied my hammock outside the chief's hut where I was bunked, but that's another story.

I picked up one of those inch-long scars, under my lower lip, one gets from putting his teeth through his own face, as a result of that 1948 automobile accident in Indianapolis. I also collected a 30-stitch, four-inch attention-getter traversing my left check from sideburn to jaw-bone, just missing both my facial nerve and jugular vein. I got this by walking through the aforementioned plate-glass window in 1973.

I was visiting Ed Kozicky, Winchester's highly esteemed conservation director, in his office in East Alton, Illinois, to discuss his Nilo tests on the relative properties of steel and lead shot. After our meeting, I bounded downstairs, bid goodbye to the receptionist and walked through the plate-glass side-panel of the main door. This, mind you, after a witnessed lunch that consisted of nothing more lethal than barbecued chicken and a draft root-beer! As they loaded me into the ambulance, I begged Ed not to tell my boss, Bill Talley, Winchester's Senior V.P., the circumstances as it would severely damage my reputation. After all, what would a young undergraduate German baron at Heidelburg give for such a dueling scar?

I have a number of mementos from Korea, including the painful memory of two broken noses, but this is hardly the place to tell war stories. Rather, I would like to remember my last major civilian scar, a two-inch, several-stitched token of Paris, the Summer of 1955, that is mostly covered by my left eyebrow. After coming back to Ohio State

University, following my discharge from the Army in August, 1954, my roommate, Dave Call, and I decided to join my sister and her husband in sailing their small 22-foot sloop from England to Spain during the next summer vacation. Since my sister had given up Buck Rogers guns, I went without fear or trepidation.

As it happened, the sailing part of the trip was just great and, outside of almost piling into a lightship and sinking in a storm, without event. After being beached in Barcelona, it came time for Dave and me to return, so we hopped a train for Paris to meet some old buddies from the ship coming over. Unfortunately, we did meet them and proceeded to see a bit of old Paree in classic American undergraduate fashion. To make a long story short, as we were fleeing at full tilt from the Arab Quarter, I turned to look over my shoulder to see if we were being pursued by some irate locals and ran into a car. I have the dubious distinction of being the only American tourist to have hit a French taxi cab instead of vice versa.

As I sit here, contemplating the years and its scars, both literal and figurative, I wonder if I am lucky or just plain clumsy. There is a lesson to be learned by all of this, but I'm not sure I'm ready to face it, at least not for another 48 years! One thing though, the pain is gone, but the bittersweet memories, the laughter and the tears, remain.

Time does heal all wounds. Well, most.

V
FICTION AND FANTASY

A Note on Part Five

This is the section where we leave behind all pretense of credibility or factual reportage. These are also the stories that were both the most fun and the hardest to write. Some took years of cogitation and, finally, hours at the typewriter. I'm not completely satisfied with any of them at any particular given time, but then, I guess, no writer ever is. I suppose any more work on them would only make problems worse. So here they are. No more comment. If the story doesn't get the message across, no amount of verbosity in this little prelude is going to help now!

The Demon Dog of Deacon's Draw

Munroe Gordon first saw Josiah Cartright's pointer dog on one of those stark, piercingly cold nights that sometimes suddenly close out Indian summer.

One day it had been pleasantly warm, the leaves just beginning to turn and the air a little lazy. Then, without warning, the first frost swept in with a vengeance. Still and clear. Full moon and no wind. Just plain, old-fashioned cold. A sound could be heard for ten miles and it seemed a man could almost see as far by the light of that moon at midnight as he might during the day.

With the first hint of frost and the bite of clear cold on his face, the young man broke out his shotgun and fetched his ancient hound, Paddle Foot, for their traditional first coon hunt of the season. Paddle Foot would never win an award for grace and beauty, but what he lacked in looks, he made up for in cagy, old-fashioned experience well tempered with natural instinct and seasoned with courage. Paddle Foot also loved his young master as only a dog grown old in service to one man can. And the affection was returned in full by his owner. Gordon owned other dogs—a young setter he doted upon and a disreputable labrador—but, as he often said, Paddle Foot had raised him from a whelp.

It was a good evening for coon hunting and man and dog soon forgot the cold in the intensity of their pursuit. They had left home after a late supper and, the brisk air invigorating every step after they left their pick-up, soon found themselves deep into the woods by 10 p.m. They had had a good run with a young coon at the end of the line and both partners were pleased with their fine beginning.

Munroe Gordon was a pleasant, open-faced man in his early twenties. Although relatively young among the sages of an ancient sport, his hunting abilities and gentle talents with hunting dogs of all breeds had won him a respect among his peers far beyond his years.

They had wandered through the woods—driven by the drive of their first chase—into areas unfamiliar to the young hunter and even his companion hound. The woods were deep and dark—even for this moon-

190

lit night—and gave little evidence of ever having had much contact with man and his tools. The wind had quieted and with it the woods. The moon had drifted behind a transient cloud and the resultant darkness cast a strange sense of detached isolation on the forest. Muroe had stopped, listening for any sound to break the uneasy silence. And then an almost alien clatter and eerie howl cut through the air to fill their ears. Paddle Foot growled and then, strangely, whimpered by his master's side.

Munroe stood, unmoving and silent, listening to the rattle of stones and snapping of twigs. The noise grew louder and more insistent. He lifted his gun and wheeled to see a deer—his tongue and eyes protruding in exhaustion and fear—bounding through the open glade beside him. And then, lunging through the brush, eyes gleaming in the night and body steaming in the cold air, a huge dog—liver and white—pounded into view. A pale glow radiated from the dog's heaving, muscled body. Swamp glow. Fox fire. All the strange and eerie phenomena sometimes seen in unlikely places ran through Munroe's mind, but this unnatural iridescence defied comparison or explanation. As the great dog started across the clearing intense on his quarry, young Gordon released his breath in a long gasp.

The dog stopped, sniffing the air and casting his head in slow, methodic rhythm from side to side. Munroe stood frozen in the shadows of the trees. Then the dog stopped and stood looking in his direction, some twenty yards away and deadly still, his obscene coat casting its sickening light into the shadows about it. The man could hear the dog's steady panting. Suddenly he remembered his gun.

He couldn't raise his arms. The dog just stood there and stared at him, seemingly weighing something in his mind. And then Munroe heard a snarling, whining growl from beside him. Before he realized what Paddle Foot was doing, the old hound had charged the intruder.

The big dog made one swift movement, quick for so large a beast, and before Munroe's stunned eyes, Paddle Foot was stretched lifeless in the eternity of one moment. A man stepped from the woods and stood behind the dog. He had made no sound, but Munroe Gordon—his mind deadened by the sudden murder of his dog—seemed unsurprised by the stranger's unexpected appearance.

He was a tall, dark wiry man with the blackest hair of any man Munroe had ever seen. But it was his eyes, riveted above a hawkish nose and suspended under one atrocious, unbroken eyebrow, that told the story. Someone once called a man's eyes "windows of the soul." Well,

191

he never met Josiah Cartwright. If he'd have looked in his eyes, he would have plumed the depths of hell itself.

"Beezy," Josiah's voice quietly drifted through the air. With a contemptuous toss of his large gargoyle-like head, the dog reluctantly turned and trotted back toward the man. The man whispered something beyond the reach of the other man's ears and slipped into the darkness of the woods. The unworldly glow had disappeared and he was lost in the night. The man turned to follow.

"Wait a minute, Mister," Munroe Gordon had found his voice as the dog departed, "What about my dog? Your dog killed my hound!" The man turned once more and looked at the young man standing before him. Munroe returned his stare, both men fixing each other's faces in their memories. The man stepped back, into the shadows without a word and was gone. The younger man looked down at the stiffening flesh that had been his dog and made no move to follow. He had not recognized man or dog, but he would never forget either. He would meet them sooner than any of them would imagine.

II

Josiah Cartwright had no wife nor kin that acknowledged him and no man called him friend. He frightened children and made grown men strangely uneasy. It had always been so and, it appeared, with good cause. Josiah lived in a forgotten area of this world, the southern "Pine Barrens" of New Jersey. South Jersey—at least the interior—is a mysterious, unknown land to those who speed through the state by turnpike and expressway. Josiah's village—his was the only shack left standing with all four walls and roof—was a ghost town called Deacon's Draw. An itinerant, philandering preacher had been hung, drawn and quartered there in the 1700's as an example to other gentlemen of the cloth of similar persuasions.

Josiah's people—the inland "Pineys"—are a curious, inbred breed, increasingly suspicious and clannish with each generation. Some say these strange people—the ones we never see—are descended from Tory "cowboys" (guerillas we'd call them now) who fled to the Barrens after the Revolutionary War and later intermarried with the remaining Indians, runaway slaves, smugglers and lord-knows-what. It is not the sort of heritage that makes for good neighbors.

It's a poor district and the people poorer. Josiah and his kind had little to call their own—scant material wealth, the barest sort of existence, a limited future. It is a hard life with little recreation as the modern world knows it. The pleasure they receive from life is based on what's at hand—drinking, wenching, brawling, fishing, trapping and, most importantly, hunting.

Hunting is important to them: they can combine business with pleasure. Game laws mean little or nothing and a good many venison steaks have landed in New York restaurants by grace of a Piney's well-placed midnight shot. As with any business, the tools of the trade are valued most highly by the people who practice the trade. A good gun—and a good dog—are valuable, cherished possessions.

Josiah cared for nothing or no one in this world—except one thing, his large liver and white pointer. They were inseparable and people said they were well matched to deserve each other. The dog was as mean—if not meaner—than its master. But even Josiah's worst enemies had to admit that the dog was almost unbelievably uncanny on game. Josiah called his dog "Beelzebub's Demonly Delight" or just plain "Beezy" for short. Only when Josiah crooned "Beezy" as the dog egg-walked into a point, it almost sounded obscene.

No one knew where Josiah had found his pointer. Everyone—at least in the Barrens—knew that Beezy was probably the best bird dog they had ever seen. The "Pineys" were lucky in one respect: they had quail and they knew how to hunt quail dogs. Strangely enough, Josiah Cartwright had never before boasted a bird dog that even touched some of the fine pointers and setters fielded by his neighbors. That is, until Beezy hoved up on the horizon one Fall night.

On that night a few of the Pineys happened by Josiah's shack—they were on their way to check a deadfall—and a large liver and white pointer came bounding out from behind the shed. He was a giant of a dog with a growl to match and even they, familiar as they were with all sorts of maverick dogs, were prudent enough to hesitate. They stood stock still while Beezy—for naturally it was he—gave them a cold once-over. When Josiah came from his shack, they saw his arm was band-aged from wrist to elbow. Josiah never volunteered any information concerning his arm or Beezy's background and people gave up asking, but not wondering.

Since it was Fall, it wasn't very long until Beezy's other talents became apparent. Hunters would occasionally run across Josiah and his dog in the field—after all, everyone knows the same quail coverts in a small locality—and it must be confessed that most times they abdicated the field to that formidable pair. Josiah had never been a creature to command undying affection; in company with Beezy, he was

193

downright fearsome. But some of the retreating hunters watched after they withdrew to the shadows and what they saw livened up many a tale around Clurgy's Franklin stove.

Beezy was some quail dog—or, for that matter, grouse, woodcock and pheasant dog as well. People reported they saw Beezy plunge into frozen, ice-topped ponds after fallen ducks with no concern whatever for ice or chilling water. There he'd be, chopping through the thin-skinned ice like some primitive icebreaker; water splashing all about and bearing down in relentless fashion on some hapless duck. Josiah didn't lose any cripples that year.

But Josiah Cartwright had secretly long coveted some sort of stature that would set him apart (in a favorable light, that is) from other men. Something that no man could take away. He knew he would never be rich or powerful, a captain of industry or respected leader of anything for that matter. But he could win the Sneaky Hollow field trial and for him that was more than enough.

III

The Sneaky Hollow Invitational was a rare trial; entries were strictly limited to handlers and dogs native to the state. As such, it wasn't prey to the big professional trainers from the South and their large stables of rich men's dogs.

As a consequence, this "purified" trial had come to mean a lot to the state's amateur dog handlers. If a man could place at Sneaky Hollow, he had arrived at the senior rank among his peers in the tight circle of New Jersey's sporting dog world. If he—glory of glories—should happen to win, his life was complete. There could be little treasure left in this world for him; everything else would be anticlimactic in his remaining years.

The great day arrived and representatives of all sections of the state joined for the one event that brought them together in single-minded purpose each year. Tall, sandy Scotch-Irish from the hills of the Northern part of the state joined the dark, smaller—and merrier—Italian-Americans of the flatlands of middle Jersey. A Hungarian refugee freedom fighter, accompanied by his aristocratic Vizsla pointer, from New Brunswick, rubbed elbows with a distinguished Anglo-Saxon, High Episcopalian doctor from Short Hills who, paradoxically, was accompanied by a rather non-descript, sturdy Brittany. Farmer, lawyer, businessman and commuter to New York, clergy and scoundrel, they were all united in one cause: sporting dogs.

And among them all—standing out like a foreign intrusion although they were perhaps of the oldest stock in the state—were the Pineys, the strange people of the southern Barrens. Awkward, withdrawn, shyly and slyly observing the goings-on with veiled eyes that darted behind their guarded eyelids, these men and their occasional woman stood apart although they were surrounded by the crowd. And, alone, even among his own, Josiah Cartwright and his great dog stood to one side under a great elm tree. They were biding their time.

A flurry of commotion stirred the crowd on one side and Josiah turned to see a handsome young man step out with a slim, racy setter by his side. The murmurs of the onlookers gave ample evidence of their esteem for both man and dog. It was Munroe Gordon and his young setter bitch, the "Jersey Belle," his standard bearer in this year's invitational. Since young Gordon was no slouch when it came to either field trials or a little judicious betting on the side, the smart money was fast drifting to the Jersey Belle, popularly known as Belle.

Although she was young and dainty, as her name might imply, she had already established an impressive record as both a shooting dog and a winner of local field trials. She was a pretty little thing—all white with a light ticking of orange sprinkled across her muzzle and down her sides plus one orange ear—and Gordon doted on her as an older man might his mistress.

Josiah and Beezy sidled up behind Munroe and Belle as they registered. Beezy appraised the young setter with a malevolent eye, bared his teeth and growled a deep, menacing snarl in his throat. Belle lazily tossed her ears as though to rid it of an itinerant flea or other loathsome object and turned away. Beezy made a lunge forward, but Josiah checked him with a yank of his lead. Munroe turned and surveyed the situation with a startled eye. He started forward, hesitated, then with his face a mask, quietly spoke.

"That's quite a pointer you've got there. I hope he's under control," he said.

"Control enough," Josiah grunted, his eyes veiled.

"He's a registered dog, I take it?" the young man questioned.

"Yes," Josiah said with a strange smile, "but not in your book—or any other you've seen!" Munroe stood looking at the pair for a second or two and then walked away with Belle at heel. Josiah turned and signed Beezy up for the Invitational.

The puppy stakes were finished well before noon. The first heats of the Invitational were run as soon as the judges had finished a short snack. Being dedicated men—and also anxious to return home some-time before midnight—the judges ran the trial straight through the day with no formal midday break for lunch.

As a result, there was a constant flow of spectators and participants between the parking areas, the grandstands and the gallery as it followed the various heats on the courses outlined. More people arrived, some drifted away. Eighteen dogs were entered for a total of nine heats, averaging thirty minutes per heat. Anyway one viewed it, it was going to be a good afternoon's work.

Although the invitational was limited to dogs native to the state, the entries were all of first-class caliber. It was apparent from the first heats that this was going to be one of the most strenuously contested competitions in the history of the event. In the third heat, Beezy and Josiah quickly established a standard that most dogs would find hard to equal.

Old "Beelzebub's Demonly Delight" was—as his name might suggest —literally hell-on-wheels when it came to birdwork. His bracemate in the third heat, one "Kentucky Sky Lou," had been regarded by many as an up and coming pointer. After Beezy got through with her, she was lucky to get a ride home. There was no doubt, Beezy was the dog to beat. As the saying goes, a miss is as good as a mile—and no-body, least of all Munroe Gordon, cared anything about coming in second. If you couldn't beat Beezy, you were done.

Entry after entry, setter and pointer, brittany and short-hair, sallied forth to do his best against the awful, awesome performance Beezy had established early in the day. A fearsome pall hung over the assembled handlers as heat after heat was completed with the hateful downstate dog still triumphant. Resignation and then despair gripped the steadily dwindling group of waiting handlers as champion dog after champion dog was ground up by Beezy's standard set in the third heat. Try as they might, the dogs couldn't measure up.

While there is usually considerable argument about even the most trifling judicial field trial decision, no one could find even the lamest excuse to question Beezy's leadership. Through it all, Munroe Gordon remained unperturbed. Sprawled in nonchalant fashion against a station wagon, he regarded the pathetic fatalists about him with contempt and amusement. The Jersey Belle was entered in the eighth heat, which was soon to start.

Well, the eighth heat was Belle's all the way. "Fancy Dan's Bo" was Belle's bracemate and it must be admitted that "Bo" was game to the

196

last. Bo refused to acknowledge what was obvious to everyone else, canine and human. He turned in an admirable performance, but the Jersey Belle, under the gentle guiding spirit of her master, capped her already winning heat with a beautiful closing point and double retrieve at the end of the course. One of the missed birds from a previous point had joined up with another and the official gun had downed one with each barrel of his Winchester double gun. It was, so to speak, the frosting on the cake.

After a moment's consultation, the judges stepped forward and their leader announced that due to Belle's superlative performance and Beezy's already established position, there would be a run-off heat between those two dogs to decide the champion of the Invitational. The gallery went wild. It appeared that the downstate demon might be vanquished by a little faith, hope and charity after all.

The remaining heat of what was now officially the first series of the Invitational was run without incident. No other dog matched the winning performances put up by Beezy and Belle and even the handlers involved seemed anxious for the run-off heat to be started. They didn't have long to wait.

Never have right and wrong, black and white, good and evil appeared so sharply delineated, especially between dogs. No one ever thinks of a dog as evil, black-hearted or wicked, but Beezy seemed all of those things to the spectators of Sneaky Hollow. Beezy was too methodical in his hunting. He didn't really enjoy it for its own sake, but rather for some fiendish satisfaction. That was it. Beezy was too perfect for a dog. He had no apparent faults; he made humans uneasy. A dog shouldn't be superior to man—who has many faults and knows it. You couldn't really "like" Beezy. Nothing worse could be said about a dog.

"Gentlemen, prepare for the breakaway. Marshall, see to the gallery," one of the judges motioned to the crowd behind him. It was the largest number of spectators the field trial had witnessed in years. "All right. Mr. Cartwright, Mr. Gordon, you may commence."

Belle and Beezy lit out in parallel bursts, quickly extinguished their initial nervous energy and settled down to business within seconds after release. Both interpreted the wind, cast accordingly and moved down field with the handlers and judges following, trailed by the gallery.

Beezy performed in his usual cool, determined, seemingly perfect fashion, but Belle was a dog possessed—not by the devil for that was

197

Beezy's domain—but by all the varied and talented ancestors that made up her bloodline. All her Laverack and Llewellin forebears must have showered their benevolent magic upon her nose and brain that day. Each forceful stride seemed to proclaim her joy in hunting; each carefully executed approach on game underlined her skillfully tutored training. If Beezy was a demonic machine, Belle was heavenly inspiration.

Beezy seemed to sense that things were different. For the first time, he had a serious challenger. His huge, powerful body tensed and he lunged forward with more determined force than he had ever before exhibited. But what Beezy supplied in sheer force and power, Belle made up in skill and tactics.

While Beezy covered ground in huge leaping bounds, determined to move through as much territory as possible as fast as he could with the hope of finding the most birds, Belle picked her way with care in a steady, calculated lope. Finally it happened; Belle picked up a bird that Beezy—impatient in his determination—had missed. In fact, as the gallery murmured, Beezy had practically walked right over the bird. Josiah's face darkened with rage; Munroe's demeanor imparted nothing but a sort of serene calm.

"That's one for old Paddle Foot," he murmured. Belle continued on her way. She never hesitated nor doubted what her instincts told her and her training dictated. Faultlessly moving through each course, the small white and orange-ticked setter picked her way from bird to bird with a sublime economy of movement. Beezy on his part became almost frantic with frustration and, it appeared, rage. It seemed as if he knew that he was losing out and it was more than he could bear. He became careless. Eager to even the score, Beezy pushed too hard on a running bird and it flushed wild ahead of him. The gallery roared. It was all over but the handing out of trophies.

The gallery had already started back to the starting point when a snarl—then a yelping cry of pain—froze them in their tracks. They turned to see Munroe rushing forward with unbelievable speed toward two struggling dogs. Beezy's huge head was fixed over Belle's, his jaws firmly, wrenchingly tearing at the slim neck of the setter. Blood coarsed down the soft white-feathered hair. Munroe Gordon raised a fist and slammed it against Beezy's head. Beezy, stunned, released his hold, staggered a moment and, shaking his head, turned on Munroe with bloody fangs. Josiah ran forward.

"Hold on, you devil! Hold on!" he shouted. Beezy stood there—his sides heaving, eyes dilated in flashing rage and madness, his mouth dripping saliva and blood.

"Get that dog out of here before I kill him. Right now! Get! And I swear I'll kill him if I ever see him again—anywhere." The younger man was breathing in slow controlled gasps. He had knelt by the Jersey Belle, who lay there, her quiet form occasionally jerking in spasmodic reaction to the shock of Beezy's brutal attack. Munroe had cleared the blood away from her neck. It appeared painfully, but not damagingly, torn. She would be well in a day or two, but it would be a long time before she—or anyone—forgot Beelzebub's Demonly Delight.

Josiah turned without a word. He walked away, up the road toward the woods, with Beezy at his heel. The gallery, judges, handlers and spectators remained silent as they watched the two leave. Josiah was the last Piney to leave. The rest—without sign or notice—had silently faded away during the first moments following Beezy's attack. Munroe Gordon straightened up and looked toward the retreating figures of Josiah and his dog. They were just cresting the hill. Without a word, Gordon—as if on some sort of premonition—started forward and, to the amazement of everyone, hastily trotted up the road to the top of the hill.

When he looked down, he saw Josiah—with Beezy at his left heel—pass down the other side of the hill until they were out of sight of the assembled crowd back at the grounds. Then Beezy stopped and seemingly with a low growl had halted Josiah Cartwright. Josiah quickly turned and faced the dog. They remained motionless for a moment or two, some deadly silent struggle coarsing over heaven knows what line of communication between them. Josiah seemed almost defiant in his stance; Beezy threatening.

Finally, Beezy gave a sharp, demanding snarl and impatiently tossed his head. Josiah's shoulders seemed to sag and with slow, agonized steps he walked back to the dog. The dog started forward, intent on its path; the man took a position at the dog's left heel and stumbled after him. It was almost dusk and Munroe Gordon was suddenly witness to a strange transition. As the sun's light faded in steady measure and the man's figure slowly blended into the shadows below, an eerie, almost phosphorescent light grew in contrasting proportion about the figure of the dog. And then . . . the little haze of light growing steadily

199

brighter but ever smaller as it moved into the darkening distance—it simply disappeared.

It was the last sight anyone—in or out of those isolated Pine Barrens —ever had of Josiah Cartwright of Deacon's Draw and his dog, Beelzebub's Demonly Delight, who was sometimes called Beezy by his master.

Remember Tolliver Guilford?

It is well known that the relationship between members of the "hunt-fish fraternity" and their wives is a delicately balanced one indeed. In fact, in a few unfortunate instances, certain wives have demanded their husbands make a choice between outdoor pursuits and indoor comforts. No one wins such a contest and the wise outdoor husband sees to it that this crisis never arises.

There was considerable surprise among the members of the Midtown Turf, Yachting and Polo Association (hunting and fishing only), therefore, when one Tolliver Guilford, a member of long standing and average good sense, revealed that he planned revenge against his legal spouse. It seems that Mrs. Guilford had decreed that Tolliver's faithful, but generally worthless, setter, Spencer Q. Dog, must depart from the family mansion forthwith.

Spencer Q., in a fit of rare enthusiasm, had skillfully removed the back screen by the simple maneuver of leaving the house without opening the door while in pursuit of a trespassing cocker spaniel. Since cocker spaniels were heartily loathed by both Spencer Q. and Tolliver, the latter considered the loss of the screen lamentable, to be sure, but the natural result of a patriotic act. Mrs. Guilford did not agree, however, and Spencer Q. was soon residing in temporary exile with a bachelor uncle on the other side of town. Mrs. Guilford—Verna by name—regarded the arrangement as permanent; Tolliver chose to regard it as a temporary expedient to be tolerated until happier days permitted the return of Spencer Q. to his proper position in society.

Months passed and there was no relaxing of Spencer Q's ban. Verna remained not only unshakeable in her opposition to the return of the exile, but horror of horrors, had interpreted her initial victory as a sign of weakness and was now pressing further demands upon the reeling Tolliver. Hints were made that he might better spend his week-ends grubbing in the flower beds and generally improving the appearance of the house and grounds. Admittedly, Tolliver's grounds would never elicit whinnies of envy from the local garden club, but they were respectable—just barely, of course—but still respectable.

He saw no point in wasting good time planting petunias or painting fences, when he could be improving his knowledge of nature by pursuing the wily trout and phantom grouse. Verna did not agree with this basic premise and it was soon apparent that trouble—real trouble, not the niggling sporadic skirmishes that accompanied each hunting and fishing expedition, but *real trouble*—was in the offing. There is nothing more horrifying than civil war and it was obvious that Tolliver was planning subversion against what Verna regarded as the law of the land.

Tolliver took to brooding. On the now rare occasions when he would steal out for a meeting of the Midtown group—known, for brevity's sake, as MTYPA, which sounds sort of like a Russian track team—the members were depressed by the change wreaked in their formerly carefree companion. As Spring progressed and the MTYPA's trout excursions gradually phased into Summer bass trips, Tolliver's absences became increasingly frequent. Certain fickle, impressionable younger members shook their heads in premature grief and ventured the opinion that "Old Tolly" was lost to mankind forever.

The older members, who had seen the rise and fall—and conversely, the fall and rise—of many under similar pressures in their day, were neither dismayed nor misled by Tolliver's apparent resignation (the unkind said surrender) to his fate. Their faith was soon justified. Tolliver appeared one day with face flushed with triumph, his old swagger signaling a return to glory.

Early that morning, Verna, cocksure in her confidence and apparent total victory, was surprised with her arms filled with fly rods, old shooting clothes and other miscellania of the chase, finny and furred. Tolliver, who was on his dutiful way to the garage to mix a new batch of crab grass killer, stopped short, stunned by the suspicion that suddenly overwhelmed him.

"Why Verna, what have you got there?" he said.

"What does it look like? It's all that old junk of yours that's been cluttering the back room, that's what it is, Tolliver," she answered. No hint of rebellion in Tolliver Guilford's eye caused any hesitation in her reply. She was firm in her conviction.

"What are you doing with it," then as suspicion fully bloomed, "what are you going to DO with it?"

"Good Will Industries and Salvation Army," she replied and made to pass, impatient with his prattle.

"Oh, no," he said, "Oh, no—I don't think so—not that."

"Don't argue with me, Tolliver Pierce Guilford, I've no time," Verna said.

"Take it back Verna," his tone stopped her interruption, "I mean it. Take it back—now."

"Now listen here—," she started.

"Verna, this is it," his course seemed suddenly very clear, "I'm not going to let you dispose of a life's collection of valuable gear. Why some of those rods are Leonards! I've worn that jacket in over twenty different states in as many hunting seasons. No, sir, you're not going to throw them away! On second thought, I'm pretty sick and tired of a lot of things you've been making me do lately."

"Oh, you are, are you," her battle voice coming to the barricades for the attack.

"Verna, before we go any further, I'm going to tell you something. I'm not taking anymore of your guff. Not only that, I'm going fishing with the boys on their annual deep sea jaunt Saturday. Now, don't interrupt," and wisely she didn't, "because I'm going to give you the alternatives. If you try to boss me around any more or try to nag me into messing around with this stupid garden of yours, I'm pulling out. You can go live with your mother, your Great Aunt Kate or anybody else you choose, but me, I'm not taking it any more. Do you understand me?"

"Yes, dear," Verna meekly replied. Audacious behavior in the face of seeming insurmountable odds had paid off in total victory. Apparently.

Hence, Tolliver Guilford was a new man or, rather, his old self. Firmly entrenched in MacSorgle's favorite basement chair, which smelled strongly of tobacco, beer and a bit of mildew, in the Mac-Sorgle rumpus room, Tolly gave a swift recapitulation of the day's campaign and then settled back to linger lovingly over the more delicate morsel of triumph itself. He discussed various aspects of tactics, propaganda, strategy and, most important, reparations with the assembled brethren of the MTYPA. It was not enough, Tolly maintained, to merely win. Verna should also pay for the misery of the past months.

She should at least suffer some small token of the months of degradation she had inforced on him. Heady with the sweet intoxication of his return to manhood, Tolly indulged himself—and the other members —with wild, intricate schemes of revenge, some of which seemed to fall just short of violating the law. As the evening wore on and Tolly's dreams began to take concrete shape, the older members, who had

203

forseen his return from Elba, began to wonder if he was facing Waterloo.

"Leave well enough alone," one veteran was heard to mumble.

"Best to quit while you're even," Uncle Jo MacSorgle flatly stated. "Tolly thinks he's ahead, but he isn't. He and Verna are just back to where they were before. In other words, they're even. No one has lost too much face—yet. Tolly had lost some, but he got it back today. He ought to leave it that way. If he pushes, he may lose what he got back. Also," Uncle Jo tapped his pipe, "Spencer Q. Dog has not returned. I consider the battle in dubious outcome until that issue is finally settled. Tolly had best mind to Spencer Q. before he commits his reserve forces in some other campaign—one, I might add, that is based purely upon vanity and revenge."

"Tolly was largely successful today because he was right—and right was on his side. Now, this other adventure—especially with Spencer Q.'s fate still uncertain—is skirting the edge of folly. Revenge ain't right. Not this year, at least. Remember Herman Hill, the zealous game warden?" A delicious shiver went down young Harry Byrne's back as a graphic picture of Herman Hill, who had unsuccessfully sought revenge that year, came to mind. Herman had attempted to gain favor in the eyes of headquarters at the expense of Uncle Jo and had suffered a fate so horrible it cannot be repeated in these pages.

Herman Hill and his fate not-with-standing, Tolly Guilford was not about to deny himself the fruits of his victory. Within a very short time, news of Tolly's folly, as it was labeled by Uncle Jo and his cohorts, began to filter into MacSorgle's rumpus room. Although he would have denied it to all, Tolliver Guilford's pattern of retribution was amazingly similar to that inflicted by his wife upon him in the recent past.

Tolly started with little things: leaving wet clothes in a pile on the bedroom floor (formerly forbidden—even in his best days, Tolly had to change clothes in the basement); tracking mud through the kitchen (equally forbidden); and, to add insult, insisting that Verna clean all game and fish, regardless of condition or smell, he might bring home. Since he sometimes indulged his noted generosity and offered to have certain bachelor companions' game cleaned as well, this last proposition was particularly odious to Verna. Uncle Jo shook his head and muttered something about the "female of the species and spontaneous combustion."

Tolly was riding rather high at this point, however, and indeed it appeared his position was secure. By September and the first shorebird

shoot, Tolly had not only restored all of his previous privileges, but had inaugurated quite a few new ones, some of which were so extreme in their latitude of married freedom that most members of the MTYPA (at least those embroiled in holy wedlock) were torn between feelings of envy and awestruck fear. He now came and went when he wanted on the week-ends and sometimes during the week. He might or might not tell Verna of his plans or departures and returns. He absolutely refused to play contract bridge or, horror of horrors, canasta, a game Verna loved. He didn't shave, mow lawns, paint, dabble in plant life, repair anything but tackle or guns, go to the store(s), attic, basement or garage (except for tackle and guns) or do almost anything Verna wanted on any weekend he might by chance be home. He was downright rude to Verna's friends, contemptuous of his neighbors (who had not experienced emancipation) and beginning to be a bit of a bore to the members of the MTYPA.

It was inevitable. Tolly had been returned to the fold with unhampered joy by a unanimity of members, but it soon became obvious that Tolliver Guilford in total victory was a different character than the old easy-going Tolly who only wanted to hunt and fish a little and let everything else well enough alone. The old Tolly was not only a good friend and fine companion on hunting and fishing trips, but also, if the truth were admitted as evidence at this late stage, a fairly decent husband and provider. Even Verna would admit that now. The contrast to her present dilemma would demand recognition of the merits of the past life.

The new Tolly, however, was something else again. As Uncle Jo stated, "We have created a Frankenstein monster—what with certain members and their encouragement," and he cast a look of undisguised disgust towards the younger members clustered around Harry Byrne. Tolly had begun to chide the more timid married members of the club with indictments of their manhood. He upheld his present status as an example—nay, a goal—for all to follow. He was the unfettered man, the noble savage returned to Rousseau's state of nature, a direct descendant of Jim Bridger, Thoreau and D. H. Lawrence, if such a combination be possible. Needless to say, it was no time at all before Tolly had become—sin of sins—patronizing.

"Well," Uncle Jo began one night after Tolly had departed their usual weekly meeting to give a lecture to the Elks on man's role in modern suburban America, "I believe it is time we began to consider our good friend Tolly Guilford. This is a subject that has been scrupulously avoided in these past weeks, but one that seriously needs discussing."

"Tolly," he paused for silence and got it, "has become a pompous ass. That we can live with, I suppose, since we already have a number and variety of that species." A few members squirmed uneasily. They weren't the ones Uncle Jo was talking about; those who sagely nodded their heads in agreement (and cast accusing looks at their companions) were more likely the subject of Uncle Jo's reference.

"But it's more important than that—him being an ass, that is. If he's —we're—not careful, he's going to end up without any friends, maybe not a job, and, most assuredly, no wife. Now, I know—I know—Verna's not exactly everyone's picture of the perfect mate. Mine either, for that matter. But who the heck is? Have any of you looked in the mirror lately? Cripes, I can't stand it myself." Everyone squirmed.

"Now, I think we're going to have to do something about all this. Things may have gone too far to bring back the status quo before all this business started with the exile of Spencer Q., but we have to save old Tolly from himself. We may end up losing him, at least for awhile, but in the long run I think we will have done the right thing. After all," and he pointedly looked in the direction of Harry Byrne and the younger members, "we have a certain responsibility in this matter. We are not completely without blame."

"Yes sir," no one could be more contrite than Harry Byrne when the occasion called for some tactical humility, "but what can we do? I mean, well, Tolly isn't going to listen to any advice. He's giving it."

"For once you're right, Harry, and I think I know what we've got to do. As a matter of fact, I think the best thing to do is not tell you what I'm going to do. If I did, the effect wouldn't be the same and the plan wouldn't work half as well. And then again, some of you couldn't keep a secret if you were locked in a bank vault on Bikini Atoll." Uncle Joe got up and carefully put his favorite tankard back in its center position over the mantle.

"Now, the rest of you, listen to me. Go on like you have before. Don't pay any more—or any less—attention to Tolly than you have in the past. And," he paused by the door, "don't pay any attention to me —any at all, regardless of what I may do. Understand? O.K., I'll be seeing you."

"Now why would Uncle Jo leave us here in his basement, and where is he going at this time of night," young Byrne asked. Since no one had an answer, the meeting was adjourned and the members silently climbed the stairs to the kitchen, said goodbye to Aunt Bridget Mac-Sorgle, cast surreptitious looks for Uncle Jo, who was nowhere in sight, and went home, some by way of Sorenson's Second Avenue Saloon.

II

As days passed, the full interest of the MTYPA was centered on the Fall hunting season. It was scarcely noticed that Uncle Jo missed the first Saturday pheasant hunt. When Uncle Jo appeared at the next bi-weekly meeting of the Association in his basement, he was meditative and singularly uncommunicative. He sat in the corner, comfortable with pipe and ale, nodding pleasantly to tales of the previous hunt, the one he had been sorry to miss. He offered advice on current projects, if asked, and generally avoided Tolly Guilford. That worthy, still soaring in obnoxious triumph, now considered himself the sage of "Hunting Hill" (his new name for his 1¼ acre lot and converted Cape Cod house) and mentor to the less enlightened—that is, the other members of the MTYPA. He had gradually usurped a dominant position in the MTYPA and those who sometimes disagreed with his pronouncements were regarded (by Tolly) as something akin to Trotskyites in Stalin's Russia.

Since Tolly now regarded the MTYPA as a captive fief, he devoted much of his time to outside organizations previously unacquainted with his uplifting example. Tolly was out to correct that situation; he was spreading the "word" as interpreted by T. P. Guilford, emancipator of men. As pointed out earlier, Tolly had already shown the way to the Elks, who had received his message in dubious fashion. It came as no surprise, therefore, when Tolly announced to the assembled MTYPA members that once again duty called. He would have to leave the meeting early; the Knights of Columbus were waiting to be freed. Tolly left; the members looked to Uncle Jo. He was carefully examining the inner working of his pipe.

Tolly's meeting ran considerably longer than he expected. He met a couple of friends he had not seen since the previous Spring and, eager to give them the complete details of his campaign, Tolly had adjourned with his comrades to a neighborhood establishment noted for its imported draft beer and reasonable prices, a rare combination in any civilization. It was well after 1:00 a.m. when Tolly got home. As he turned into the driveway, he switched off his lights, cut the motor and silently rolled into the garage. He eased both the car and garage doors shut, gently picked his way to the kitchen door and, with the dexterity of years of experience in similar situations, quietly unlocked it. He glided into the darkened kitchen and then, as he bent to remove his shoes, he stopped.

Tolly straightened up. He walked over to the wall, switched on the light and turned to the refrigerator. Whistling, he proceeded to relieve the box of a variety of foods. When he had what he wanted, he slammed its door shut with a careless gesture and sat down at the breakfast table. His chair made its usual scraping sound, but its harsh grating was magnified outrageously in the silence of the night. Tolly couldn't have cared less. He turned on the radio.

Fat and happy, as the saying goes, he tromped upstairs, his way well lit by every light he encountered. After a rather noisy session at the bathroom washstand, Tolly strolled into his and Verna's bedroom. He switched on the light; Verna appeared to be asleep. He dropped a shoe. Another shoe. No comment. Sighing, Tolly rose, put on his pajamas and put out the light. He climbed into bed, snuggled deep and contented into the covers, the pillow cradling his head.

"Good night, dear," Verna said.

Tolly slept the deep sleep of those with peace of mind and a stomach full of beer and sandwiches. Hours passed and he found himself in that curious half-world between sleep and consciousness, a limbo where he was neither asleep nor yet awake. He was vaguely aware of his surroundings and his mind seemed clear, but he was unable—or, rather unwilling—to physically carry out any activity. He seemed to hear a weird crying, almost a despairing wail. It would begin low, rise

208

in pitch and finally end with a raucous entreaty. Then it would turn to a maddened scold, a piercing challenge, a shrieking demand for combat to the death.

It wasn't a dream. As Tolly brought himself back to complete, though somewhat fuzzy, consciousness, he glanced at Verna's bed. It was empty. Another shriek jerked him to a sitting position among his covers. There, hiding crouched behind the window drape was Verna, intent on the small clump of woods across the road behind the house. The early light of dawn filtered through the window. She held a bulbous wooden tube to her mouth. Her cheeks puffed and another wild call impaled the air.

"Great Caesar's ghost woman—what are you doing!"

"Blowing my crow call," Verna replied, her attention still riveted on some unseen activity across the road.

"What did you say?"

"I'm blowing my crow call—sh-h," Verna impatiently waved with her free hand, "I think they're going to light in that big oak."

"Who for heavens sake?" his tone was hushed.

"Why the crows, of course," Verna said and turned back to the window.

Tolly sank back on the bed. For sometime he regarded Verna with a speculative eye. She continued to stand behind the drape. Verna was oblivious to his existence. After awhile Tolly got up, dressed and went downstairs. He sat down in the kitchen and waited. When Verna didn't come downstairs, he absentmindedly put the coffee pot on the stove and turned on the burner. When the pot started to bubble and Verna still hadn't come down, he fixed himself breakfast, quietly ate and left for work. As he pulled out of the drive, he heard a low screeching call from the back of the house. He looked up. A lone crow was gliding phantom-like in lazy circles about the oak tree across the road. Another, perched on a high limb, tentatively flapped its wings and settled back on its roost.

It was not a good day for Tolly. He had a vague uneasy feeling that something had begun which would not end well. Worse, he also intuitively felt that the process of coming to that inevitable end would be a perilous one indeed. Verna's morning behavior was completely beyond his comprehension; there was nothing in fifteen years of married life to provide any comparison or clue to her dawn activities. He determined that he would straighten things as soon as he got home that evening. He had made a big mistake in not forcing the subject that morning, but his stupefaction had been so complete it had not entered his head.

Filled with determination to "nip this thing in the bud" (whatever it might be that was budding), Tolly left work early, raced home and strode purposely into the house. No one was there; a note was on the kitchen table. "Dear Tolly" it said (Verna never called him Tolly, only Tolliver) "I'm going to a meeting of the Women's League to Preserve our Woods and Waterways . . . I won't be back till late as some of the girls are stopping off afterwards for a little refreshment . . . Don't wait up . . . Verna . . . P. S. There are some cold cuts and macaroni in the refrigerator."

Tolly looked around. The sink was full of dishes; a greasy frying pan was on the stove. As he sat down, his foot kicked a magazine under the kitchen table. He picked it up; it was the latest edition of "J. J. McSween's Olde North Woods Catalog for Outdoorsmen." Fascinated, he flipped the pages. The order coupon in the back had been carefully clipped from its page.

"So that's it!" Tolly exclaimed, "Comes the dawn . . . well, whatayaknow about that." Tolly shook his head and chuckled. Good ole Verna. She had really seen the light all right, all right. Not only had she cast aside her old nagging ways and silly interests, but she was actually making an effort to mold herself to his way of life. What more could a man ask? To top it off, she was going to get him something for his birthday that he wanted for a change—something from J. J. McSween and not some crazy velvet smoking jacket. Happy as only a man can be who is gifted with rare insight into the female mind, Tolly Guilford went to bed. Shortly after midnight, Verna Guilford returned home. After a noisy farewell to the ladies who had driven her home, Verna went to the kitchen and fixed herself a sandwich to carry upstairs. Later, after a bit of unnecessary commotion at the washstand, she flipped off the light and sank into bed with a sigh.

"Good night, dear," Tolly said.

The next morning and for a number of mornings after, Tolly got up, found that Verna made no similar effort and made his own breakfast. He said nothing. He could give a little. After all, Verna was busy; it wasn't easy to run a house and try to learn a whole new way of life at the same time. Tolly was tolerant. He felt it was worth it; the boys would really stand up and take notice when they saw this miracle in action.

Verna's nose was stuck in outdoor books most of her free time, which was considerable now that she had largely discarded her work

210

habits. Tolly noticed that the house was a little more dusty than usual but when he saw Verna's face buried in Caleb Storke's "Practical Trapping for Boys," he knew it was worth it.

It appeared that Verna's interest in cooking—always one of her prides in the past—had considerably diminished as well until Tolly returned one night to find a huge smudge cloud of smoke rising from the backyard. Rushing forward with the portable fire extinguisher from the garage, he found Verna intensely ministering to an odd, box-like contraption of galvanized tin huddled over a hole filled with charcoal and wood. She was smoking venison according to a method described in the latest issue of "Outdoor Man." The side of the garage was black with soot.

The next Saturday Tolly skipped the MTYPA morning pheasant hunt and scrubbed the side of the garage. It was no use; the heat had blistered the paint. Tolly had a glimpse of the following Spring; it was filled with paint·buckets. He shuddered and went back to the house. Verna was nowhere to be seen. Irritated, Tolly tramped into the kitchen, which was its now usual mess, and looked around for some lunch material. There wasn't any cold meat; a half-molded hunk of cheese defied consumption. He decided to make a fried egg sandwich. No eggs. The bread box yielded a loaf of stale bread saved to make dressing. He heard a car pull into the drive. Furious, he slammed the kitchen door shut and hurried to the garage.

Uncle Jo MacSorgle's old Chevy station wagon was parked in the driveway. Verna and Uncle Jo were at the tailgate with another figure squirming with excitement at the back window. Uncle Jo looked up as Tolly bore down upon them.

"We've got a little surprise for you Tolly. We've brought Spencer Q. back," Uncle Jo said quietly. Verna stood silent at his side. Tolly came to an abrupt halt, transfixed by Uncle Jo's words. It was almost as if he didn't understand. Spencer Q., quivering in ecstasy as only a spoiled, high-strung English setter can, let out a low crooning wail of greeting.

"Spence—Spence old boy—come here old fella—that's right—heck, let him loose—that's all right boy—that's all right—down fella—down—that's a good boy," Tolly's monologue ignored the others. Spencer Q. reciprocated in kind; he knew a good deal when he saw it. Things had been pretty lean at his temporary berth with the bachelor uncle on the other side of town.

"Verna—Uncle Jo—I don't know what to say . . . this is the greatest," Tolly wheezed, wiping his nose in emotion. "The family's back together again, by golly." He gave Verna a squeeze.

211

"Yes, isn't it wonderful," Verna gave Uncle Jo a strange sideways look.

"Well, I gotta go now," Uncle Jo said, "by the way, Tolly, we've got another surprise for you. Verna and I have been working the dog the last couple of weeks and old Spence has really come along. I mean it. I think it's just what he needed. I mean work every day, instead of just on weekends. Verna did most of the work, actually."

"No kidding! Well, how's he doing?"

"Good enough to be the club's entry in the Sneaky Hollow Invitational Field Trial for Sporting Dogs next week," Uncle Jo dropped his bombshell.

"What! Are you kidding? Spence?," Tolly gaped.

"Just that," Uncle Jo said, climbing in the car, "but Verna will have to run him—it will take a lot of work to get him in shape in time—and Verna's the only one who can give him some field work every day," which was a bit of a white lie since Uncle Jo was retired and had every intention of training Spencer himself.

"Heck, that's all right," Tolly was so addled by the twin fortunes, Spencer's return and Spencer's quick graduation to championship status, that he missed the obvious weak points in Uncle Jo's logic. Uncle Jo had counted on that.

"Well, goodbye—gotta run now," Uncle Jo slipped the brake and backed from the driveway into the street. Tolly, Verna and Spencer Q. stood watching him go. Tolly was a picture of the complete male, filled with ego and joy. Verna's expression betrayed nothing; the eyes, perhaps a bit, but that would be hard to say. Spencer Q., for his part, scratched his ear vigorously.

"Sometimes I feel like a dirty low-down heel," Uncle Jo muttered to himself, but then, brightening, "but I can't think of anyone who deserves it more—and, besides, I'm probably saving his marriage. And he got Spencer Q. back. Come to think of it, maybe I'm a heel after all. Oh well." The old station wagon meandered on down the street.

III

The next two weeks passed rapidly, highlighted only by one event. As it happened, the opening of duck season landed on Tolly's birthday and he was looking forward to it with great anticipation. He considered his birthday to be a good omen; he would have a great opening day. He made much preparation and when the eve of the great day arrived, he went to bed early. Since Verna had been busy with Spencer Q. and her new outside activities with the Women's League to Preserve our Woods and Waterways, they had seen little of each other. In fact Verna was out to a meeting that night and Tolly retired before her return, but he went to bed happy. When he had emptied the garbage that night, he had found a large crumpled ball of wrapping paper in the trash. Curious, he smoothed it out. There was a label emblazoned across one surface; it read, J. J. MacSween—Pride of the North Country." Verna had not forgotten. All was well with the world.

The next morning, still dark in its pre-dawn hours, Tolly rose from his bed, groped through the inky black of the bedroom out to the hall and downstairs. His duck hunting gear was piled in the hall. Quietly, but swiftly, he dressed. He gulped a fast glass of milk, grabbed his thermos and lunch and slipped out to the car. In a few minutes he parked in back of young Harry Byrne's house. A sliver of light in the kitchen alerted Tolly to Harry's awakened presence. Harry ducked out of the back door and climbed in the car.

"It looks like a good day, Tolly. Miserable for most folks, but great for ducks."

"And duck hunters," Tolly said happily.

"By the way, happy birthday."

"Thanks," Tolly's world was a benevolent, joy-filled universe.

They drove a half-hour or so, chatting pleasantly about the morning's miserable, but wonderful, weather, how the ducks would be moving around and, hopefully, offering themselves to that hardy breed, the duck hunter who thrived on rain, sleet and cold. They drove through the silent streets, passed into the country. A few minutes more and they turned down a dirt road. The snow tires dug in and they careened toward a distant lake just discernible in the first glimmers of dawn. They pulled to a halt by a ramshackle boat house. An old Chevy station wagon was parked behind it. Uncle Jo's Chevy.

"What the h---," Tolly began and stopped. They got out of the car and walked over to the boathouse. The door swung open as Tolly groped for his key. He pushed it wider and they looked down at the empty berth in the floor. A few words—needless to repeat—were uttered quickly and in some violence. Later, as the morning passed and their conversation was punctuated with the sound of not-too-distant gunfire, equally harsh words were spoken, slowly and with quiet determination. About ten o'clock a boat appeared off the point and steadily chugged towards the boat house. It was the missing duck boat.

213

Decoys were piled high in the box and Uncle Jo was easily identifiable in the stern, tending the motor.

But a second figure, back to bow and swaddled in a shining new rain parka, was huddled in the middle. The boat, its motor cut to idling, came up to the boathouse and glided into its berth. A full limit of blacks and mallards were piled by the decoys. Uncle Jo beamed his welcome.

"Hi, fellows, been here long," he turned to his companion. "Why, Verna, you didn't tell me Tolly and Harry were going to hunt today. Too bad. The ducks were really flying—up to about fifteen minutes ago. The sun came out and they just disappeared. Why, what's wrong, boys—," Uncle Jo's voice drifted away.

"Give me a hand with these ducks, will you, Tolly," Verna said. "We certainly did wonderfully, didn't we? Uncle Jo is a fine guide and a great shotgun coach. Why, I got two of those mallard drakes myself. Thanks, Harry." Young Harry Byrne had taken the ducks. Tolly stood silent and unbelieving, but his surprise was fast changing to more potent feeling. He opened his mouth.

"How do you like my outfit, Tolly?" Verna interrupted. "It's really very practical, you know. I got it from J. J. MacSween. Look—boots, pants and all. I had to use the egg money, but it was worth it." That did it. Tolly whirled on his heel and stamped from the boathouse. In a few moments, they could hear a car motor and then wheels spinning as the car churned away. Young Harry stood awkwardly to one side, his arms filled with stiffening ducks.

"Well, Verna. Harry. Let's go home. We've done a day's work this morning," Uncle Joe said pleasantly.

The next week rapidly passed. Tolly made no mention of the events of the opening day of duck season; indeed, he had little to say to Verna about anything. Verna was busy with Uncle Jo and Spencer Q. in anticipation of the Sneaky Hollow Invitational the next Saturday.

Tolly, for his part, largely ignored these preparations. As almost a counter-balance, he devoted his time to his outside lecture activities to the exclusion of all else. It might be said there was a guarded truce between the Guilfords. The house was a mess; meals were rushed, from a can and unscheduled. Tolly's laundry went undone; his bed was unmade. He remained strangely silent through it all.

When the great day arrived and the MTYPA journeyed to the Sneaky Hollow Invitational, there was considerable speculation among the members whether or not Tolly would show up. Their fears were groundless, however, for soon Uncle Jo's station wagon rolled into view with a full complement of personnel: Uncle Joe, Verna, young Harry Byrne, Tolly and, of course, Spencer Q. Dog. The contest was on.

Spencer Q. was magnificent. When Verna and Spencer's heat was called, Verna ran the club's entry with all the polished poise of a professional. (Tolly followed with the spectators in the gallery.) Spencer Q. quartered the field with that rare combination of efficiency and style that make champion dogs stand out from their less talented brethren. With cool determination and a certain expert flair, Spencer Q. would without fail locate the quail, approach it with great care in a delicate "egg-walking" stalk and slam on a perfect point, inches from the bird. He never flushed the bird wild before locking into point and the bird never succeeded in running out ahead of him.

"That's some dog. Yessir, it isn't often you get a dog up here that can handle quail like that. Yessir, some dog," young Harry Byrne shook his head.

"I know," Tolly said in a funny little voice.

"Old Spence, he sure never acted like that before," Harry muttered.

Tolly turned and walked back to the parking area. When the trial was over and Verna and Spencer Q. had collected the top honors that were without question theirs, they found Tolly asleep in the backseat of the station wagon. At least he appeared to be asleep.

When the car pulled into the Guilford driveway, Tolly got out of the car and went into the house without a word. Uncle Jo switched off the ignition, took out his pipe and lit it without looking at Verna.

"Well, Verna, I believe that about does it. I think your problems are over. I imagine Tolly got the message. It must be pretty obvious to him that one partner's self-centered interests shouldn't be allowed to dominate a marriage—or, for that matter, any relationship between two human beings. It's pretty easy for a person to justify his own selfish attitudes when he does it in the name of healthy sport, educational hobby or some such nonsense, but I think Tolly realizes now that there's a limit to everything, including a person's patience. I guess he'll be waiting to negotiate a surrender of sorts when you get in there. Verna, be charitable. It's an easy thing to do in victory."

"I guess he'll be waiting all right," Verna interrupted. "Boy, am I going to fix his red wagon. He'll wish he never started this, I guarantee you. Good-bye, Uncle Jo. Harry."

"Goodbye, Verna," Uncle Jo said, sadly watching her forceful stride toward the house.

215

"Gee, Uncle Jo, she doesn't sound very charitable or merciful to me," young Harry Byrne said from the back seat. "I don't think we're going to see Tolly for awhile, do you?"

"I don't know, Harry. I don't know. In fact, I'm not even sure I did the right thing, but somehow I *feel* I did. It might be tough on Tolly for awhile, but he'll survive and, in the long run, he'll *probably* realize he's the better for it. As for us? Well, I think we can all survive without Tolliver Guilford's guiding hand and shining example for a spell. Come on, let's go home. I've got some Canadian ale in the cooler that might spoil or something if we don't take care of it." The old station wagon slowly backed from the drive, turned and wandered down the street.

Our only sight of Tolliver Guilford is an agonizing one—that of a captive, emasculated suburban bond servant, garden trowel in hand, kneeling in a position of classical subservience among the gladiolas and tulips. We turn our heads away without a word; we will not intensify the innate tragedy of the man by acknowledgement of his humiliation. We prefer to remember him as he once was—without peer on stream or lake; expert with fly rod or bait casting rig; among the best with a shotgun; more than passable with rifle; fearless with knife and fork; formidable with beer can opener and corkscrew. Rest in Peace, noble companion of ribald wit and lazy smile. We knew you when.

The Man with the Cardboard Suitcase

He was, as the Irish say, a wee small man. Hardly one to draw a casual glance, let alone strike fear in anyone. He arrived late one afternoon, lugging a cheap fiber-board suitcase tied with two cracked leather straps and a piece of old cord. Since our room was on the third floor of the Pension, it had taken him a bit of time to manage the three steep flights of ancient stairs with the suitcase that appeared to weigh more than its carrier. He was perspiring in the August Spanish heat and his old-fashioned rimless glasses were actually fogged over. A faint beading of moisture covered the almost adolescent fuzz of his upper lip and a trickle of perspiration trailed down one side of his left cheek from an odd little pork-pie hat perched squarely on his close-cropped head. As hot as the day was, he had kept his ill-fitting suit, a very business-like dark blue, tightly buttoned. His tie was unloosened, tight against a collar stiff and too small for his ruddy neck. A most unprepossessing man, indeed. He also was the first terrorist I had ever met.

It was the Summer of 1955. I had returned from Korea the previous Summer, gone back to Ohio State the Fall of '54 and, in company with my roommate, Dave Call, had hitched a ride to Quebec and taken passage (roundtrip $273) on a Greek ship with a German crew under a Panamanian flag for England. We landed with $3.36 between us and joined my sister and brother-in-law. They planned to sail a 22-foot sloop from England to Spain via the internal waterways of France. Two months later we ended up in Barcelona. Tired, half-broke, and with just a few days left until we had to head back to the States, we found an inexpensive (in those days, the American buck still commanded attention) pension in the working-class district. Breakfast and one other meal were included in our daily rate of $10 each. That rate was based on three people sharing one room. Dave and I were to have a roommate, an Irish teacher on holiday, who was due the next day.

His name was Daniel O'Donnell or so he said. He was an odd one from the first and I never believed that was his name. Well, maybe the Daniel part because he responded to that in a natural fashion, but

217

he didn't look like an O'Donnell to me. More of a Smythe or Browne. Anyway, his story was that he was on holiday and being a poor, but dedicated, school teacher, he had chosen to take his annual holiday in the sun, in Spain, a country then both poorer and almost as religious as Ireland. The exception that proves the proverbial rule, he did not exemplify the traditional concept of the happy-go-lucky, extroverted, outgoing Irishman. Quite the contrary, he was a painfully dull, colorless man of seemingly frugal nature, abstremious habit and boring wit. That is until he had, as the Irish also say, the odd jar or two.

I must admit that Dave and I were somewhat taken aback by our new roommate, but deciding to make the best of the situation, attempted to welcome him with some measure of cordiality. In his fashion, he returned our overtures, but with a certain suspicion until he was satisfied that we really were two American undergraduates bumming through Europe. Mumbling incomprehensible Irish expressions of what I believe he took to be pleasantries, he wrestled his suitcase under the bed. When Dave and I offered to help him, he quickly demurred and allowed as how he would handle it himself, thank you. Later, in retrospect, we were to think it more than passing strange that for a man who never changed his suit in the four days we knew him, he should have such a heavy suitcase.

Since our last days were crowded with activities, we saw little of our roommate until our last night in Spain. Then, overcome with a little camaraderie left over from the Sunday bullfights, we invited him to go out to dinner, which never got off the ground until about ten in the evening. By the time we finished our paella, our friend Daniel had done a pretty good job of playing catch-up in the wine department, especially since we were picking up the tab. Amazingly, he had also undergone a remarkable transformation. Our Hibernian Mr. Chips had become quite the pugnacious, boistrous classical Irish pub crawler. He insisted we have Irish coffee and, failing to find that, a number of Fundador brandies. In no time flat, he had embarked into raging tirades centered on those two favorite Irish subjects, which other people try to avoid at all costs, namely politics and religion. His opinions, let it suffice to say, were more than a little bizarre.

It was Mr. O'Donnell's quite sincere belief that the world's troubles could be laid to two doorsteps—the English Empire and International Zionism. On second thought, maybe it was a mixture of both. Considering the British policy in Palestine after the war, I thought this a rather odd evaluation, but prudently kept my mouth shut. Having a

218

tad of Irish blood in my streams myself, I am sympathetic to Ireland's historic beefs against England, but I found it hard to stomach Daniel O'Donnell's fervently held belief that the Nazis should have won the war because it would have toppled the British Empire and wiped out world Jewry. I looked at Dave and his glance confirmed my suspicions —we had a genuine certified nut on our hands. Worse, we had to bundle him up out of the bar—just prior to being thrown out after one of his more outrageous outbursts—and literally carry him up three flights of stairs.

Unfortunately, the passage to the third floor gave our friend his second wind and he was soon launched into several I.R.A. songs, seemingly simultaneously. We managed to quiet him down with the promise of more whiskey (which we watered) and, chameleon-like, his mood changed from his outgoing personality back to his old, introverted, depressed character. It was then that a few words, interspersed here and there in his rambling, slurred monologue of mumbles, started to trigger a faint alarm in the back of my mind. I had done a lot of research on the Irish troubles for a term paper. Too many things were falling into place to be a mere drunken blowhard's rambling. It didn't fit the man but, yet strangely, it did. We had more than a vacationing school teacher on our hands and I was willing to bet that the suitcase under the bed held more than a change of socks and McGuffey's Reader. Meanwhile Danny Boy had lapsed into silence, leaning back against the wall with his eyes wide-open and unblinking behind glasses. There was finally nothing more to say and Dave and I, knowing we had a full day the next, reluctantly retired to our respective cots. O'Donnell was still staring when, half-alarmed but desperate for rest, I went to sleep.

When we awoke next morning, Daniel O'Donnell and his suitcase were gone. Although he had been scheduled to spend another week at the pension, he had simply disappeared without a trace. When we casually questioned the pension's proprietor, he ignored our inquiry and changed the subject. Later we were to find that his establishment had many Irish "guests" of peculiar politics. Since there were also other pensions that catered to certain types—Breton and Basque as well as Irish—we had no doubt that our friend had found friendly, discreet accommodation elsewhere. Barcelona, the center of the Catalan independence movement, was sympathetic ground for splinter groups.

After we returned home, I kept pace with the ups and downs of the Irish Republican Army. The Movement almost collapsed after the Sec-

219

ond World War, but then as the Northern Irish problem continued without solution, it thrived on that adversity on unto, as we sadly know, this very day. I never heard or saw Mr. O'Donnell again, of course, but I can fairly well guess his destiny. Contrary to popular belief, gunmen don't usually die by the gun. On the contrary, they end up being cabinet or even prime ministers. Sometimes they become presidents and, on the odd occasion, vest-pocket emperors. As for Irish terrorists, many end up running country pubs or even teaching schools.

Since my first contact with the likes of Danny O'Donnell, I have been fortunate (or unfortunate, depending on your viewpoint) in meeting a number of gentlemen who embraced terrorism as a legitimate political extension. Many are quite respectable citizens now. An ambassador to Washington. A president of a University. A noted business leader. And so on. In most cases, they were soft-spoken, quietly mannered, conservatively dressed. Only their eyes betrayed their past. The eyes were almost uniformly coldly dead, except that every once in awhile a casual question or isolated statement would conjure up a flash of madness that would make a frightening passage through those eyes and then the veil would drop again and the conversation would continue on its bland way.

I have often pondered the question raised by the terrorist in society. How do we cope with political terrorism in a democratic society? How do we keep the tools of terrorism—the Danny O'Donnell suitcases, if you will—from hands that have no compunction in using guns and bombs against defenseless civilians of any age, creed or color? One doesn't do it by disarming the citizenry, because you can't disarm a determined terrorist. The network of illegal weapons is too organized, too widespread and too available. I don't mean the so-called "Saturday Night Special," the stolen .45 from an Army arsenal, the odd bootlegged rifle or sawed-off shotgun. I'm talking about Russian burp guns, "plastique" explosives, fragmentation grenades, recoilless rifles and handy mortars. The full bag, sophisticated way beyond Danny O'Donnell's wildest dreams, is easily obtained in almost any large city of most Western countries.

For those who constantly cry for increased legislation to ban the transport—and even the manufacture and ownership—of firearms, I would remind them that the Imperial Russian government had all sorts of laws and a highly effective secret police, but it didn't prevent Russian anarchists from blowing up Czar Alexander II . Needless to say, modern history is replete with examples of political terrorism and assassination, all in the face of stringent prohibitive and punitive laws forbidding same. Palestine, Cyprus, Algeria, Northern Ireland, Rhodesia, Kenya, Indo-China and Viet Nam, Malaya, Argentina, Mexico— countless other areas come to mind. Even Nazi Germany couldn't prevent the assassination of Reinhard Heydrich in Prague in the middle of the Second World War when the Gestapo held Czechoslovakia in an iron grip.

The United States had had its share of recent political terrorism, though fortunately not on the level "enjoyed" in other areas of the Western world. We have seen the Black Panthers, the Weathermen, the Symbionese Peoples' Army, Puerto Rican Nationalists and various other odd-ball splinter groups, but their level of activity has never had enough of a support base or an effective enough leadership to sustain the sort of terrorist program seen in other countries in the last thirty years.

It is unlikely that conditions in the United States will nurture such terrorist activity—unless there is a dramatic economic downturn that, in turn, creates a socio-political crisis. Then, it is entirely possible that certain groups—with either real or fancied wrongs—will take direct violent action in the face of what appears to be political indecision or stalemate. When—and if, of course—that happens, the pressure for restrictive legislation concerning *all* firearms, explosives and other potential weapons, will be tremendous and very difficult to withstand on traditional grounds.

As we have already noted the difficulty in preventing terrorism itself, it is apparent that the prevention of restrictive legislation—directed at the general citizen and ineffective against the terrorist—is equally elusive. The best we can do is to maintain our traditional defenses—the maintenance of constant vigilance through our legislative watch-dogs, backed by communication with our constituency, the firearms-owning citizens—*but* perhaps broadened to educate as much of society as possible on the true nature of the terrorist and, most important, the means by which he obtains and maintains his arsenals.

When the facts are brought to light, it will be readily obvious to all but the most biased anti-gun groups that *any* law passed governing the legitimate commerce, ownership and use of private firearms by conventional citizens will have absolutely no effect on the acquisition, transport and illegal use of contraband materials by outlaw terrorist groups. On the contrary, the existence of a well-armed—and motivated —citizenry has always historically acted as a check on the overt activities of clandestine private armies. Again witness in recent times the experiences of Kenyan, Malayan and Rhodesian settlers, not-to-speak of the most well-known example of home defense in Israeli kibbutz.

In the last analysis, there will always be little obcure men carrying old battered suitcases up darkened staircases in some time in every land. Their motives are murky, the methods murderous, the minds morbid, but they will be there and, occasionally, their actions will demand all of our attention at least for a headline. One of their tasks, along with undermining society in general, is the specific disarming of the general populace so that its citizens will be even more at their mercy. Quite simply, we can never allow that to happen or our lives will not be worth living on any level.

The New Year's Entry

One shadow detached itself from a deeper darkness nestled under the broken fence-line and clustered brush bordering Ransom's Creek. As the first dawn's light filtered over the ridgeline of the neighboring Wasteland Mountains and steadily infiltrated the weather-broken cornfield, the silently gliding shadow took on an indentitiy of life and purpose—and finally form. The old dog fox moved carefully, yet with an assured swiftness nurtured by both instinct and experience, over the frost-tinted ground. He had hunted long and well. His stomach was full of a young but foolish rabbit and he was heading for the warmth and security of his home ground earth—an enlarged woodchuck burrow neatly usurped from its first tenant two seasons before.

Down past the Brunsville Road and over by Cherrytown Corners, Simon Patchett was making his early dawn patrol of stables and kennels. It was a routine unchanged for each fox hunting day since he had first observed the accumulated wisdom of his predecessor as professional huntsman of the Carval Valley Hounds some 16 years before when he had been a fledgling whipper-in to the hunt.

Midway between the Carval's kennels at Cherryton and Bowers Bridge and a bit to the West of Brunsville Road, another—younger, but perhaps more determined—foxhunter was setting about her established pre-hunting routine. Instead of checking hounds for hunting fitness for the day's work ahead, Miss Alexandra Waddell Smith was busy trying to keep an 8-week Labrador puppy locked in the tack room of her father's barn while she attempted to wrestle out the burrs and other miscellaneous vegetation that had impregnated her pony Tuppence's tail and mane.

Tuppence was long and shaggy in his winter coat as her father had held off clipping the pony in hopes that Sandy would allow her favorite old friend a long rest during the hunting season. Tuppence had been—and still was, it appeared—Miss Smith's first pony and had been a trusted dependable companion since both had started hunting three years before. Unfortunately, while Sandy had continued to outgrow both boots and britches, to her father's economic frustration, poor old

223

Tuppence had stayed just the same—well, maybe a little rounder and sleepier, but certainly no taller or stronger. After all, Tup was, maybe, 16—or was it 21?

Sandy was simply too big for the gallant old pony to take on a four-hour hunt over 20 miles of rough country and a possible 30 or 40 jumps of varying height and difficulty. By the end of the previous season, Tuppence was dragging at the rear by the finish of the hunt when in years before he was giving his young mistress an arm-straining fight.

Jack Smith had been adamant throughout the season and Sandy had been reluctantly—but slowly—transferred to the attentions of one Hercules Kerrigan—a large pinto pony with a watch-eye and a disposition to jump anything in his somewhat dubious vision. While Kerrigan's disposition and notorious escape tactics from barn and paddock did little to sooth the suspicions of fleeting acquaintances, those who knew his history were full of awe for his instinctive expertize in the hunt field. It was said—and perhaps rightly—that he was the truest hunting pony in Carval County.

But Sandy's heart apparently was not to be won so easily by new faces; she was equally adamant in her fidelity to her old pony and, while she begrudged Kerrigan his prowess in the field, her affections remained staunchly affixed to her first pony, the noble and rotund Tuppence. Finally, after a season of flying fences and galloping long runs on her new black-and-white charger, Sandy chose her battle-ground carefully and well—not for her the direct assault, but rather a typical female outflanking maneuver when her enemy was at his weakest moment—as for instance when her father was stretched supine and stuffed on his favorite sofa after a hearty Christmas dinner. Surrounded by some carefully chosen presents, his admiring (he thought) family and the smell of holly, pine needles, turkey, eggnog and wood-smoke from the Yule log, Jackson Smith was a set-up for any determined female of single-minded purpose. Before he could drag himself out of his complacent sense of well being and sleepy security, he found that he had given his consent—even his promise—that Sandy could take out Tuppence for the traditional New Year's Day hunt, the last big holiday hunt of the year.

Well, the day had arrived and, her father's belated misgivings notwithstanding, Sandy and Tuppence were reunited. It was a scene guaranteed to bring a nostalgic tear to even the most hardened old groom, but there weren't any grooms to be so melted in the Smith barn, only a disgruntled, mumbling father, half-asleep and clumsy in the early

224

morning half-light. Sleep-clouded mental processes were quickly cleared as every instinct reacted in a negative fashion to the bargain that he had been lured into on Christmas Day. He knew—simply just felt in the inner core of his being—that it was all wrong.

He quickly walked up to his daughter, intent on her ministrations to the softly dozing Tuppence, and placed a gentle hand on her shoulder. She looked up, but with a look of steadfast stubbornness, not returned affection for the gesture. He started to open the argument once more, but knew he was defeated short of breaking his word and perhaps invoking more ingrained problems than the situation was worth.

Simon Patchett caught the eye of the Field Master, Loring Torrington, Esq., received an almost imperceptible affirmative nod and then raised his huntsman's horn to his lips for the first call to his milling hounds. It was exactly 9 a.m. and woe to any late comer.

Simon moved his mount, surrounded by the 20-odd couples of hounds and flanked by his two oldest whips—Taddy O'Byrne, late of County Galway, and his cousin, Douglas Patchett—and trailed by first his oldest son, Michael, as junior whip, and then the Field Master, the honorary secretary of the hunt, Mr. Stephan MacGregor, and approximately—no, exactly, he never miscounted—37 members of the field, including 13 children. Thirteen is a bad number, he vaguely considered as he moved briskly off at an extended trot.

"Come along—Come along, boys—Come along," he gently urged as he moved down the road toward Brunsville and the old Ransom place. The hounds—already steaming and anxious in the morning's briskness —eagerly trotted along, close but always evading the steady, regimented placement of strong hooves clacking down among them.

The old huntsman moved only a quarter mile or so before he broke off the road and bordered a plowed field toward a small grove of trees at the north corner of the field. The hunt followed at a respectable pace and finally halted behind the field master some 50 yards from the covert as Simon cast the hounds into the underbrush.

The whips—all three—had long since fanned out in flanking movements a considerable distance away from the huntsman and his hounds and were now standing silent vigil at points commanding interlocking fields of vision covering the escape routes from the covert. If a fox broke from covert ahead and out of sight of hounds and huntsman, one of the whips had better view it from his favored position or answer to old Simon that night when all the day's tactics would be reviewed

225

with scrupulous and unwavering fidelity for the truth, regardless of whose fault was involved.

Then, as Simon was about to pull hounds out of a clump of briars and berry bushes atop a small hillock overlooking the fence-line bordering Ransom's Creek, Senator gave one long mournful yelp, followed by the quickening short yips of the younger hounds until finally all of them were making busy, inquisitive music.

Senator took a straight line, head down, tail back and drooping mouth happily open, crooning his awesome moans of satisfaction in his accomplishments. After all, leadership and talent will out, he seemed to be reaffirming with each positive cry.

Simon waited, silent still on his bay gelding, Habardash, with the field clustured behind Mr. Torrington some 20 yards away. The field was quiet and intent on the hounds running some two—now three—hundred yards away and picking up speed as they gained confidence in their line. All small talk, idle flirtation and plain gossip were forgotten and even the trailriding types—who came mainly for the riding and jumping rather than the hunting—were centered on the chase.

Simon's eyes swept the countryside, swiftly evaluating the lay of the land and the possible routes a fox might take, both when idling along on its own or when pushed by an eager pack. He quickly established the whereabouts of his whips and registered silent satisfaction that they were strategically established in exactly the right positions to visually command the sloping valley running through the Ransom ground. As his eye passed over his cousin Douglas, far to the right forward on the Parrish farm, he saw his relative stand in his stirrups and then—as Simon intuitively guessed a split second before the actual action—raise his hunt cap three times before waving it about his head. Simon gathered together his reins and with a gentle squeeze moved Habardash off into a slow walk as Douglas then indicated with outstretched arm a distant object moving steadily along the outside furrow of a broken-down stubble field. At the same time, Senator and friends came boiling out of the creek bed and, gaining a temporary ascendancy on the rising ground, gave a collective swelling roar of glee and—it must be admitted —blood lust.

Simon started off at a brisk trot, mindful of the suppressed excitement and ill-concealed impatience behind him. With a slow, almost impish smile, he savored his small trot for a few more yards, relishing the compressed power and rising pulse-beats held back behind him.

It was a moment of ultimate control and power. He turned slightly in his saddle as he brought his silver hunting horn to his lips and once more briefly caught the Field Master's eye before he blew the beautiful, exquisitely descriptive notes of "Gone Away."

As Habardash went through a fast transition to a hand-gallop with Simon upright and forward in his stirrups, the huntsman's pleasure in starting the run was compounded by the memory of the flushed excitement coursing through Loring Torrington's face, similar to all the field behind him. The Field Master touched his own mount with more than casual action and the horse leaped forward, signalling the field behind that the symbolic command to charge had been given.

The bolder riders on the fittest, fastest, best-bred mounts quickly established their positions in the front rank shortly behind the Field Master, whom they were forbidden to pass without permission, an unlikely possibility in most situations. The rest of the adult field settled down to places in the run suitable to both their ability and bravery— and the same qualities of their horses. The children in imitation of their elders rapidly assumed the same sort of flying procession behind the main body.

Poor old Tuppence, conditioned to his perogatives of first rank privileges in past years, made a determined effort to keep up, but—to his puzzlement, then frustration, and finally desperation—he found that the rest of the ponies kept passing him until he and Sandy were biting dust in the rear rank. The old pony gallantly plunged on but the distance kept widening.

"Take it easy, Tup—Take it easy," she murmured, "It's o.k.—slow down now." But the pony seemed oblivious to all outside stimulation except the maddening sight of their companions lengthening the distance from them. Vaguely heard in the distance, the sound of hounds running and making music as one primeval instrument further forced the pony forward. Sandy tried to pull her reins back in tentative signals to check Tup's frantic speed, but his mouth seemed almost deadened in his determination and single-minded purpose. The first jump—a small log obstacle—appeared in front and Sandy and Tuppence flew it much too fast and almost too close.

The pony ran on, occasionally offstride and almost stumbling over rougher terrain, but still running with every ounce of strength and will left in his body. Another jump—this time a post and rail about 3' 6"— and the pony sailed over, but this time his hind legs dragged over the

227

top rail as they descended and Sandy almost went over his head as Tuppence lurched forward in a fast stumbling motion before gathering momentum to rush onward.

The hounds could just be glanced as they dipped over the ridge-line behind the old Parrish orchard a half-mile ahead. Sandy sat back in her saddle and pulled in her shortened reins, but Tuppence went on as if possessed by some sort of equine demon. Part of the field had clustered in a bunch by a fence line and, as Sandy raced on, she realized they were taking their turns at the big new chicken-coop jump by the Parrish farm road. It was a solid jump about 4′ 6″ that had not had time to sink a few inches in the softening ground that would come in Spring. By the time Tuppence came into the approach, the remainder of the field had made it over with the exception of two children whose ponies were too small to navigate such a formidable fence.

Sandy faintly heard her father shouting as if from some distant room in another time as Tuppence charged into the jump. She could not distinguish his words and, if she had, she would not have answered for she knew what he was saying. And she would not have stopped Tuppence even if it would have been possible. The jump seemed to tower ahead of her and she felt the pony gather his legs under himself for one last effort. They were in the air for what seemed like minutes—and then they came down in a crumpled, tumbling mass of tack, flying hooves, tossing heads and flailing arms. Sandy rolled clear—and, strangely enough, her senses were equally clear—but Tuppence simply lay where he had finally fallen. Sandy remained still for a moment where she had come to rest some yards distant from her pony.

Later, after Mr. Parrish had come with his shotgun and did what he had to do, Jackson Smith took his daughter home. She had insisted on staying while Tuppence was gently and swiftly sent to what sentimentalists call "Fiddler's Green," and, in proper tradition, she had kept a fairly tight mouth and her eyes merely dimmed. She said nothing, however, and after they had driven a mile or so, her father turned to his daughter. Before he could voice his concern, sympathy or whatever there was in his mind and heart, Sandy turned away toward the window and made the only statement she ever tendered about that New Year's hunt.

"It was my fault—I know it—but you don't have to worry anymore—I won't be riding ponies anymore—I'm too old for them now—I grew up today."

Over West of the Wasteland Mountains, the hounds were being gathered in by the whips as old Simon waited by the hounds truck on Brunsville Road. Deep in his earth, panting and sweat-caked, the old fox gathered his strength and waited until fatigue finally relaxed his joints and sinews and then finally lured him into an almost narcotic sleep. It had been a good night's hunting and an exciting day's sport. He would have to do it again some time—but not for awhile.

The Friday the Thirteenth Hunt

If one were to pick the most idyllic surroundings and timing for the ultimate grouse and woodcock hunting trip, you would be hard put to beat a fine Indian summer day in October in Southern Vermont. On the other hand—unless one made a practice of flaunting the gods and getting away with it—if the date picked for that trip were Friday the thirteenth of October, 1978, perhaps the judgement exercised might be considered not the best.

As it happened, a certain "Visiting Sport" made his first bird hunting expedition to Vermont this October last after an initial pass through New Brunswick. It seems this fellow, accompanied by an aged, half-deaf and almost all-blind, English Setter, managed a decent hunt for a few days, even taking the odd bird or two. Flushed with success—some of the birds had even been on the wing—the Sport then moved south to inflict his presence on some long-suffering friends.

As the sport approached the old town of Grafton, he was reminded of the legendary *Tranquillity* stories by the late Colonel Sheldon, who had taken a similar Vermont village and turned it into the Camelot of grouse lore. "Tranquillity," patterned after Sheldon's home at Fair Haven, boasted as fine a set of characters as ever graced a hunting series. "The Captain," "The Judge" and, of course. "The Dark-Haired Lady" lived in a world where gentleness, courtesy, courtly manners and day-by-day sportsmanship were still important. It was a land where it was always October with the autumn leaves, blazoned in color, just starting to fall. The Visiting Sport was to find that "Tranquillity" and its inhabitants were still not too far away in either time or place.

Arriving the early evening of the twelfth, the Sport was soon introduced to a number of local grouse and woodcock enthusiasts. There was the "Old Sailor," who had shepherded an airplane rather than a ship in the South Pacific in the Second World War, and who had made his lasting peace in his beloved Vermont hills with his even more-cherished wife.

Counter-balancing the Old Sailor was the "Village Pro," the youngest member of the group, but according to both fact and fiction, appar-

230

ently without question the premier grouse and woodcock hunter in the area. Every rural New England community has its resident "guru"—the man, usually up in years, who knows every spring hole for trout, grouse covert within fifty miles, when the woodcock are in and the geese have left, when to hunt and when to lay abed.

Well, Grafton's "Village Pro" was all of this and, worse, only in his late twenties to boot. It was almost too much to bear, but those who wanted to wheedle some of his coverts out of him were prepared to pay the price for it. Besides, the Village Pro was a nice chap, which made his continued, unbroken success at least tolerable.

The "Tarpon Fisherman" was a relatively recent addition to the group. A dedicated saltwater flyfisherman, as his nick-name might indicate, he had lately become almost equally enamored of the Vermont Mountains, its skiing, its bird hunting and, of course, its people—perhaps some more than others. In temporary exile from the more constricted confines of suburban Connecticut, the Tarpon Fisherman was sort of camped out in a rented house. Not renowned for his culinary ability, but highly respected for his gastronomic intake, he ate out a lot.

Lastly, as all tranquil Vermont villages must have, there was a "Dark-Haired Lady" who, with little effort, was the hub about which a great deal of sporting activity centered. A fine skier and horsewoman, the Dark-Haired Lady also carried a Holland and Holland side-by-side shotgun in the field each Fall. If a bird flushed, one, we are told, should not be over-long in exercising any gentlemanly courtesy toward the Lady Companion as she was not troubled by such considerations. She took her share of birds.

The group soon moved out for refreshments, dinner and a planning session for the next morning's campaign. It was agreed that everyone would meet at the Old Sailor's house outside of town at nine a.m. The Village Pro wanted to start at seven, but the Old Sailor, recoiling in horror, exercised his prerogative as senior hunter and vetoed that idea. The Tarpon Fisherman, who had had nothing but bad luck since the season had opened the first of the month, said he would agree to anything as long as he got at least a shot. The Village Pro, mentally counting how many birds he *already* had hanging in the garage, quietly agreed.

The Dark-Haired Lady, who had been toting around one of those bad bugs that lay one low for several weeks, sighed and said she would have to skip the morning hunt, but would have lunch for the hunters if they were prompt and really did show up at twelve noon as they always promised. She would also have to miss the afternoon hunt as

231

she was campaigning for "Mother of the Year" and it was parent's week-end at her son's prep school in Massachusetts. The Visiting Sport offered sympathy, having gone through the same sort of week-end a couple of weeks previous, but secretly gloated that there would be one less local gun to contend with. It was noted that the next day was Friday the Thirteenth, which inspired a good deal of good-natured rib-poking and funny comment about gun safety and such.

The morning of Friday, October thirteenth, was perfect. At least, the weather was ideal. Not too cold for comfortable hunting and not too warm for good dog work. The classic Fall grouse day in New England. On rising and contemplating the day, The Visiting Sport suddenly realized he held no hunting license for Vermont. The headlines loomed in his imagination: "Visiting Sport Hauled Off to Slammer," with sub-head, "Locals Held as Accessories to Transient Poacher!" Not to worry. The local town clerk—who, of course, was somebody's cousin and well known by everyone else—would open her office at nine a.m., and, yes, she would even take an out-of-town check.

The Old Sailor was informed that the Sport would be a little late but should arrive about nine-thirty. They were told that it made little difference as the Pro was already there and, in fact, was out making a run through the Cemetery covert with Katy, the Sailor's young Chesapeake retriever. The Tarpon Fisherman, who was soaking up his usual rations with the Sport, looked stricken. That was one covert he might miss.

There being little left to eat, the party moved out to their cars. The Visiting Sport's car didn't work. The battery—or something—was very ill. The ignition system didn't even click or sputter when the key was turned. All the way from New Jersey to New Brunswick and back to Vermont with no trouble and now disaster. Again, not to worry. The local Grafton Garage—again owned by someone's cousin who everyone knew—came highly recommended and would solve the problem while the Sport hitched a ride with the Fisherman.

The license being duly collected and the garage suitably informed, the Fisherman and the Sport finally arrived at the Sailor's home about nine forty-five to find that the Pro was still out kicking up birds. A half hour later, he and Katy were still gone so the Sailor finally went outside and shot in the air a couple of times. In short order, the Village Pro was back. He and Katy had gone through the Cemetery covert and flown several grouse and woodcock, but he hadn't had a shot. The

232

Fisherman looked relieved. They would hit that covert again later in the day.

It was ten-thirty a.m. when they finally moved out. The Sailor had been talking to the local barber—who was either the garageman's, the town clerk's or someone's cousin—and *he* had reported taking a limit of grouse the previous day and leaving a lot of other birds at Windsor's Castle. Windsor's what, the Sport inquired? It seems one of the old settlers was named Windsor and, having a somewhat paranoid sense of humor and value, had dubbed his farm house (long since disappeared) "Windsor's Castle." Well, why not?

The problem was that Windsor's Castle was, one, fairly far away and, two, a pretty large covert that took a bit of time to cover. As the Sailor pointed out, they wouldn't have time to cover any other ground if the hunters went to Windsor's as they had promised the Dark-Haired Lady the group would be back promptly at noon. The Tarpon Fisherman was a study in mixed emotions—possibly good grouse shooting versus definitely fine food. The Pro was biding his time: he hadn't recommended the Windsor covert so he was reserving judgement. The Visiting Sport went along with the Sailor in his old jeep while the Tarpon Fisherman went in the Pro's truck.

As it happened, the Fisherman's setter was out of action with a nail split to the quick and Katy was off to the vet for a chronic swallowing problem, so the only dog was the Sport's old English setter, Jimmy. The Sport was secretly worried that the old dog was on his last trip. Jimmy was somewhere between ten and fourteen. No one knew exactly how old he was as he had been bought from an itinerant Cherokee construction worker who, after making his sale, had then disappeared.

The dog had performed in fine fashion for some six years, but his eyes were clouded over with cataracts, his hearing had increasingly faded and his heart had a murmur. While Jimmy had "done it all," as they say, in New Brunswick the previous few days, it was doubtful he would be doing very well for very much longer. The Dark-Haired Lady had not said much when she first saw him, but had murmured something about "the old boy being in his twilight." She had guessed it was probably his only trip to Vermont.

One would like to report that the trip to Windsor's Castle passed without event, but it would hardly be true, nor would it be in keeping with a chronicle on a "Friday the Thirteenth Hunt." Without elaboration, let it suffice to say that while wiping off the inside of the wind-

233

shield, the Old Sailor very nearly went into a ditch. He was not overly helped by the Sport, who, being a guest, was reluctant to make a suggestion regarding the impending accident until almost the last moment. Luckily, the ditch was avoided but not without some comment being made as to the not-so-funny string of little disasters that seemed to be shaping up for the day.

Safely arrived, guns and dog broken out, the four hunters moved out through what appeared a beautiful spot for grouse and, intermittent with patches of alders, woodcock as well. There were old apple trees, briars, water—but not too much—stone walls, all the traditional ingredients for the best of New England hunting landscapes. The hunters pushed on. The dog—still fresh—quartered the ground with both knowledge and instinct. Being old, Jimmy worked closely. No birds were flushed by dog or hunter. Indeed, the dog showed no interest at all. Perhaps he made a little game or was "birdy" for a momentary second, but that was it. Finally, as they approached the edge of one side of the cover, they came upon an old orchard with a number of apples on the ground. A few, a very few, had been pecked, but the dog indicated that the feeding hadn't been very recent as there was no scent to stimulate his interest.

The Pro suggested that the birds had to be somewhere and perhaps they were across the road in the heavier cover laying on the hillside opposite. The hunters moved across and fanned abreast covering the hill parallel to the old road. They worked their way back toward the parked cars, but nothing wild—not even a passing squirrel—intruded in their path. Finally, at last, the dog simply went to the rear of the jeep and waited for the group to return. He knew there weren't any birds in that covert, regardless of what the barber had reported.

It was about eleven-fifteen and the Sailor suggested that they had best be on their way or they would be late for their lunch. He also pointed out that the Dark-Haired Lady, while one of the pleasantest persons alive, was still "all business" when it came to certain things— like being on time for lunch so she could be off in time to see her son's soccer game. The Pro said that he knew a little covert just down the road that would take about five minutes to get to and maybe ten minutes to hunt. He was sure there was a "drummer" there. The Tarpon Fisherman's eyes gleamed. The Sport said he was neutral, but what the heck was fifteen more minutes? After all, they could drive a little faster on the way back. It was a bit of logic he had often used to find more time to hunt and fish when he shouldn't. Protesting very weakly, the Sailor agreed to this argument and the party soon found itself in a small covert immediately adjacent to the road and opening into a sort of wide triangle between two open fields.

Within a few minutes of entering the covert, the Sport thought he heard a bird flush. Seconds later, the dog came up to the flushing area and made game. Another hundred feet or so and the Tarpon Fisherman yelled the bird had re-flushed in front of him. The group moved forward, strung in even line across the narrow cover, the dog moving in front. Suddenly, the bird flushed again, out of sight to most, but not to the Tarpon Fisherman. A shot sounded, the first of the day, soon followed by a triumphant shout. The Tarpon Fisherman had his first bird of the season and Friday the Thirteenth was looking up. Jimmy proudly brought the bird back to hand, but not as gently as the Fisherman would have liked, as the tail-feathers were mussed. Still, he was more than happy—he had his bird and they were heading for lunch!

Even with laying on more speed than the old jeep liked, they were still about a half-hour late for lunch. The Sport, who had lingered in the rear until the others had entered to bear the brunt of any indignation that might be around, then had piously announced to the Dark-Haired Lady that "Lord knows he had told them all that they should have left earlier, but no one had listened." She had replied that she had well known they wouldn't be on time and had accordingly baked in an extra half-hour in her planning. The lunch was superb, the conversation somewhat grandiose in regard to certain shooting prowess, both displayed and promised, and more time was spent than anticipated. Finally, it was time for the afternoon hunt. The Old Sailor had to leave to take Katy to her vet and volunteered to take the Fisherman's setter as well.

Since it was mid-afternoon, the three remaining hunters decided they would make a run through the Cemetery Covert the Pro had visited that morning. (It should perhaps be pointed out here and now that no one is divulging any secret coverts in the Grafton area so that predatory foreign shooting types can go up and ravish the local birds. "Windsor's Castle" is another fictional name for a real place. As for the "Cemetery Covert," well, any self-respecting New England village worth its salt has *at least* one and maybe two cemetery coverts. And that goes for "Church" and "old Sawmill" coverts too. And that doesn't even cover "old orchards" and the like.)

After parking by a graveyard that chronicled the rise and fall of hundreds of years of Grafton folk, the hunters spread into the adjacent

235

alders and hardwoods. As they moved down a tumbled stone wall, the Fisherman on one side, the Sport in the middle on the other and the Pro to the far right, a grouse flushed and the Fisherman fired. He informed the others that he knew he had knocked down the bird, but he couldn't find it. The three hunters searched the area around the stone wall some thirty yards ahead, but with no success. Meanwhile, Jimmy was most interested in the nooks and crannies of the wall. Sniffing the rocks and winding the air, the old dog started methodically, but most interestingly, working down the wall. The hunters were still searching the area when suddenly the Fisherman looked up and announced that "here he comes with the bird in his mouth." The Fisherman allowed as how he might forgive the dog for chewing the tail-feathers on the first bird after all.

Well, what can one say to add to the day. What had started as a dismal Friday the Thirteenth, prone to accident and error, turned into a fine hunt with good new friends. In the next hour or so before twilight, the Fisherman had still another shot (actually two) at a grouse; the Pro took feathers out of the same bird, and then took a woodcock. The Sport missed a woodcock while crossing over to help the Fisherman look for the grouse he might have hit. Later, they all flushed another grouse and a woodcock. A lot of action for an unlucky day and a short afternoon in a season that—up til then and with the exception of the Village Pro's efforts and the barber's fantasies—had been a pretty grim one for most of the area's grouse hunters.

The Fisherman had a brace of grouse, the Village Pro had the satisfaction of guiding his friends into birds, the Visiting Sport had the pleasure of seeing his old dog have one more fine day in the field, the Old Sailor had the bitter-sweet knowledge that *he* could have gotten some of those birds his friends had missed if he had only been there instead of nobly taking his friend's pooch to the vet.

And what of the Dark-Haired Lady? What did she get out of all these shenanigans? As the saying goes, what was a nice lady like her doing with such a mixed bag of disreputable characters running around in old torn hunting clothes, accompanied by smelly dogs and muddy boots? Well, I suppose, like Colonel Sheldon's "Dark-Haired Lady," maybe she just likes the company and the surroundings.

As the Visiting Sport was giving Jimmy one last run before leaving for home, she watched him carefully lift the old aching dog back into the station wagon. With all the care being given, the dog still quietly

whimpered as joints, aged tendons and strained muscles responded in pain. Without anything being said, she must have known what was going through the Visiting Sport's mind for her last words were: "Don't do anything rash. Promise, you won't do anything rash."

The Sport promised he wouldn't and it is a safe guess he won't. Who knows? Maybe it will be Fall again in Vermont and they will all gather again—the Old Sailor, the Tarpon Fisherman, the Village Pro, the

237

Dark-Haired Lady and the Visiting Sport, who, hopefully, will have old Jimmy with him to cover the ground, ever so carefully, in the land where it is always October with the leaves, so brilliantly colored, just beginning to fall.

EPILOGUE

A Note on the Epilogue

This is one of the few articles in this volume that have appeared in another book. Some years ago, when I was head of Winchester Press, Eric Peper and I commissioned two anthologies, *Fishing Moments of Truth* and *Hunting Moments of Truth*. They were both excellent collections of some of the best writing on the two subjects by then living outdoor writers of the first rank.

While both books were superb and well accepted by the general sporting public, I always felt that somehow the hunting book was too full of blood and guts. When I finished reading the manuscript after all of the articles were submitted by our authors, I had the feeling that, while the individual pieces were just fine, the sum total effect wasn't the whole story of what hunting means, both abstractly and to the individual hunter.

Anyway, I sat down and wrote *Epilogue to a Hunting Moment of Truth* in the hope that somehow I could express and, more important, get across what hunting and being a hunter means.

Now, some six years later, this essay still seems as good a way to end this book as any.

Epilogue to a Hunting Moment of Truth

Someone once said the killing of an animal during a hunt is really anti-climatic and certainly it is a time of paradox—regret mixed with triumph. There is a curious post-hunting depression that usually evolves into a sustained elation. Lastly, there is the quiet satisfaction in a job well-done and a trophy well-taken—if one has played the game as rules, both written and unwritten, tell us it should be played. This is the time of reflection, of remembrances of experiences shared, of victories and defeats—equally rewarding as viewed through the prism of time.

What about all that time between the planning of a hunt and the so-called moment of truth—the trigger-pulling, if you will—and what about the period after the kill before the trip is over? Well, I can tell you a big game hunt is a mixed bag indeed—some fun, a little misery, a lot of hard work, but all rewarding. Anyone who has ever packed into the high country or struggled through the almost obscene undergrowth of jungle lowlands or drifted across a heat-stricken midday desert knows that one pays for one's trophies in many coins. I have hung, exhausted and bone-weary, on the side of a mountain while a driving, freezing rain pounded its way through every dry crevice of my clothing and wondered why am I—who fear heights and despise being wet and cold—at that particular spot at that specific time?

The answer is simple. I am there because I want to be there—not for that miserable experience, but for the possible moment that *may be* before that trip is done. I may not even know what that moment will be—one of "truth" or not—but, I search for it, drive myself toward it, and am irresistibly drawn toward it. In the last analysis, I not only want to be there—hanging on the side of that mountain, wandering across that desert or slogging through that jungle—but, if the truth were to be admitted, I probably need to be there too. And in that, perhaps, we have the real meaning of the "Moment of Truth" as it applies to hunters, if not all men. We are hunters hunting because that is what we are supposed to do, have always done, and—hopefully —will always try to do in the future. I am reminded of Theodore Roosevelt's fine words that describe hunting much better than my attempts:

No one but he who has partaken thereof, can understand the keen delight of hunting in lonely lands. For him is the joy of the horse well ridden and the rifle well held; for him the long days of toil and hardship, resolutely endured, and crowned at the end with triumph. In after-years there shall come forever to his mind the memory of endless prairies shimmering in the bright sun; of vast snow-clad wastes lying desolate under gray skies; of the melancholy marshes; of the rush of mighty rivers; of the breath of the evergreen forest in summer; of the crooning of ice-armored pines at the touch of the winds of winter; of cataracts roaring between hoary mountain masses; of all the innumerable sights and sounds of the wilderness; of its immensity and mystery; and of the silences that brood in its still depths.

It has always amazed me when those opposed to hunting have condemned the practice as unholy, immoral and alien to man's finer purposes. What utter disregard of all the facts of history, folklore, natural history and the overwhelming evidence of life and death about us. What complete poppycock. The only thing unholy, immoral and alien to man and all nature is that which is simply unnatural—false, contrived, artificial, forced, constricted and twisted against nature's innate systems and balances. Since man is a hunter by nature, the act of hunting can hardly be an "unnatural" act, let alone immoral, unethical or unholy. There are those who rather desperately attempt to deny man as a hunter, but I would consign them to argument with more qualified men than me—namely, the overwhelming majority of anthropologists.

When man is denied his hunting instincts and the natural aggressive drives that have preserved this rather puny animal down through the centuries, he often finds himself in very deep trouble. On the one hand, man becomes weakened as he is frustrated in his instincts, his society softens and his civilization wastes away in the face of stronger challenges. On an individual basis, certain men channel their thwarted aggression into anti-social behavior: ruthless business practice, predatory sexual conquest and even criminal action—either through personal assault or in collective war.

Certain self-appointed voices of so-called modern civilized thought decry hunting as an out-moded, discredited and incompatible pastime in modern society. These seers—usually urban-bred and based—abhor the country sports as, indeed, they really fear the country. They hope to conquer by ridicule and involuted logic the strength of the country-

243

side, its mores and morality, its basic standards and its very validity.

When our critics condemn hunting as uncivilized, they ignore the historical fact that hunting was the catalyst of man's coming together in any form of organized society in the first place. They ignore the fact that hunting provided both the backdrop and the impetus to our first art forms—from cave paintings, to lyric songs of the chase, to panoramic tapestries on castle walls, to epic poems singing the praises of Odysseus and Beowulf. Lastly, they ignore the facts of scientific life —man is a predator; perhaps the most efficient and magnificent predator the world has ever seen.

The love of hunting is nothing to instill shame in the human race. It was once popular to condemn all predation but now at least we have come to recognize and admire the necessary role of the predator in the lower forms of animal life. The eagle is now protected—well, almost protected—throughout the land and the hawks and falcons are coming into their own, although a little late for the saving in some instances. The great cats—many endangered species—are wondered over and looked upon as symbols of grace, power and authority over the world. Paradoxically, it has been the hunter who has led the battle for the protection of his fellow predators in many cases.

Consequently, predator and predation are no longer "scare" words in the classic sense with the general populace. Predatory animals and their importance to the proper balance of nature are recognized as key factors in the ecosystem. Their interdependence with prey species in our environment is accepted, protected and even encouraged. Even preservationists have come to realize that certain prey species experience population explosions—with all their attendant disasters of starvation and disease—when they are allowed to expand without the check imposed by traditional predators in their home range.

A great many animal protectionists are not only sincere, but sensible people. They recognize the problems of over-population and nature's role in taking care of the situation. Many animal lovers have come to accept—even venerate—the role of the animal predator. Unfortunately, few protection-oriented animal enthusiasts can accept the fact of life that in many cases man is the only logical and acceptable predator available to accomplish the job that needs and must be done to insure the sound survival of certain prey species adjacent to settled areas.

Man—either in urban or agricultural communities—is unprepared to accept certain of the large predators in close proximity to either his family or his livestock. Nothing any of us—hunter or protectionist—can

244

say will convince the suburban and exurban towns of New Jersey that the Somerset county deer herd needs a good pack of timber wolves or an occasional family of eastern panthers to keep it in healthy balance. Understandable and completely justified. Likewise, but less justified, no one is going to convince a Montana sheepman or cattleman that grizzlies are not the devil's own creatures.

So there you are. What do you do about the fantastic over-population of deer in many areas of the continental United States? Who is going to harvest the surplus elk herd in the Yellowstone Park? Man in his traditional role of the hunter is the obvious, logical and only acceptable solution, but he is violently rejected—and the animals involved often condemned to biological disaster—by the very people who fiercely declare their unswerving dedication to those same four-footed creatures of the forest.

Strangely, there are those among the anti-hunting faction who have actually endorsed the elimination of animal herds rather than allow them to be hunted. I have actually heard this proposition seriously advanced by so-called well-meaning and sensible people: the fact is granted that animals will breed and increase beyond their food supply; that further they cannot be trimmed back except by human control; that, lastly, this is intolerable from an ethical standpoint because it turns man into a killer who kills for pleasure and this must be prevented at all cost—in this case, the lives of the very animals involved! In the last analysis then, the animals don't really count and in that I think we have at least a hint to the key of the anti-hunting phenomena.

245

This element in the anti-hunting movement advances the following argument for their position. There are animals—both wild and domestic—that must and, indeed, should be harvested for the good of mankind. These anti-hunters accept this because it is an economic and biological necessity. Certain animals are taken for food and other products; others are eliminated for less palatable, but equally justified, reasons—they are dangerous or simply obnoxious to man—or they compete with man for land and water, probably the most heinous crime of all. Ergo, wild animals must go, but they must be dispatched as domestic animals are slaughtered—dispassionately, impersonally and, hopefully, by surrogate killers who will do the dirty deed quickly, efficiently, and discreetly out of everyone's view. In order to quell any twinges of conscience and salve any lingering doubts, the killing must not give pleasure to anyone—no sport or satisfaction in an animal taken in fair chase. There must be no chance of the animal surviving or the whole program would be pointless. After all, the idea is to save man from himself and his base hunter's nature. There is only one way to do that—remove the cause and chance of temptation, the animals themselves.

As you can see, this particular odd lot of anti-hunters could really care less about animals; they are concerned with salvation as they see it and heaven help the poor benighted heathen—in this case, you and me—who doesn't agree to be saved. The key to their position is simply this: they cannot accept the facts of life and death that we men are animals as any other and as we now live, so shall we one day die as all life must. Albert Schweitzer developed the "reverence for life" theory, the cornerstone of this philosophy, and it simply holds all life is sacred and must be preserved at all costs. (Schweitzer sort of selectively chose which life he thought was sacred around the pea-patches of his African medical compound.) Modern advocates of "reverence for life" have become even more discriminating in their implementation of Schweitzer's philosophy and, by and large, take a sort of puritan's view that the only killing to be stopped is that involved with sports hunting. God deliver us all from well-meaning, divinely-inspired crusaders. Perhaps they simply are incapable of understanding what again Theodore Roosevelt knew and expressed so well:

In hunting, the finding and killing of the game is after all but a part of the whole. The free, the self-reliant, adventurous life, with its rugged and stalwart democracy; the wild surroundings, the grand beauty of the scenery, the chance to study the ways and habits of the woodland creatures—all these unite to give to the career of the wilderness hunter its peculiar charm. The chase is among the best of all national pastimes; it cultivates that vigorous manliness for the lack of which in a nation, as in an individual, the possession of no other qualities can possibly atone.

President Roosevelt had no problem assuming the dual roles of "the mighty hunter" and America's father of conservation. With an almost uncanny foresight, his words of the turn of the century have as much meaning now as they did then:

In order to preserve the wildlife of the wilderness at all, some middle ground must be found between brutal and senseless slaughter and the unhealthy sentimentalism which would just as surely defeat its own end by bringing about the eventual total extinction of the game. It is impossible to preserve the larger wild animals in regions thoroughly fit for agriculture; and it is perhaps too much to hope that the larger carnivores can be preserved for merely aesthetic reasons. But throughout our country there are large regions entirely unsuited for agriculture, where if people only have foresight, they can, through the power of the state, keep the game in perpetuity.

I am sure it must seem singularly strange to many non-hunters—and, of course, anti-hunters—that a group of men and women who have obviously spent a great deal of time and effort pursuing and often killing wild animals should be so concerned with their continued well-being.

Perhaps, as Oscar Wilde once said, "Each man kills the thing he loves" but I would prefer to think that our dedication both as individuals and collectively runs a much deeper course than that rather paradoxical quotation might indicate.

While there is scarcely time to delve further into the philosophical and pragmatic justifications of sport hunting, let it suffice to say that the record speaks for itself on the question of who has largely paid the bills for conservation through the years. As an example, there would be no wildlife management—or, indeed, wildlife populations of any size —in the United States if the hunter had not provided the economic wherewithal in the form of licenses, fees and special taxes on arms and ammunition to both the Federal government and the various state agencies concerned with wildlife. There was a time not too distant when conservationists and their societies—and their concern for wild-life—were regarded by the great mass of people as some sort of freaks who ran around in tennis shoes carrying signs and generally making nuisances of themselves. Now, with the newly awakened interest in ecology and the total environment, the sportsman is receiving a much needed and welcomed assist from a broad spectrum of the body politic —hopefully, on a lasting basis and not only as a sometime fad to be abandoned when other, more alluring, siren songs sound in the future.

The time, treasure and talent offered up—freely and willingly—over the past half century by organizations like Ducks Unlimited, the Izaak Walton League, The Campfire Club, The Boone & Crockett Club, The National Wildlife Federation and countless state and local organizations cannot be measured in materialistic terms alone.

The vast game herds that have been brought back from near extinction in North America bring pleasure to all Americans, hunter or not, and who can say how much money or time went into the effort and what it is worth in dollars and cents. We, as hunters, bear a responsibility beyond the ordinary citizen. Since we have taken the privilege of hunting individual wild animals, we must accept the custodianship of their overall well-being as various species. We must never take an animal without reason—and good reason—or we have committed the worst sin of all—for to kill without meaning degrades an animal for it means its life meant nothing. In the last analysis, we might all keep a few things in mind as we venture forth on our various hunts, large and small, through the world:

> A ravaged hillside is an affront to all men's eyes,
> A polluted stream knows no boundaries and flows by
> everyman's village.
> A poisoned atmosphere is breathed into the lungs of
> all men, black or white, rich or poor, young or old.
> And lastly, a slaughtered game population is a crime
> against all living creatures.

Perhaps one day there will no longer be hunting as we know it now and animals will only be seen in somewhat artificial circumstances in game preserves and zoos. I hope not, but if it be so, let those who are left to enjoy this sequestered wildlife remember those who did so much to guarantee its survival. And if we hunters leave any epitaph let it be that future generations will say: They gave more than they took. That will be our "Moment of Truth."

248

FIREARMS ASSEMBLY

A two-volume set, outstanding in its field. Each article gives a brief history of a specific firearm, identifies all parts in an exploded-view illustration and explains takedown and assembly in captions and line drawings. Contains all significant American Rifleman exploded-view articles through September 1980.

Firearms Assembly 3: The NRA Guide to Rifles and Shotguns. A big 256 pages, soft cover. ASB10021. Retail $8.95. NRA Member's Discount Price **$7.50.**

Firearms Assembly 4: The NRA Guide to Pistols and Revolvers. A large 264-page edition. ASB10022. Retail $8.95. NRA Member's Discount Price **$7.50**

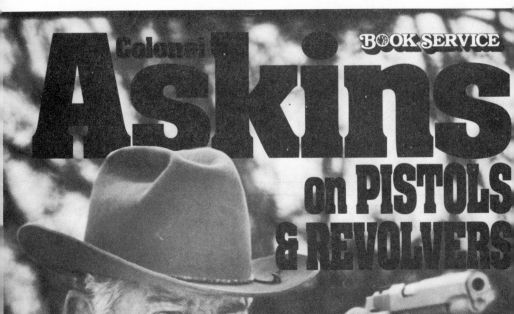

BOOK SERVICE

FIREARMS ASSEMBLY

A two-volume set, outstanding in its field. Each article gives a brief history of a specific firearm, identifies all parts in an exploded-view illustration and explains takedown and assembly in captions and line drawings. Contains all significant American Rifleman exploded-view articles through September 1980.

Firearms Assembly 3: The NRA Guide to Rifles and Shotguns. A big 256 pages, soft cover. ASB10021. Retail $8.95. NRA Member's Discount Price **$7.50.**

Firearms Assembly 4: The NRA Guide to Pistols and Revolvers. A large 264-page edition. ASB10022. Retail $8.95. NRA Member's Discount Price **$7.50**

FIREARMS ASSEMBLY

A two-volume set, outstanding in its field. Each article gives a brief history of a specific firearm, identifies all parts in an exploded-view illustration and explains takedown and assembly in captions and line drawings. Contains all significant American Rifleman exploded-view articles through September 1980.

Firearms Assembly 3: The NRA Guide to Rifles and Shotguns. A big 256 pages, soft cover. ASB10021. Retail $8.95. NRA Member's Discount Price **$7.50.**

Firearms Assembly 4: The NRA Guide to Pistols and Revolvers. A large 264-page edition. ASB10022. Retail $8.95. NRA Member's Discount Price **$7.50**